W9-DHT-882

Karel Englis

ECONOMICS:
A PURPOSE ORIENTED APPROACH

**translated by
Ivo Moravcik**

EAST EUROPEAN MONOGRAPHS, BOULDER
DISTRIBUTED BY COLUMBIA UNIVERSITY PRESS,
NEW YORK
1992

EAST EUROPEAN MONOGRAPHS, NO. CCCXIII

TABLE OF CONTENTS

Introduction to Karel Englis'
Economics:
A Purpose Oriented Approach
Frantisek Vencovsky

No social science has experienced a development so rich in diversity and conflict as has political economy. Its history continues to be the history of searching, groping, and conflict between theory and practice.

Within a single century–from the middle of the eighteenth to the middle of the nineteenth–political economy was established as a separate scientific discipline, thanks, essentially, to the pioneering work of three great figures: Francois Quesnay, Adam Smith, and David Ricardo. The legacy of their thought–carried on [developed further] in particular by Jean-Baptiste Say, and John Stuart Mill has formed the foundation of the system of economic laws of classical liberalism. However, this was far from sufficient for the understanding of the always more complex economic phenomena of the end of the nineteenth and first half of the twentieth century.

A major scientific re-orientation of economic thought took place, and from criticism of classical political economy emerged gradually attempts and efforts to see things in a different light. The foundation of alternative views was on the one had a new teaching about economic value based upon various modifications of the classical theory of objective value (different tendencies and shades of socialist schools of thought, in particular Karl Marx), and on the other hand a transition to subjective theories of value (in particular the Austrian marginal utility school–Karl Menger, Eugen Bohm-Bawerk).

Serious economic problems of the inter-War period led to focusing of the attention of theorists on a search for macro-economic relationships between economic phenomena and their ability of being controlled by government policy (John Maynard Keynes and a number of analogous thinkers–Paul Samuelson, John Kenneth Galbraith). Simultaneously, also on the basis of analysis of macro-economic factors–emerged theories and models of economic growth (Roy F. Harrod, Nicholas Kaldor, Joan Robinson, and others). Economics was also enriched by detailed work in specific areas–such as prices (Irving Fisher) and monetary factors (Gustav Cassel, Jacques Rueff, Milton Friedman).

This rich–often chaotic–stream of economic thought was entered during the first half of this century, in an original way, by the Czech economist, Karel Englis, originator and developer of the teleological theory of economics. His point of departure was a logical-noetic critique of existing economic theories and schools that were characterized by a lack of a correct and reliable noetic orientation an complex cognitive synthesis suited to economic thinking.

The lumping together of heterogeneous–causal and purposive–concepts and cognitions in economics, the lack of understanding the purposive view of economic phenomena, and in particular the ignoring of the agent, his interests and his approaches–overshadowed especially in the theoretical schools of this century by a superficial macro-economic causal view–prevented the understanding and satisfactory explanation of the principles and the functioning of individual economic systems and of their mechanisms. Karel Englis approached this serious problem of logical-noetic instability and hence unreliability of the empirical application of political economy by constructing an altogether novel teleological orientation.

Englis was born in 1880 in Hrabyn, Czech Silesia. He studied economics at the Faculty of Law of Charles University in Prague and began his career in the central statistical offices of the Austro-Hungarian monarchy in Prague and Vienna. His scientific activity and interests led to the chair of political economy at the Czech Technical University in Brno. When Czechoslovakia was established he became in 1919 the first president (rector) of the newly founded Masaryk University in Brno. There followed a time filled not only with scientific work, when Professor Englis elaborated the basic elements and laws of teleological thinking and applied them to the science of economics and finance, but also of public activity. Economic and political problems of the new state necessarily guided Englis' interest to practical questions. He held the portfolio of finance in most of the Czechoslovak cabinets and from 1934 until the critical time of 1939 he was governor of the Czechoslovak National Bank. he had therefore a unique opportunity to verify in practice and to successfully apply the actual perceptions of the new teleological theory. After the Second World War and the liberation of Czechoslovakia he was invited in 1945 to join the Faculty of Law of Charles University in Prague and in 1947 he was elected its president (rector). His activity as university teacher ended in February 1948. The last period of his creative scientific work was devoted to a new conception of logical noetics. He died in his native Hrabyn in 1961.

Professor Englis' scientific literary activity was immensely rich. he wrote of course in Czech, some of his works were written in German, many were translated into other languages. Scientific works of crucial importance for the teleological theory of economics include above all: *Zaklady hospodarskeho mysleni [Foundations of Economic Thought]*, Prague, 1922, 165 pages; *Financni veda [The Science of Finance]*, Prague, 1929, 408 pages; *Theorie statniho hospodarstvi [The Theory of the Public Sector]*, Prague 1932, 230 pages; *Hospodarske soustavy [An Essay on Economic Systems: A Teleological Approach]*, Prague 1946, 148 pages; English translation, Boulder-New York, 1986, and finally his magnum opus *Soustava narodniho hospodarstvi [The System of National Economy]*, two volumes, Prague, 1938, 1617 pages. Englis' chief economic insights are contained in [the present work] his brief text, *Narodni hospodarstvi*, Prague 1940 and 1946, 304 pages; translated as *Economics: A Purpose Oriented Approach*, Boulder-New York, 1991. In addition to these pivotal works he published numerous works on particular subjects, polemical works, and especially works dealing with economic problems of the times in which he propagated his economic and financial policies. The result of his work in the field of the new logical noetics (theory of the system of thinking) was his *Mala logika [Lesser Logic]* (Prague, 1947 511 pages; also published in German, *Die Lehre von der Denkordnung*, Wien, 1961, 279 pages, and *Das Problem der Logik*, 1960, 67 pages) as well as a number of other as yet not published works, in particular a large work in several volumes *Velka logika [Master Logic]*.

Englis' theoretical conception starts out from the view that the causal method of perceiving and comprehending phenomena–which basically sees chains of causes and effects–is inadequate for the science of economics. Economic processes can be fully understood and explained only when we start with the agent, when we view human activity as purposive activity whose origins are certain objectives and which seeks the means to accomplish them. Englis' economic theory therefore fits in with his new and original conception of logical noetics according to which we can comprehend and understand reality in only three ways or forms: the ontological, when we view all phenomena as merely being and relationships as causal; the teleological, when we view all phenomena as wanted and relationships as purposive or guided by the objective; and finally the normological, when we view phenomena as derived from obligations and relationships as following from obligations.

Each of these methods of cognition has its system of formal concepts (ontology: cause and effect, etc.; teleology: purpose, means, utility, cost, return, etc.; normology: norms, obligations, etc.) with which the perceiving agent approaches reality as object of cognition. Every insight into reality, every empirical judgment therefore has content (the object of cognition) and form. A given reality can be perceived in a different form (e.g., a particular event may be viewed ontologically–one inquires about its cause; or teleologically–one inquires about its purpose, sense, etc.). Everything that we state about reality has already been elaborated by one of our cognitive approaches which in their totality constitute our system of thinking. Hence "reality on its own"–without a system of thinking and its cognitive approaches is incomprehensible. Englis' noetic stands therefore fully on the side of critical idealism; in fact it expands Kant's cognitive approaches to include the teleological.

Application of the teleological approach of cognition to the economy leads to the teleological theory of economics. Englis points out of course that there is no noetic objection to an ontological theory of economics. Human activity too can be seen as merely existing and it can be explained causally–just as the activity of ants and bees. However, such explanation would not be scientifically satisfactory, because we desire to comprehend the meaning and the purposive nature of behavior, of the relationships of specific actions, briefly of economic behavior. Hence the science of economics must be teleological. One can therefore state that the purpose of the teleological theory of economics is the discovery of an order, a system in the activity of obtaining and using the means for various purposes in life. Accordingly purposive behavior does not concern only man as a psycho-physical being, but also to every organization: association, state, church, etc.

The ontological conception of the economy which seeks relationships of causality is merely a complement of the teleological approach. Here belongs e.g., the history of various economic phenomena, economic statistics, etc. We can discover laws of economic development historically and therefore causally, but systemic principles of economic order and their internal functional relationships can only be grasped and comprehended teleologically. Economics cannot be both causal and end-oriented. This has been, until now, and continues to be a shortcoming of all economic theories and schools, and these theories and schools have therefore been incapable to comprehend economic processes satisfactorily and guide them reliably. Englis has demonstrated the scientific potency and reliable practical applicability of teleological cognition in all spheres of the economy. His teleological approach to solving empirical questions continues to be relevant.

It turns out, above all, that many elements of Englis' teleology represent a contribution to modern theory of management. Englis analyzed the process of decision making which proceeds in accordance with the principle of rationality both in the acquisition and use of means, given a particular objective. He discovered the formal-logical substance of this process, he "de-psychologized" the principle of rationality, showing it to be an approach that can have different contents depending on the objective, whether the latter is subjective satisfaction of the individual, making money for a business enterprise, or some particular deal of society for public policy. Several modern sciences of management and decision making–cybernetics, praxeology, and others lag far behind Englis insight concerning the formal nature of teleological concepts.

Englis' teleological theory delineates also with great precision the different economic systems, uncovers their systemic principles, and specifies the elements that are appropriate for each particular economic system. It shows that ever economic system possesses its own characteristic set of functional relationships which corresponds exclusively to that system alone.

Thus to capitalism corresponds economic behavior of producers and consumers guided by their own subjective valuation, as well as the complex of the market mechanism, private ownership, etc.

To the socialist system of social cooperation corresponds public organization of production which secures the right to work and the right to full return for work; it includes state regulation of production but individual operation of consuming economic units, etc.

To the solidarist or communist system corresponds state regulation of production as well as consumption based on objective central valuation which secures the right to a living, etc.

Accordingly Englis' theoretical approach solves the question of an appropriate relationship between particular political and economic systems as well as the always acute question of the "purity" of economic systems. One cannot transplant to a particular system those elements which are in fundamental conflict with it. We continue to encounter a lack of understanding of systemic principles among many politicians and economists which leads to well known speculation about systemic convergence, about the possibilities and the conditions of transformation of one economic system into another, such as the "gradual transformation of capitalism into socialism," or "the gradual coming together of capitalism and socialism," etc.

On the basis of his analysis of the distinct principles of economic systems, Englis worked out also a teleological theory of the public sector. He analyzed the methods, possibilities and limits of government intervention in the economy. He showed that public policy actually rests on solidarist foundations, that it represents a solidarist superstructure built rests on the underlying individualistic order. By making precise the fundamental elements of particular economic systems, by uncovering the appropriateness of these elements for each system, Englis laid the foundations of a very relevant science of public economic policy, especially the science of state intervention.

Of equal significance for the theory for the guidance of the national economy is Englis' contribution to the theory of prices especially his specification of factors that affect relative prices and those that affect the movement of the price level. His insights concerning movements of the price level resulting from inflation and deflation [of the monetary base???] as distinct from those resulting from expensiveness and cheapness (v dusledku drahoty a lace) are original.

Just as inspiring, both theoretically and practically, is Englis' theory of the controlled economy. He sees its essence to be government intervention in the price mechanism, the displacement of prices from their equilibrium function (i.e., of prices in the broadest sense of the word, not only of goods but also interest rates [price of capital], wage rates [price of labour] and exchange rates [price of foreign exchange]). Similarly he demonstrates, purely teleologically, why only prices that emerge from a purely competitive market bring about maximum productivity and maximum output at minimum cost.

Equally stimulating from the viewpoint of the teleological approach to modern economic policy are Englis' insights in a number of other fields, especially the theory of wages, interest rates, exchange rates, credit and money supply policy.

Englis' teleological elaboration of these problems is contained in the work which is here presented to the expert public. The English translation of Englis' brief text, *Economics* was originally published in 1946. Neither the author nor those who have assumed the care of his rich scientific legacy should be blamed for this delay. External circumstances were stronger. However, the intervening years did nothing to diminish the scientific contribution of Englis' pioneering work. In Ivo Moravcik's translation and with the support of the author's son, Karel Englis Jr., those interested in economic thought will find a book whose originality of economic thought stands out. What is more, the history of recent years and current economic events in the world confirm sufficiently the necessity of a consistently teleological approach in guiding economic policy.

Prague, September 1988

Dr. KAREL ENGLIS

PRAGUE 1946

Printed by ORBIS, Prague XII

FOREWORD
to the second edition

The second edition of this book appears at the request of the Faculty of Law of Masaryk University in Brno. The first was intended as a text for senior students of secondary schools. However, since economics is not yet taught in secondary schools, it may also serve for initial orientation, at the university level.

The first edition appeared in 1940, in war time and during the German occupation. The second appears now, in 1945, in a once again free country. It is identical with the first edition which was itself intended for a time when our country would again be free. It contains therefore no "Einstellung zum Reich" [Inclusion in the German Reich] which was then required–particularly in textbooks. This fact escaped notice of the Germans but not of Czechs. A book containing a critique of my book appeared in 1941. Its author wrote that one had to take exception to Englis' text "because it concentrated so much on the development of concepts that it avoided real problems of the day." What problems did he have in mind? Before the above quote he wrote: "Another reason was to present a text that would facilitate comprehension of problems created by the new realities of political and economic life." What were, in 1940, the new realities in the political and economic life of our country which a book on economics was to address? No one will have any doubt that it was precisely those realities and problems which I purposely avoided. I will return to this unusual critique elsewhere and another time.

In 1938 appeared (in Czech, German, French, and English) my critical study of German [National] Socialism as programme of the Sudeten German Party. The book was confiscated by the Germans immediately after the occupation. I am happy, however, that in 1940 I escaped being forced to "glorify" our absorption in the German Reich and German National Socialism.

The fact that the second edition is identical with the first (there are reasons for that) explains why–when the text mentions the World War, it refers to the First World War. That is why there is no discussion of the particular set of problems associated with currency reform that arises following a period of controlled economy, such as we face after the Second World War. This will be done in the next edition where I shall also deal with the International Monetary Fund and with an interpretation of our social revolution.

Dr. Eng. Zdenko Blazej compiled, at his own initiative and with diligence, a subject index. I with to thank him from my heart. The index appears at the end of the book.*

I also wish to thank Dr. Z. Blazej, Docent Dr. J. Siblik and Dr. F. Stranecky for their help in correcting proofs.

I dedicate the book to my wife, Valerie Englis, loyal companion of my sunny as well as dark days.

Prague, 20 December 1945   Dr. Englis

---

* Translator's Note: I have not attempted to translate the index.

INTRODUCTION TO THE SCIENCE OF ECONOMICS

Man is part of the animal world. His body, organs, life, birth and death represent part of the field of inquiry of natural science (zoology, physiology, biology, etc.). In common with other animals he too confronts nature in struggling to preserve and improve his life. In common with other animals he seeks food and shelter from cold and inclement weather. Some animals (bees, badgers) store food for winter just as he does. Unlike man, other animals are not concerned about winter clothing. They hibernate, migrate to warmer regions, or perhaps nature itself provides them with warmer, thicker fur. How animals obtain food, how they strive to survive and improve life, is the concern of natural science. How man provides for preserving and improving his life is not the concern of natural science but a special science, the science of economics or national economy.

Why is the question of how man strives to preserve and improve his life not part of natural science? If he were to strive to accomplish these objectives as other animals do, economics would be simply a part of natural science. But this is not the case. We marvel at the handiwork and the order of bees in the beehive, how the bees make use of space (hexagonal honey-combs) etc. However, the evolution of the bees' "ingenuity" appears to have come to an end. For thousands of years, at all times and everywhere, ever since man has observed them, the work and the order of the beehive have not changed. There has

1

been no change, no evolution, as if bees followed some order, as if they were "driven" by a compulsion called "instinct."

We observe–in fossils preserved in amber–that countless millennia ago, ants kept aphids as they do today, that for ages cuckoos have been laying their eggs in the nests of other birds, etc. By contrast man's efforts to preserve and improve life change daily. Every man is different in this respect and all the time these efforts are being improved and perfected before our very eyes. Man improves himself through education and training. His productivity improves. Means of production (machines, engines) are being perfected, as are the means of transport (from wheelbarrows to railroads, to automobiles and airplanes) and the means of communication (from sound and light signals to telegraph, telephone, radio, and television). Order among men is being improved as well (from tribal warfare to the organized state). The difference is crystal clear. On one hand the unchanging beehive, on the other the continuously evolving workshop of human labour.

The age-long absence of change of the drive to preserve and improve life of animals (other than man) include that drive, in our mind, among phenomena that "obey" natural law, a law also obeyed by the structure of the animal organism, its birth, life and death. Among the causes of these organic changes is instinct which determines the nature of animals' drive to preserve and improve life. All that animals do, all that happens to them, follows natural laws and natural causes. The natural cause of the animals' drive to preserve life is what we call instinct. It is for this reason that the study of that drive is part of natural science.

However, change is not totally absent, not even in the natural world. It is only that we, human beings whose life span is short and who can only perceive (even when we look back) only a brief segment of the life of the universe, see many things as immutable though in reality they are not. This is because change is too slow and we do not perceive it. When we observe the hour hand of a watch we do not notice its movement. But if we extend it a distance of twenty kilometers we would soon be out of breath if we attempted to walk fast enough to keep up with its tip. The point is that what we observe in nature and what we admire as ingenious arrangements (e.g., the order and handiwork of the bees in the beehive) has not existed from time immemorial but has evolved over a very long period of time, as has all creation in its enormous variety and multiformity. We do not know the cause of evolution. However when we perceive it not as mere change but as development toward something better and more perfect it necessarily appears as purposive, intended, wanted by someone. This lies outside the framework of the objective of our inquiry. However when evolution is perceived as a purposive and intended process it becomes creation. As such it necessarily assumes someone, an agent, to whom we must logically attribute purposiveness, whether we refer to its Nature, God, or something else. Fish have air bladders which enable them to swim, wild game grows winter coats, the bones of birds are hallow making them very sturdy and at the same time making flight easy because they are light. Blades of grass have hallow, segmented stems which are sturdy and do not break in the wind, etc. But fish did not create their air bladders, nor did wild game its winter coat. In fact fish and game are not even aware that this equipment facilitates their life. Nor are all men aware that their two eyes provide a stereoscopic view, nor do we as yet quite understand the interrelated functioning of our glands. By the same token, bees are not aware how expedient is the arrangement of the beehive, that the hexagon represents the best utilization of space (unlike the square which has unused corners, while other configurations do not fit into each other). Only exceptionally, on a higher level of development, can we attribute to the animal itself the development of a useful instrument (e.g., primates use strong branches as sticks for support as well as to fight).

In contrast with all this stands the creative activity of man that can be attributed to him, as his intended, purposeful work guided by his thought (intellect) and his will. It has attained a marvelous level of development and is being constantly improved and perfected in all respects. In his creative activity man is also bound by the order that rules all nature and which he perceives as natural law. He cannot violate it but he came make use of it, in acting upon external nature, to affect it in accordance with his purposes. If he wants to engage in cattle husbandry he must respect the animals' nature. He cannot feed them meat, just as he cannot feed grass to dogs or cats. But he can use the animals' strength, its fertility, its milk, its body (meat, bones, etc.). He may use hybridization to develop breeds better suited to his purposes (e.g., milk yields). If he wishes to grow trees he must take into account that soil, sun, and air are the determinants of tree life. But he may improve the soil so that trees will do well, he can improve the quality of fruit by pruning or hybridization, etc. He cannot change physical forces, but he can chain them in a motor or engine, so that they may better serve his purposes. He cannot avoid the aging and death of his own organism, but–having explored the natural laws by which his organism is governed–he can act to bring about improvement, healing, etc. In creating new species himself, man even appears to be "replacing" the Creator who has brought forth on earth various species of plants and animals. But man merely employs nature's creative powers, guiding them in the face of particular conditions and forcing the species to live and be active under those conditions. There are therefore limits and conditions to man's creative activity which he must take into account. Nevertheless his activity is creative activity. It purposefully transforms and molds nature (including himself as part of nature) into something different than it would be without his intellect and will. It brings about constant improvement and greater perfection which must be attributed to his intellect and his will.

Man does all this to preserve and improve his life. His striving to preserve and improve his life is therefore different from the instinctive and unchanging drive of other animals. It cannot be explained in terms of an immutable natural order, and its study is not natural science (as is the study of bees, ants or other animals). The special nature of man's creative activity and his striving to preserve and improve life–as distinct from the analogous drive of other animals–is due to his intellect. His intellect may only be a gradation, a higher degree of the intellect with which other animals are also endowed (in smaller measure). But the difference is enormous. The reason why other species, even those closest to man and who have lived on earth for as long as he has, have lagged so far behind, and what exactly is the role of speech (which man alone possesses) in his intellect, is also outside the framework of our inquiry. We take it as given that human intellect differs so much from the intellect of other animals as man's striving to preserve life differs from the analogous drive of other animals.

PART ONE

GENERAL

A. BASIC CONCEPTS OF PURPOSIVE THINKING

A. How the Practically Acting Individual Views the World

Practically acting men think purposively. How do they view the world (external phenomena: minerals, trees, animals, etc.)? They view them in a different way than the natural scientist. The natural scientist wishes to explore phenomena as they are, as they exist. He observes a tree spring up from seed, form roots, trunk and crown, blossom, bear fruit, reproduce, grow, and die. That is how he views everything. As far as he is concerned there is nothing either good or bad, useful or harmful. But the practically acting man, sees the world in a different light, in accordance with what he finds useful. He sees some things as pleasant, agreeable, welcome, beautiful. He desires them and acquires them. He finds other things unpleasant, repulsive, ugly. He does not want them and gets rid of them. And so he views everything as either wanted or not wanted. He sees the tree as wanted by someone for its wood, blossoms, fruit, or shade. The tree, something that simply exists (a botanical entity) as far as the natural scientist is concerned, becomes at that point a good. Let us take off the glasses with which we saw the tree as wanted by someone. The good disappears and what is left is the tree as a botanical entity.

And so, if we wish to understand the practically acting man, we must join him in viewing everything as wanted or not wanted–with his eyes (his eye glasses) which are different from those with which nature is seen by the natural scientist. This gives rise to a special way of observation that is indispensable to understand purposive thinking. It is its postulate that we view everything as wanted by someone. That is how we observe the behaviour of the practical man. And now we also wish to understand it.

B. Method of Comprehension. Purpose and Means

When we wish to comprehend something that we have observed, we ask the question: Why? We wish to understand phenomena that we have observed. A child sees that it rains and asks its father: Why does it rain? If the father is a physicist who sees everything as natural scientist (i.e., as simply existing) his answer will be: It is the effect of the cooling of water vapour. The cooling which preceded and brought on the rain is the cause, and the rain is the effect of that cause. If the father is a pastor who views nature as wanted by the Creator, his answer will be: God wishes rain because he wishes that it should irrigate the fields and gardens. That is the purpose of rain and rain is the means to that purpose. The same phenomenon has been observed in two different ways: Once as simply existing; the second time as wanted by someone. To each of the two ways of observation corresponds a particular method of comprehension (and thus of interpretation) that is suited to it.

When we observe a phenomenon as simply existing (as the natural scientist does), we ask: Why does the phenomenon exist (or occur, e.g., why does it rain)? And the answer is: Because something (the cause) preceded it and brought it about (as necessary effect). In his mind the observer links one phenomenon with a second and the second with a third. He forms a chain in which each link is a cause and each subsequent one an effect. The same phenomenon is an effect relative to the previous one and a cause relative to the subsequent one. Because this approach to comprehension (the casual method) is necessarily associated with a particular method of observation (everything is seen as simply existing) we know that phenomena, seen simply as existing, can only be understood and explained causally, and vice versa, that causal explanation requires seeing phenomena as simply existing. We possess a great deal of knowledge of what exists. We classify such knowledge in our mind as chains of causal sequences, into classes that have common causes, etc. E.g., classification of animal species is based on the common origin of one or the other class. It is a causal classification. The principle of exposition and comprehension is the principle whereby the observer orders all his observations generated by a given method of observation.

When we regard phenomena, objects and actions as wanted (by someone) and when we wish to understand them, we ask: Why are they wanted? And the answer is: Because something else is wanted as purpose. Therefore we thus explain one wanted thing–the means–by another wanted thing–the purpose. We want grain because we want flour. Both ends and means are "postulates," something that is wanted. A postulate that is an end (we want flour) in relation to another postulate that is a means (we want grain), may in turn be the means in relation to another postulate (we want flour because we want bread). Here too there is consistency (functional, as between the circle and its diameter) between the method of observation (we view everything as wanted) and the method of comprehension and exposition that is suited to it (we explain the wanted means by the wanted ends).

The relationship of cause and effect is called causality; the relationship of means and ends is called finality (finis–end, purpose; in Greek–telos). Hence is we view phenomena as wanted (by someone) we must comprehend and explain them in terms of finality; logically an explanation that uses the principle of finality necessarily requires that we order phenomena as ends and means, as wanted by someone.[1] We possess much knowledge about what is wanted and we order it in our mind by arranging and grouping it according to the principle of finality. One thing is a means (a spoon) another is a purpose (eating); several objects serve the same purpose (a set of silverware, writing utensils, the equipment of an enterprise). It is a teleological or finality system.

There is one more "Why." Thus far we have associated the question Why? with observed phenomena which we explained and related to each other, and we arrived at two kinds of relationship, causality and finality. However, the question Why? may also be asked with respect to a conclusion that we wish to have explained logically (not factually). For example, consider the statement that the mass of a room will be maximized if objects are brought into the room according to their specific mass, with those that have the largest specific mass being brought in first. Now let us ask, "Why?" What is it that we wish to comprehend by asking the question? The logical correctness (validity) of this statement! Because we answer the question by analysing the statement. Specific mass is the relationship of mass to space, and when the objects that are

---

[1]   The German philosopher Wundt (and following him, many others) is therefore in error when he states that finality is reversed causality, explaining the matter by the example of the heart and the circulation of blood: Why does blood circulate, asks Wundt, and his answer is: Because the heart beats. He then reverses the question: Why does the heart beat? And he alleges: So that blood may circulate! But that is not so. It is because something occurs in the muscles and nerves which causes the heart to beat. To obtain the answer, "so that blood may circulate" (that is, a purpose) we must change our method of observation and ask: Why is the beating of the heart wanted (by someone)? Only then do we get the anwer: Because what is wanted is the circulation of blood, or–which is the same thing–so that blood may circulate.

brought in are ranked according to specific mass, this implies the best utilisation of space as far as maximizing the mass of the room is concerned. Now we understand the correctness (validity) of the statement which we asked to have explained. Here we do not relate phenomena but statements; we do not learn about the truth concerning phenomena but about the correctness of statements. The answer to this kind of Why? is called a logical reason (for the validity of the statement). Mathematics and geometry are filled with such logical conclusions. Causes and purposes are frequently confused with logical reasons. For example, in statements such as: The reason why it rains is the condensation of water vapour, or: The reason why grain is milled is to obtain flour. This is logically incorrect.

It is therefore proper to distinguish the three kinds of Why? and the three kinds of answers. Either we explain the correctness of conclusions by other conclusions, by logical reasons, or we explain the truth of phenomena and the relationships between them. In the latter case we either explain an existing phenomenon by another phenomenon that gave rise to it (as a consequence) and we thus arrive at the cause (relationship of causality) or we explain a thing that is wanted (the means) in terms of another thing that is wanted and which the means tends to bring about, the purpose (relationship of finality). The practical man acts purposively, and we therefore comprehend his actions in terms of the relationship of finality (teleologically).[2]

C. Other Correlative Concepts of Purpose Thinking

I. Needs

We have learned the first two concepts of purposive thinking: Means and purpose. They are correlative concepts, like

---

[2]   Here I omit normological reasoning used in explaining the validity of norms, e.g., legislative norms.

father and son. There is no purpose without a means, there is no means without a purpose (there is no father without a child). Between these two focal points of teleological thinking cluster a number of other correlative concepts. If we consider a means from the viewpoint of a purpose we note that it is expressed by the concept of need. A need is a want (postulate) of something as means to attain a purpose. When we say that we need something, it is logically necessary to add, for what purpose. If one cannot say why he wants a thing, he cannot say that he needs it. Thus one can say that he wants to be happy but he cannot say that he needs to be happy because he cannot state any further purpose of his happiness. Such postulate may be an end, but it cannot be a means, because there is no other, higher end for which it could serve as a means: It is a final, original purpose.

The content of the purpose (what we desire as an end) imparts the character of the needs. If the desired end is culture then the needs are cultural; if the desired end is defence, then the needs are defence needs; if the desired end is health, then the needs are health needs.

Sometimes the agent projects his own (active) need to the object and to the means. He may say, e.g., that the cattle need fattening. Does the cattle have a need to be fattened? No. It is the farmer who wants the fattening so that he may get more money for the cattle. The active need of the agent is projected to the means and one could speak in this case of the passive need of the cattle. This is the usual case, especially when a person is the object of someone else's care. A father may state: The child needs books more than toys (though the child is of the opposite opinion). The father who desires the ideal of an educated child as an end, wants the book for the child as a means. It is the father's active need which explains the way he brings up the child, his actions, and which the father projects to the object of his care. We could say that the child is in need of the book, that it has a passive need of the book. The state declares: Goods are to be distributed according to the citizen's needs. Does that mean, according to the citizen's wishes? No. It means according to what the state decides are their needs from the viewpoint of ideal toward which it desires to lead the citizens. The passive need of the object of care is the active need of the agent who exercises care.

2. Utility, usefulness, disutility, harmfulness

Another view of the means and ends is provided by the concept of utility and usefulness. The means is capable of realizing the end in part or in whole (bring about health, defence, culture); realization of the end is utility. The means is useful (it possesses the characteristic of being useful) because it is capable of bringing about utility.

It is not actually the objects that are means, but the actions of using them as means. The means to restore health is not medication but taking medication. The means to achieve culture are not books but reading books. The means to defence are not rifles but using them to shoot. It is only for short that we refer to an object directly as the means and we shall do so as well. A useful object is a good; it is thus an object wanted by someone as means to an end.

The character of utility is also derived from the content of the objective; from culture as an objective follows cultural utility etc.; a good that yields cultural utility is culturally useful. From the point of view of culture we attribute usefulness to a book. We describe the book as useful. Usefulness is a characteristic that we attribute to an object when we think purposively, i.e., when we consider the purpose that it may serve. Without purpose there is neither usefulness nor harmfulness [skodlivost]. Suppose we see a mushroom in the forest; is it useful? We must immediately consider whether it could be wanted by someone for some purpose. In nature nothing is of itself useful. Only man regards plants, animals, minerals as useful from the viewpoint of his purpose.

However certain actions and objects not only are not useful (not suitable for the purpose), but actually capable to displace the attainment of the end, to diminish health, culture, or

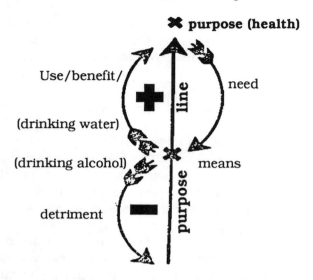

defence, to act in the opposite sense, against the purpose, to bring about the opposite of the purpose, a diminution of the purpose, a loss. That is why they are harmful. The purpose classifies things and actions not only as useful but also harmful. Something can be useful from the viewpoint of a particular end (smoking from the point of view of pleasure as an end) but the same thing may be harmful from the viewpoint of another end (smoking is bad for health). It is therefore a good from the viewpoint of one end, but from the viewpoint of another. We may visualize the matter graphically (see above).

Usefulness and harmfulness are thus positive and negative characteristics that correspond to positive change (utility) and negative change (disutility) along the "purpose line." Teleological characteristics are polarised (they correspond to opposite poles) because they express the relationship to that which men desire. Objects and actions are either suited to it or else opposed to it (they can of course be also different). Qualities that are found in nature cannot be polarised: hardness and softness, heat and cold express merely different degrees of the same quality, not a plus or minus.

3. About goods in particular

A good is a useful object. It is useful because it is wanted for some purpose. Water is useful because it is used for drinking, for water transport, to drive mill wheels, etc. The nature of a good depends on the purpose which it serves. A table is a table in relation to the purpose of being furniture and being used as furniture. When there is a fuel shortage it can be chopped up and used as fuel; it becomes a fuel and serves a different purpose than before. Grain too may serve as milling material or seed, etc. It depends on how one sees an object with regard to its usefulness and its purpose. The nature of a good thus derives from the content of the purpose which it serves, and if this purpose changes then the nature of the good changes as well.

In order that a good may serve a particular purpose it must possess certain natural qualities that we call–in relation to a given purpose–the usefulness of the good. Usefulness of a good is therefore the set of its qualities from the viewpoint of a particular purpose, and does not include all the qualities which the good possesses. The object "table" possesses various qualities but when we refer to the good "table" we do not consider all of them but only those that make it suitable as furniture. I.e., we do not consider its combustibility which transforms the same object into another good, namely fuel. The same object is thus a different good relative to different kinds of usefulness. A good expresses a certain usefulness whose carrier is the object. It arises, stands and falls with that usefulness.

The usefulness of a good is a technical characteristic and describes its ability to serve some special (technical) end; it is based primarily on its natural characteristics, its material and its spatial form. The usefulness of wood is determined by the natural characteristics of the material; the usefulness of a table is also determined also by the characteristic of spatial form. Usefulness based on the inherent characteristics of an object is direct usefulness. However, when goods are generally tradeable we consider not only their direct useableness (derived from their natural qualities) but also the usefulness of goods belonging to others that we can obtain for our goods through exchange. The usefulness of goods belonging to others and obtained through exchange is called indirect usefulness. A ring can be viewed as a directly useful ornament, because of its material and its shape. Alternatively it can be viewed as possessing indirect usefulness, e.g., as the usefulness of meat that can be obtained for the ring. What we do with the ring depends on which usefulness is more important to us. We shall either wear it or trade it.

Indirect usefulness can be concrete and definite or it can be abstract and general. A train ticket is not directly useful in its material and its spatial form. Its usefulness, the train ride, is indirect, but it is concrete and definite–it cannot be used for any other purpose. On the other hand, the material and spatial form of money also has no direct usefulness. The usefulness of money is the usefulness of the goods that can be bought with it. But this usefulness is not specific, it is the usefulness of all kinds of goods that can be bought with money and that we need. Money is thus an indirect abstract good while a train ticket is an indirect concrete good.

Special classes of goods include those that wear out, those that are used up or consumed. The distinction consists of the fact that the former are useful because of the state in which they are (e.g., a suit of clothes) while the latter are useful because of their change. Wine, food, raw materials that are used up in production such as ores, iron, lumber, and fibre are goods that are consumed. A suit of clothes, a machine, an engine, or a building are goods that wear our.

What is meant by goods that are substitutable? No two grains of sand are completely identical. However, one may require for one's purpose that an object should possess certain qualities, and all objects are suitable if they possess these qualities regardless of whether they also possess other qualities that are different. When we need something to write with we may be indifferent whether it is a pencil, an ordinary pen or a fountain pen. For the moment these goods are substitutable.

Other goods too may then be substitutable. For example, wheat at a commodity exchange[3] is a substitutable good because shades of quality are irrelevant; what matters is only that it is wheat and that it is of certain purity and weight. Securities, money, and commodities are therefore certainly substitutable goods for the purposes of commerce.

People do not always associate their image of a given usefulness with a give physical object. They refer for example to health, education, etc. as assets. Quite analogously they consider certain rights, such as the names of firms, e.g., the Skoda Works,[4] etc., to be an asset (goodwill) that assures profitable operation. An established firm inspires confidence among its customers who know the enterprise as a solid, honest and tried firm. The firm (goodwill) may therefore be bought and sold. What is involved here are certain facts of social contact, organisational facts that are associated with a certain name or symbol (firm, logo) considered to be a useful asset. Assets of this type will be called organizational assets. As opposed to physical goods they are also called nontangible assets.

4. Return, cost

At times attaining a useful end (acquisition or use of an asset) is inseparably connected with incurring a loss. In such a case one undertakes what is simultaneously useful and harmful only when the useful outcome outweighs the loss. For example a field commander may improve a defensive position by occupying a height, but this involves a cost (loss) of men. In that case the loss is called a cost and the quantity by which the

---

[3]   Wheat bought and sold–though not physically present–in a commodity exchange (bourse–a central market).

[4]   Translator's Note: The Skoda Company of Czechoslovakia has been a major producer of heavy machinery, automobiles, and weapons since before the First World War. It was national-ised after the Second World War.

useful outcome outweighs the loss is called a return. A loss is a cost when it is incurred because it is inseparably connected with an activity that leads to a primarily useful outcome. Cost exists only in relation to possible return, and return only exists in relation to cost.

Once again, these are correlative concepts. We must not forget that cost always means loss, i.e., diminution of the desired end, a real decrease, a worsening of the status quo. Cost is therefore a function of purpose, as is loss. If the objective is health then loss is diminution of health and cost is therefore also diminution of health. When toxic medication is used the cost is the impairment of health that results, but the impairment is incurred to gain the improvement of health which is even greater and the excess of the latter over the loss (the return). What is cost depends on the objective. To health objectives correspond health returns and health costs, and to monetary objectives (making money) correspond money returns and a money costs.

5. *Purposive valuation*

Seen from the viewpoint of the objective, objects and actions are classified as useful or harmful. Usefulness and harmfulness are purposive (teleological) qualities of things (goods) and actions. Different means (actions and things) may possess different degrees of usefulness from the viewpoint of an objective, because they are capable of realising that objective to a greater or smaller degree. Attributing to resources a certain degree (measure) of usefulness or harmfulness is valuation. When we refer to an object as useful from the viewpoint of an objective, we qualify it, i.e., we assign it some quality. When we say that it is more useful than another object or that it possesses such and such usefulness, we assign to it quality of a certain degree, we value it. Value is an expression of the degree of an attribute, a quality, in short it is the magnitude of quality.

This is so not only in purposive thinking. In natural science too there are qualities such as luminosity and calidity of a source, hardness, atomic weight, electric voltage, sensitivity of a photographic plate, etc. And there are values, based on assignment of numerical values, i.e., quantitative expressions, to these qualities. Of course, the qualities of natural science are different from those of teleology where (as we have seen on p. [16]) all qualities of things and actions arise from the relationship to the objective and therefore are polarised as positive and negative.

Because value in purposive thinking represents some of usefulness, all that we said about value applies also to usefulness, in particular that there is no usefulness, and hence no value, without an objective and that the nature of usefulness and of value is derived from the nature of the objective. Cultural usefulness and cultural value are derived from culture as an objective; health usefulness and health value are derived from health as an objective.

To the magnitude of usefulness (value) corresponds the intensity of need. It is proportionate to it. Just as need is a correlate (correlative concept) of usefulness and use, so is intensity of need a correlate of the degree of usefulness, value. We need more of what is more useful than what is less useful and vice versa.

Attributing certain usefulness to resources (objects or actions) means to estimate value. When an agent seeks a means to his end he obtains it because he attributes to it the capability to realise a greater or smaller measure of the objective (even though it may not actually possess that capability–e.g., ineffective medication). He thus attributes to it a certain usefulness, i.e., value for the objective in question. Estimation of value by the agent precedes the acquisition of the means. The connection between means and and exists in his mind, in his human intellect, in his estimation of value, not in some external natural circumstance or necessary consequence (as in the connection of cause and effect, such as the condensation of water vapour and rain). Man may believe that something is a means, and he may acquire it, possibly at higher cost, though it is not at all capable of bringing about his end.

However, this will be revealed, and there exists a certain store of knowledge about means that should be used to realise specific ends and for what particular means are suited. And so everyone knows that consuming milk promotes health whereas consuming alcohol is detrimental to health. Experience has taught us what means are required to bake bread, to weave fabric, to grow grain, to raise human beings who are healthy and cultured, etc. All this store of knowledge makes it therefore possible to make generally valid and therefore objective estimates of value (about suitable means, from the viewpoint of ends, and about possible ends from the viewpoint of means). Where a generally valid, i.e., objective estimate of value is possible, value too is objective.

However there exists ends where this is not, in principle, possible. They are ends whose content cannot be communicated by one individual to another, because it is not conceptually possible, ends such as, "I desire to see a beautiful painting" or "I wish to be happy." Another individual understands what I have in mind, because his own ends are analogous. However, he does not know the precise content of my objective and he is therefore unable to make a value estimate–whether I will find this or that painting more beautiful, or whether this or that thing will give me more pleasure. I alone, depending on my objective, am capable to make an estimate of value. And my value estimate, which is valid from the viewpoint of my objective (which cannot be communicated to other individuals) is not valid for anyone else. It is not generally valid, it is not objective, but subjective, and value derived from it is subjective value.

Telleological qualities are polarized (usefulness stands in opposition to harmfulness). Usefulness is positive and harmfulness is negative (cf. p. [16]). If teleological value is a measure of teleological quality, we may also speak of negative value (as measure of harmfulness).

D. Maximum and Optimum Objectives*

Maximisation is not necessarily included in the concept of purpose since we can conceive of purposes that do not involve maximisation. (E.g., many objects will do as weight to keep paper from being blown away by wind.) Maximisation concerns the content of the objective, of that which is wanted. We want a large harvest, the most culture, a maximum of defence, etc. Maximisation may be absolute (the largest harvest), i.e., without regard to something else, or relative, with regard to something else (a maximum crop per hectare).

Maximisation may be simple when the content of the objective is simple (e.g., placing the most weight in a room) or complex when the content of the objective is complex (e.g., achieving simultaneously the largest bearing capacity of a bridge and the smallest cost of construction). The two are mutually related (to each bearing capacity corresponds a different cost–given the material and construction cost required by a given bearing capacity). If it were not so, there would be two objectives (e.g., maximum bearing capacity and maximum width: Different widths can be associated with each bearing capacity). From complex objectives follows the relationship between their constituents (to each degree of bearing capacity corresponds a given construction cost).

If all constituents of the maximum of a complex objective are to be satisfied, one must seek the optimum relationship among them (e.g., such design of a bridge that will yield a maximum bearing capacity per unit of cost, or–which is the same thing–such that a unity of bearing capacity is constructed at a minimum cost). In case of complex objectives we speak therefore of optimisation of the objective. Optimisation is merely a special case of maximisation. Just as we speak of maximising an

---

* The Latin *maximus* means largest, *optimus* means best. To maximise an objective means that one desires to have as much as possible of something, e.g., wealth.

objective, we could speak negatively of miniminising an objective. There is no point to speak of minimising unculture rather than maximising culture, but it does make sense to speak of minimising the costs of culture.

Maximisation of objectives makes possible classification of means according to the degree of their usefulness or the cost of acquiring them. If we require an object as a weight to keep paper from being blown away, we are indifferent whether it is of a particular shape, colour, material, weight, etc., as long as it is sufficient for protection against wind. However, to maximise the weight placed in a particular space one must choose objects of greater specific weight over those of a smaller one. The former are more useful for the purpose. The objective of maximising culture leads to classification of various cultural means in accordance with their cultural usefulness and value. The same applies to maximisation of defence, of personal satisfaction (a subjective end), etc. Maximisation of an objective also leads to classification of means for that objective according to the level of their cost–if the acquisition of useful means involves different costs. Maximisation of an objective makes possible choosing different means, using and acquiring means in accordance with positive value (usefulness) and negative value (cost).

E. Purpose as Motivating Force of Purposive Activity

The concept of purpose implies that is attainment is desired, that it is wanted. Means (assets) must first be acquired (if one does not possess them) which implies cost (diminution of attainment of the purpose). The means can then be used which implies utility. Purposes therefore give rise to activities which are of two kinds: Acquisition of means and use of means. At the center of this activity are means which are acquired (sought, produced, etc.) and then used.

B. THE PRINCIPLE OF ECONOMISING

A. General Statement of the Principle of Economising

When an individual who strives to maximising an objective (such as satisfaction) tries to maximise utility (pleasure) by using means (e.g., money), while trying to minimise the cost (disutility) of obtaining the means (again, money), he actually tries to gain maximum utility (pleasure) at minimum cost (disutility). He thus tries to maximise the difference between utility and cost, i.e., to maximise his return. His effort is known as the principle of economising. It follows from striving to achieve a maximum of an objective.

The principle is applicable to any objective. Consider the objective of making money. Increments of money are revenues, and decrements are costs. Resources include labour, machinery, or other assests of an establishment operated to make money, a business enterprise. If the objective is to maximise profit, then the principle of economising states: Maximise revenue (by using resources) while minimising money costs (in obtaining resources), i.e., maximise the difference between revenue and cost, to maximise money return.

Acquisition of resources may be separated from their use and the principle of economising is then divided. The household of an individual retired on a fixed pension only maximises utility while using resources (money, pension). Here the principle of economising involves only the effort to maximise utility with given means. There is no cost.

It is therefore better to make the general statement that the principle of economising expresses striving to maximise utility (using resources) and striving to minimise the cost of obtaining resources. (Only when the two are united can we speak of the difference between utility and cost and about returns.)

Sometimes it is erroneously stated (even by learned men) that the principle of economising means to maximise utility and to minimise the use of resources ((utility is opposed to resources rather than costs). It is then argued that available resources should be used to maximise utility (e.g., that a pension should be used to buy the most useful items for the household), or that a certain utility should be obtained with a minimum or resources (e.g., that households should buy goods as cheaply as possible). Both statements express the same idea–maximisation of utility with given resources–seen from two perspectives. Starting from a given utility, one tries to minimise the use of resources; starting from given resources, one tries to maximise utility. But that is still only one aspect of the principle of economising, the utility aspect, striving to maximise utility by using resources, but the cost aspect is ignored. Such formulation therefore does not fully cover the principle of economising. Complete formulation of the principle includes maximisation of utility and administration of cost. What is utility and what is cost depends on the content of the objective (it may be pleasure and pain when the objective is satisfaction, it may be increment and decrement of money when the objective is to make money, etc.).

B. The Principle of Relative Utility and Relative Cost

We need a more specific rule concerning, maximisation of utility with given resources and, minimisation of cost in obtaining such resources. We consider first utility maximisation using available resources. If there is only one good (e.g., a unity of money, a kilogram of flour, an egg), it is an easy task. One simply uses it for such purpose–of all possible purposes–that yields the most utility. When each use (of all possible ones) always involves only one unit (an equal amount) of a good, it continues to be a simple matter: As with the first unit used for a purpose that yields the most utility, one proceeds with every subsequent unit of goods and uses.

The matter becomes more complicated when different uses involve unequal quantities of resources. Comparison of utilities becomes more difficult because different utilities derived from different uses are associated with unequal quantities of resources. It is as if one were to decide which was more expensive, rye or barley, when a bundle of barley (weighing 500 kg) costs 600 crowns and a bundle of rye (weighing 700 kg) costs 700 crowns. The bundle of barley costs less than the bundle of rye (disregarding their weights). Does it mean that barley is cheaper than rye? To answer this question we must relate the price of a bundle to the weight of the grain in the bundle, and we see that 100 kg of barley costs 120 crowns and 100 kg of rye costs 100 crowns, i.e., that barley is more expensive than rye. The prices of barley and rye are relative prices, relative to quantities. This is analogous to saying that a table is heavier than a pair of scissors. However, relatively–when weight is related to space, or (which is the same) when space is excluded from consideration–the scissors are heavier than the table. Relative weight (relative to space) is known as specific weight. An individual who seeks to purchase the least expensive grain (who wants the most grain for his money) must therefore enquire what the price is relative to quantity (100 kg, 1 hl, etc.) or (which is the same) what quantity can be purchased with a unit of money. If one's objective is to place a maximum weight in a given space one will not place there objects with the largest absolute weight but those with the largest specific weight (weight relative to space). Only then will the use of available space be optimal.

And there is also the way it is when an individual seeks to maximise utility with available resources, e.g., when he wants to obtain the most utility by buying goods for the household, and when different goods yielding different utilities sell at different prices. Suppose that an individual could choose whatever he liked in the market but that the total cold not weight more than 100 kg. What would he choose? Not the goods that are most useful without other consideration, i.e., in accordance with absolute utility, but goods that yield the most utility relative to weight, i.e., in accordance with relative utility of a unit of weight (goods yielding the most utility and weighing the least). If another time his total was constrained by space, say a cubic meter, his choice would be guided by the relative utility per unit of space. E.g., when food could be sent to soldiers during the First World War in packages weighing no more than 5kg, everyone tried to include within that limit a maximum of nutrients by sending chocolate and Hungarian salami, etc., rather than potatoes. And that is also how it is when money is used to make purchases, i.e., when choice is constrained by the fact that the total amount of purchases cannot exceed a certain of sum of money (income) available each month or each year. Each good has weight, volume, and price.

Depending on how an individual's choice is constrained he chooses that which yields the most utility according to weight, volume or price. Utility is maximised, when available resources are used according to the relative utility of the resource unit.

Resources are at the centre of the purposive sequence. One aspect is the acquisition of resources, the other their use. When resources are used utility si sought and maximum utility is attained by progressing in accordance with the relative utility of the resource unit. When resources are acquired there is a completely analogous consideration that concerns the associated costs. There are to be minimised. Once again there is a difficulty when obtaining resources involves bundles of resources with different total costs. And once again one proceeds quite analogously: Resources are obtained at minimum cost when acquisition choices are made in accordance with relative costs of the resource unit. When we make money we are concerned with using relatively less effort to do so.

The principle of economising which follows from maximisation of an objective therefore implies maximisation of utility and minimisation of cost and this can also be stated as follows: That maximisation (optimisation) of an objective leads to choices based on relative utilities and relative costs of the resources unit.

C. The Boundary of Rationality Resource Constraint

When all uses of a resources are ordered sequentially, then every subsequent use yields per resource unit (e.g., per unit of money) a relative utility that is lower than that obtained from the previously employed unit. This results in a curve of relative utility which slopes downward as more resource units are employed. It can be pictured, in simplified form, as follows:

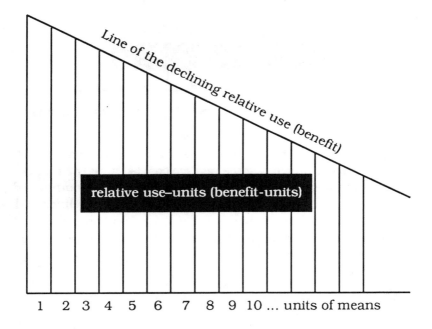

On the other hand acquisition of resources leads to an analogous sequence of upward sloping relative costs. It can be pictured, in simplified form, as follows:

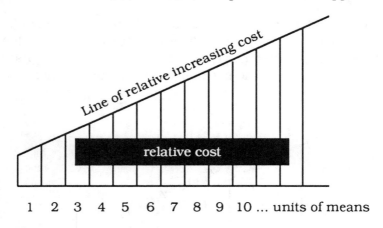

1 2 3 4 5 6 7 8 9 10 ... units of means

Each resource unit employed is therefore associated with some relative utility and some relative cost. At first the relative utility greatly exceeds the relative cost, but as the number of resource units employed increases, relative utility declines and relative cost rises. When we include both costs and utilities in the same graph we note that the curves get closer to each other until they intersect:

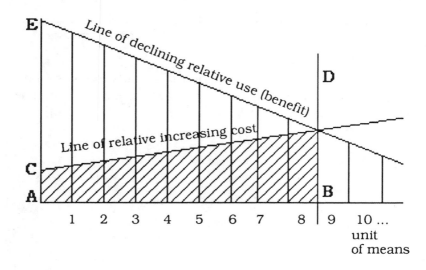

The shaded area ABCD shows by how much the utility that results from the resources acquired is diminished by the cost of acquiring them, so that what is left of total utility (area ABDE) is return shown as the difference between total utility and total cost (area CDE). The graph also shows clearly the intersection at point D of the downward sloping curve of relative utility and that the upward sloping curve of relative cost, and also that at that point relative utility, which prior to that exceed relative cost is the same as relative cost. If another resource unit was acquired it would result in a larger increment of cost than of utility. Therefore this would not be reasonable, rational. It follows that point D, where the downward sloping curve of relative utility intersects the upward sloping curve of relative cost, i.e., where relative utility and relative cost are the same, is the boundary of rationality in obtaining and employing resources. Relative utility and relative cost are marginal at that point. They are equal to each other.

It follows from the fact that further acquisition and employment of resources at this boundary ceases, that employment of resources is limited; it does not pay to acquire more resources. We shall refer to this limit as relative limit to be distinguished from the limit that results not from purposive considerations but from physical impossibility (unique goods, genuine antiques, etc.). The latter will be referred to as absolute limit. Absolute limit is of interest in purposive thinking only to the extent that it is encountered before the boundary of rationality. If it exists beyond that boundary if is of no interest because the purposive progression does not reach it and stops before reaching it.[5]

---

[5]   The graph shows that relative utility is at a maximum when relative cost is at a minimum, and that relative utility is at a minimum when relative cost is at a maximum (at the margin). It also shows that the purposive progression ceases because minimum relative utility occurs at maximum relative cost. If we turned the thing around and devoted the resource unit obtained at the curve of declining relative cost under the

D. Complex Purposive Sets. Balanced Satisfaction of Wants

1. The nature of a complex purposive set

Maximisation (optimisation) of some objective, such as personal satisfaction, calls for (requires) different means–food, clothing, housing.etc. Each becomes in turn a lower level objective (subordinate to the central objective which is being maximised) and which requires means to be realised (preparation of food, production of clothing, etc.). And so arises a complex purposive set. Subordinate objectives are also commonly known as needs, because their realisation is needed from the viewpoint of the central objective. An individual needs food, housing, etc, for his satisfaction.

Let us suppose now that there is one resource which can be used to obtain all other needs of the purposive set. Such means is e.g., labour and, at an advanced level of development, money. Individuals can use money to obtain all the various needs (subordinate objectives) and the acquisition of the various needs involves different uses of money. Every expenditure of money, acquisition of every need (food, clothing, etc.), brings utility. Individuals evaluate subjectively how much utility they obtain by spending money on food, on housing, on clothing and other needs.

---

curve of declining relative utility, it could turn out that at point D there would be an incentive to continue to acquire and employ resources because at that point the utility (of unit 7) would still be larger than the cost (of unit 1 in the graph). Why do we not do so? Because total return obtained by such progression would be less than by progressing in the way just indicated which results in maximum return. More resource units would yield a smaller total return than would fewer units.

2. Declining utility

One can proceed to different lengths to satisfy various wants: To buy more food or less food, simple food or expensive food, more clothes or fewer clothes, simple clothes or expensive clothes, etc. Let us imagine, for simplicity, that a specific good corresponds to each want, that satisfaction of wants increases as more goods are used, and that satisfaction is restricted by cessation of purchasing. Experience teaches that buying more and more of a good to satisfy a particular want results in smaller increments of utility. To get some bread is extremely desirable; however, beyond a certain point, an individual would not eat bread, even if it was free. A naked person would pay a very high price for a suit of clothes but a tenth or twentieth suit would yield to him smaller increments of utility. To be deprived of one's twentieth suit would be less painful than to be deprived of one's only suit. The incremental utility of every good is therefore declining relative to the degree of satisfaction of the corresponding want. Incremental utility may decline faster beyond a certain level of satisfaction, e.g., in the case of bread, or more slowly, e.g., in the case of housing. One can always desire a larger and better house. (Another question is whether one can afford it.)

This can be represented graphically for goods A and B and the corresponding wants:

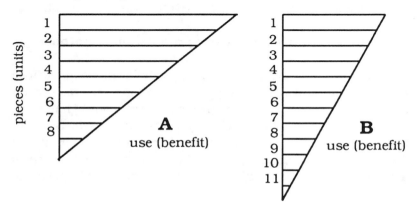

Units of each good used are shown vertically, and increments of utility of the first, second, etc., unit of good A and good
B are shown horizontally. The incremental utility of the first
unit of A is greater than that of the first unit of B but declines
more rapidly with subsequent units than the incremental
utility of B. To become fully satisfied the individual needs only
8 units of A and he is not interested in having more than that.
In the case of B he desires more, up to 14 units. The question
is: How will individuals use their limited resources (labour,
money) to satisfy different wants; how far will they proceed in
satisfying each want.

3. Competition among wants

Everyone knows from experience that an individual with a
certain monthly income is unlikely to spend it all on food
without paying attention to clothing, housing, heating, light,
etc. Thus when he takes care of one want, he must keep in mind
all other wants an satisfy each while paying attention to all the
others. He knows that if he is to provide for other wants he
cannot spend on one as much as he could if he had no others.
No individual has sufficient resources to fully satisfy all his
(unlimited) wants. It is therefore clear that in satisfying wants
with the resources available to him–labour, money–each want
must compete with ever other so that all might be satisfied in
some measure (which we seek) given by the resource constraint.

4. Marginal utilities and their proportionate balancing

Suppose that an individual buys different goods whose
units are units of weight, kilograms. Suppose also that each
good has a price per kilogram, and that the individual has some
amount of money with which he makes purchases. Because
utility obtained by buying additional kilograms is different and
declining, relative utility obtained (utility in relation to price) is
also different. The price of a kilogram of each good is the same

but the utility of each additional kilogram is declining. Therefore the relative utility added is also declining.

Graphically:

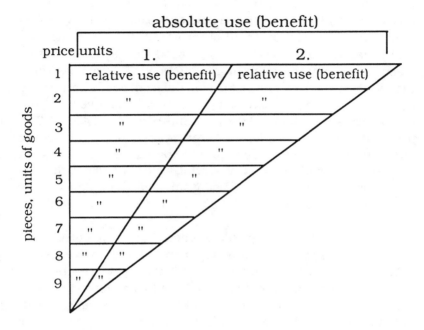

The diminishing utility bands of additional units of the good
represent their absolute utility. They are intersected by a line
that corresponds to the fact that each unit costs two units of
money. This divides the utility of the first, second, etc. unit of
the good into two parts. Each shows how much utility is
obtained per unit of money when one buys the first, second, etc.
unit, i.e., the relative utility of the first, second, etc. unit of the
good.

In this way we could show for ever good a series of units
(kilograms) exhibiting diminishing relative utility. It could
happen that the relative utility of the fifth unit of the first good,
whose utility declines more rapidly (see p. 12), would be smaller
than the relative utility of the sixth unit of a second good, the

tenth unit of a third good, etc. We know however that to maximise utility an individual chooses to buy units of goods according to their relative utility per unit of money. Therefore he would not buy more of the first good if he could obtain more relative utility by buying the second or third good. This applies to ever good in relation to all other goods. It follows that the individual will continue to buy each good as long as there is no incentive for him to switch to another good. This occurs when the relative utilities of the last unit of different goods bought are equal. This is the principle of equalisation of relative marginal utilities (relative utilities of the last units of different goods). The principle demonstrates how different wants within the set are interconnected and interdependent in being satisfied. We shall refer to this relationship of material solidarity. The principle also shows that all wants are being satisfied in a balanced way expressed by relative utility. We also show this graphically (p. 00).

This is true for every purposive set. E.g., if the objective of a secondary school is to maximise general education (consisting of 15 subjects) within a constraint of 30 hours of instruction per week it does not mean that two hours of instruction should be devoted to each subject. One cannot proceed to the smallest unimportant detail in one subject at the expense of another subject where even important matters would have to be neglected. One cannot proceed to provide more instruction in one subject if it appears to be more important to devote instruction hours to another subject.

Instruction time devoted to different subjects will be determined so that the relative marginal utilities of instruction in different subjects per hour of instruction are equalised.

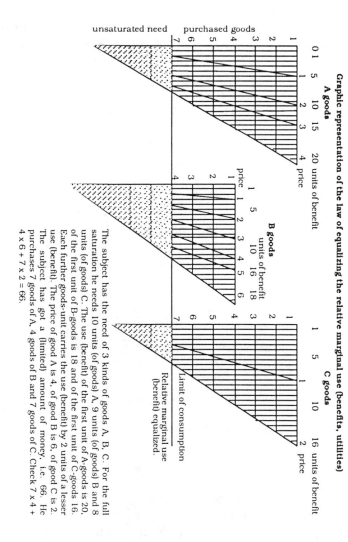

Graphic representation of the law of equalizing the relative marginal use (benefits, utilities)

The subject has the need of 3 kinds of goods A, B, C. For the full saturation he needs 10 units (of goods) A, 9 units (of goods) B and 8 units (of goods) C. The use (benefit) of the first unit of A-goods is 20, of the first unit of B-goods is 18 and of the first unit of C-goods 16. Each further goods-unit carries the use (benefit) by 2 units of a lesser use (benefit). The price of good A is 4, of good B is 6, of good C is 2. The subject has got a (limited) amount of money, i.e. 66. He purchases 7 goods of A, 4 goods of B and 7 goods of C. Check 7 x 4 + 4 x 6 + 7 x 2 = 66.

5. The relationship between prices and marginal utilities different goods

The same idea–equalisation of relative marginal utilities–may also be expressed in another way. Let there be goods

$$g_1 , g_2 , g_3 , \cdots g_n.$$

Let the marginal utilities of the last units bought by an individual be

$$u_1 , u_2 , u_3 , \cdots u_n$$

Let the prices per unit of these goods be

$$p_1 , p_2 , p_3 \cdots p_n$$

The relative marginal utilities of these different goods per price unit are therefore:

$$u_1/p_1, u_2/p_2, u_3/p_3 , \cdots u/p_n.$$

If relative marginal utilities are equalised, then it holds for the first pair and for every other pair that

$$u_1/p_1 = u_2/p_2$$

which can be also expressed as

$$u_1/u_2 = p_1/p_2$$

In words, marginal utilities are proportionate to prices and the relationship between marginal utilities of different goods corresponds to the relationship of their prices. An individual will therefore continue to buy different goods to satisfy different wants until the marginal utilities derived from satisfying different wants by buying different goods are proportionate to their prices. What was shown here for prices also holds for any other resource, e.g., labour, etc.

6. Complex purposive set must possess united ordering purposes

A complex purposive set in which several objectives (needs) compete for limited resources must have a common central purpose that stands above those ends. How else could one compare e.g., the food objective with the clothing objective? They have different contents. Therefore the utilities derived from them have different contents as well. They are magnitudes that differ in kind, noncomparable, nonadditive and nonsubtractive. Just as the contents of weight and luminescence represent different magnitudes, so do the utilities of culture and of defence. However, if an individual is to switch among objectives, when he buys goods for different purposes according to relative utilities, he must be able to compare utilities, to decide e.g., that it has become relatively more useful to buy clothing rather than food. He cannot compare the food objective and the housing objective because they have different contents and are incomparable. He must compare the utility common to all of them. But there is no usefulness and no utility without an objective. If the individual is to decide between using resources for different purposes according to relative utilities, there must be a higher objective, standing above all others, in relation to which the competing objectives become once again means valued from its viewpoint. Their realisation is valued from the viewpoint of the higher objective.

Such an objective is e.g., personal satisfaction, which is superior to subobjectives such as food, clothing, entertainment, etc. In accordance with such objective an individual decides how much of the given resources (money) he will devote to each subobjective. In doing so he compares the utility of different increments of satisfaction associated with satisfying different subobjectives. The individual resolves the conflict of interests and the competition of subobjectives for limited resources form the viewpoint of this superior objective. The complex purposive set must possess a common superior objective.

C. Economy, Form and Content

A. Concept of Economy

Man's (humanity's) care to preserve and improve life is purposive activity and it takes therefore place within purposive complexes. Each independent purposive complex within which occurs the care to preserve and improve human life, is an economic organisation. In general, economic organisations are not identical. They differ in various ways, in personal and material aspects.

In the personal respect they differ according to who they care for, whether for individuals, groups of individuals or entire nations. Men may live as isolated individuals, entire families may exercise care to preserve and improve life, and individuals or families may join to help each other in obtaining resources, such as particular goods and services, assistance to fire fighting, joint construction of roads, joint ownership of a threshing machine, joint money making enterprises, communal water works or communal hospitals. Entire nations may do so as well.

In its material aspect, an economic organisation may be restricted to a particular resource needed to preserve and improve life. Alternatively, it may exercise total care. The family (household) is concerned with total care (care for all needs); a municipality is concerned with only some resources and needs (roads, transport, water, gas, electricity, hospitals), business enterprises serve participating individuals only as far as making money is concerned. We may visualise it as if the territory inhabited by a nation was covered by scattered tents, some taller and wider, others smaller and narrower, tents of different colour and design. Each tent represents an economic organisation and persons who live in them exercise care to preserve life–either jointly or each on his own, either total care or only care for some resources and needs.

B. What We See When We Observe An Economic Organisation With Our Eyes

Let us take a look at an economic organisation. With our physical eyes we observe objects and persons, their movements and changes, their actions and transformations. This is how an economic organisation is seen by a natural scientist observing the workshop of a producing enterprise. A physicist would recognise the objects as levers, shafts, gears, steam engines, electric motors, telephones, light fixtures. He would note the energy outputs of men, draft animals, machines. He would note the chemical processes of fermentation, melting, decomposition of matter. Biologists and physiologists would note the growth of plants and animals, botanists and zoologists would observe the origins of new species of plants and animals, etc. Each would see something else. But even if all observed jointly with their eyes, they would not discern the interrelationship of all these things, whether it was just a random combination of persons, objects and activities, or whether there was some relationship, some order, some uniformity. They would see the technical content, but not the economic order. The latter cannot be seen with eyes alone.

C. The Purposive View Discloses the Economic Order (It includes a united agent and united purpose.)

To see and comprehend economic order we must take a different view. We must ask who directs the economic organisation, what ideas he has, and what objectives he pursues. If we establish, e.g., that the objective of an economic organisation is to produce sugar and to make money, etc., we begin to understand that no object and no activity is accidental, that they are arranged and ordered so as to realise the objective. The purpose determines the order of everything that comprises the organisation. We shall then understand that everything in the organisation is a means, that the purpose determines the need for various means, that they possess usefulness, that certain activities can be useful and harmful at the same time. (E.g., sugar beet is used up and disappears as sugar is made.) In short, we begin to understand that an economic organisation is a purposive complex, a purposive whole with a specific purposive order.

Every purposive complex (economic organisation) must have an agent whose will endows the organisation with a specific order and a specific purpose that determines that order. It must have a unified will and unified purpose. When several individuals associate in an economic organisation to jointly exercise, total or partial, care for their lives, they must agree that no one should act as he pleases: Either all should obey one (e.g., the head of a household) or else they should agree how to reach decisions, or they should let the majority to decide. When an economic organisation thus includes a number of individuals, but possesses a unifying will and order, we think of it and of the will as having a single agent. We give it a name (municipality, state, society, joint-stock company) and regard it as a single entity, though it consists of many physical persons. Every economic organisation has therefore a single agent, a single purpose, and a single purposive order.

D. Form and Content of Economic Organisations

Every economic organisation therefore represents a unified purposive order of means (objects and activities). We are familiar with the concepts and rules of purposive thinking and purposive order, proceeding according to relative utility in employing resources, according to relative cost in obtaining them, etc. Purposive order is therefore common to all economic organisations. They all proceed (from their viewpoint) according to the principle of economising, they have their needs, utilities, value, their boundaries of rationality, etc. Their purposive framework consists of interrelated purposive concepts (as its spine) and processes guided by the principle of economising (as its vital essence). The framework is therefore common to all economic organisations. It represents their common form. Of course, the content of that form is not always the same, and economic organisations differ from each other materially according to this content. The content is primarily the content of the purpose which rules the entire economic organisation and spreads throughout the pipeline of interrelated concepts. When the content of the organisation's purpose is personal satisfaction, an increase of satisfaction represents (subjective) utility, and a decrease (effort, pain) represents (subjective) cost. In accordance with these, the securing and employment of resources then proceeds up to the boundary of rationality. When the end is the ideal of human improvement, utility is represented by increments of life, health and culture and cost by their decrease. Resources are acquired and employed in accordance with the latter. All economic organisations have a common form (framework and structure of purpose) but they differ with respect to their contents, i.e., the contents of the purposes which rule them, and the utilities, costs, etc., that follows from them.

We must be thoroughly aware that the content of an economic organisation are not objects, goods, etc., but the content of the objectives that they serve, the content of their usefulness. With a different objective and a different usefulness, the same objects may turn into different goods. E.g., a book in the home may serve to entertain, in a public library to educate, and in a bookstore to make money. In one economic organisation it serves as means to make money, in another as means of entertainment or instruction. When we speak of the content of an economic organisation we have in mind money making and other contents of its objective and its utility.

Different ways of managing resources follow from different contents of objectives. When we organise a library for best appearance, we arrange books differently than when we wish to achieve easy access to books. A national government obtains revenues and makes expenditures differently than a small businessman, because it pursues different ends. Further study of economic organisations leads therefore to classifying the contents of objectives which these organisations strive to attain. There are no differences in form which is common to them all.

E. Complete and Partial Economic Organisations

A complete economic organisation is engaged in both the acquisition and the employment of resources. An illustration is the self-sufficient economic organisation of an individual who buys and sells nothing and acquires everything that he consumes by himself, in his economic organisation. But acquisition an employment of resources may be separated and this gives rise to partial economies. That is what happens when money is introduced. A craftsman makes money in his workshop (a partial, money making organisation, an enterprise) turns it over to his household (a partial, consuming organisation) to be used further (for consumption expenditures, not for making money). The economic organisation of a retired person who no longer works and collects a pension is only a consuming organisation, a household where money is used only for consumption purchases (he incurs no cost and spends money in accordance with relative utility).

D. MAN AS AGENT AND OBJECT OF CARE
Individualism–solidarism

A. Care to Preserve and Improve Life is a Complex Purposive Set

In exercising care to preserve and improve life man pursues many different ends, which compete for limited resources. Ends may be on the same level (health, education, entertainment) or else superordinate and subordinate (sowing grain–producing alcohol; milling flour–baking bread, feeding grain). Each in itself would lead to a different ordering of resources. If the objective were concerned only with food we would use money differently than when we also use it to buy housing, clothing, and other needs. If care to preserve and improve life includes all various possible human ends, and if it represents a unifying order rather than a random cluster, it must be ruled–as we already know–by a single common and paramount objective that makes it possible for us to understand that order.

B. The Individual as Agent Exercising Care for Himself

Here there is a fundamental difference between the individual as agent exercising care for himself and as object of care exercised by someone else. A man cares for himself–the father cares for a child. Accordingly there exists a duality, a polarity, of the paramount objectives of care. When exercising care for himself, acting as care-exercising agent, the individual orders everything according to his will, and in accordance with his personal satisfaction, as the ultimate objective of his actions and of his ordering of means. Here the end is subjective and from it are derived subjective needs, goods, utilities, costs, values, etc. Utility is then represented by increases of satisfaction (pleasure) and disutility by decreases of satisfaction (pain). No ultimate purposive explanation exists for the behaviour of two individuals, the first giving up food in order to see a play, and the second giving up food in order to get better clothes, other than that they choose to behave as they do, rather than behaving differently, that they conclude that their behaviour yields more subjective utility to them. If an individual is to exercise care for himself he must be free to acquire resources (i.e., to engage in productive activity), to use his resources (i.e., to consume), and he must have control of his resources. (Control of things is ownership.)

C. The Individual as Object of Someone Else's Care

When the individual is object of someone else's care (as a child is object of care by its parents) he can be endowed neither with control of goods nor with freedom to obtain resources or to use them (to produce, to consume). This is so because everything now happens, not in accordance with his wishes, but in accordance with the will of the agent who exercises care for him. It no longer happens in accordance with the objective of his personal (and subjective) satisfaction as governing purpose but according to what the care-exercising agent desires. The latter cannot pay attention to the satisfaction of the individual who is the object of his care. Otherwise he could only do what the latter desired. Instead he must pursue, as the purpose of his care, some improvement objective. He must be concerned with the physical, educational, and moral qualities, and their harmonious relationship, which he desires that the object of his care should attain, in other words, he must have an image of the ideal of a healthy, cultured, and moral individual. He will compel the object of his care, regardless of what the latter desires, to obtain an to use resources according to that ideal, which is objective (its content is communicable), and from which are derived objective needs, goods, utilities, disutilities, costs, and values.

Utility is represented here by improvement of life, health and culture, and disutility by their diminution. Accordingly resources are valued from the objective purposive focal point of the care-exercising agent, i.e., differently than from the focal point of subjective satisfaction of the object of care. A young person may derive satisfaction from smoking, while his father may view it as harmful. A father may decide that a book is more useful than a toy, even though subjectively the child values the toy more than the book. From this objective purposive viewpoint is derived a different order of acquiring and employing resources. Some goods that the object of care would prefer will not be available, others will be ranked higher than they would be in the subjective valuation of the object of care. The object of care cannot be endowed with economic freedom (freedom to consume and freedom to produce). His is subject to someone else's will and cannot control resources. It is the care-exercising agent who must control resources (ownership).

D. Two Distinct Orders Derive from This

No other possibility exists. The individual either exercises care for himself or someone else exercises care for him (he is either an agent of self-care or an object of someone else's care). In the first case the individual's central purpose is personal satisfaction which orders all his care to preserve and improve his life. In the second case it is the improvement ideal of a healthy and cultured man which rules and orders one individual's care for another. The first purpose is subjective, the second is objective. Different contents of utility, disutility, value, etc., correspond to each.

With different contents of the objective, resources are ordered differently. As a result, to each of the central purposes of care and of preserving and improving man's life (either his own or someone else's) correspond different orders.

When the individual exercises self-care, when he is the agent who exercises care for himself, he must be endowed with resource ownership. He must be free and unconstrained to acquire them (by producing) and to use them (by consuming). When he is the object of care, he cannot be economically free and unconstrained. He is subject to the will of someone else who exercises care for him, the will of the care-exercising agent. He cannot have control of resources. They are controlled by the care-exercising agent.

Both these purposes are primary, original. They cannot be subordinate to any other purpose. They are neither needs nor means because we cannot conceive of any higher purpose that they could serve. An individual may say that he wishes to be satisfied or happy but he cannot say that he needs to be satisfied because he cannot say for what purpose.

E. The Individualist Economic System

Let us now visualise an entire nation's care to preserve and improve life, organised systematically according to one or the other principle. Either all citizens are agents of self-care or all are objects of state care. In the first case–when everyone exercises care for himself, when he is the care-exercising agent–the nation's care to preserve and improve life will not constitute a unified order, a unified economy, instead it will consist of as many economic organisations as there are citizens (except that some will associate in joint economic organisations, such as households or enterprises). Each organisation will allocate resources as it wishes, in accordance with its subjective valuation of resources, in accordance with the satisfaction of individual citizens. Each individual exercises care for himself in his own way, in accordance with his objective of personal satisfaction. He has his economic organisation and he controls resources (ownership). He is unconstrained and free to acquire and use them.

Relations among such organisations develop in accordance with their interests (utilities). We shall see below that they engage in mutual lending and borrowing, trade, etc. There are as many allocation centres for the care to preserve and improve life as there are agents. Each allocates resources differently, since each is subjectively and individually distinct.

All of the nation's care to preserve and improve life is thus also ordered, but not uniformly, not in accordance with a single objective purpose, but according to individuals (individual persons), differently for each individual, in accordance with subjective utilities. That is why we refer to such order of a nation's care to preserve and improve its life as individualist and we speak of the individualist economic system.

F. The Solidarist Economic System

1. The entire nation as object of state care

And now let us consider the second case, when all the citizens of the nation, i.e., the whole nation, are objects of care exercised by the state which represents an authority superior to all. This takes place in accordance with the objective of attaining the ideal of man, and–if the object of care is the nation–the ideal of a healthy and cultured nation.

Care to preserve an improve the life of an entire nation then becomes a unified order, a unified economy (with a single agent–the state, and a single allocative purpose). Because all citizens are objects of that care, none is endowed with control of goods (ownership) and none is free and unconstrained to acquire and use resources (freedom to produce and freedom to consume). Control of goods is in the hands of the state. And the state guides production and consumption of all in accordance with the objective that it pursues.

2. The content and structure of production and consumption

The state would acquire resources by using the labour of its citizens in accordance with its plan. It would acquire resources of the kind and in quantities such as would appear most useful for preserving and improving the nation's life from the viewpoint of the ideal of its life, health and culture. It would therefore produce what was objectively necessary, objectively most useful, from this viewpoint, rather than what was subjectively desired by individual citizens. It would act like a father acts with his children. This is how production and consumption are determined in the aggregate. The structure of production and consumption would therefore differ from the structure of production and consumption in an individualist economy where it is determined by the subjective utilities of thousands of decision makers. Many goods, other than those included there, would be produced, and their quantities too would be different. Objectively harmful goods, such as luxuries, and inferior literature would disappear.

However, such economy would also face the question how to allocate production (in obtaining resources) and consumption (in using resources) among all citizens. Its task would be to minimize the costs of obtaining resources and allocating labour, and to maximise the utility in using and distributing resources among the citizens. And what constitutes utility and cost in such economy? Utility is represented by increments of life, health and culture which the state tries to achieve for the object of its care (as a father does for his children) and cost is represented by diminution of culture, health and life which the state causes to its citizens when it assigns to them various kinds of labour.

3. *Goods would be distributed according to objective (passive) needs of the citizens*

When a consumer good is allocated to different individuals it yields different utilities because different individuals do not have the same (passive) need of it. The sick need medication and the young need education. The closer an individual is to the ideal of health and culture, the less does he need the care. The weaker he is, the farther away from the ideal, the more does he need the care. To save the life of an individual when it is in jeopardy is more important than to provide more cultural goods to an educated individual. To assist the weakest individuals is the most useful employment of resources. The need to assist the weak represents a need of the care-exercising agent (the state) which projects it, as passive need, to the object of its care (cf. p. 00). Utility is obtained from such assistance (increment of life and health) represents utility of the care-exercising agent (the state). In that case we say that goods are distributed according to "need" but not the subjective need of the object of care but the objective need of the state pursuing the ideal of man. At the same time this represents distribution according to objective utility.

In this connections arises the concept of a set of goods required to sustain bare existence to which we refer as a subsistence minimum (some quantity of food, shelter, clothing). When we extend our postulates from merely sustaining the life of individuals to the postulate of individuals who are cultured, then the need for goods required for that purpose is also extended to include cultural needs. Existence has priority before culture. Compared to more important needs, less important ones are non-essential, luxuries. One cannot provide luxuries for some when the lives of others are in danger.

Such employment of resources—according to relative objective utility, measured by life, health, and culture, and expressed as passive objective needs—leads to balanced development of all individuals. It does not imply equal consumption but unequal consumption, leading to balanced qualitative development of individuals. Each unit of a good consumed is allocated to yield maximum utility (increment of life, health, and culture). All this follows from the principle of relative utility and leads to maximisation of utility from the viewpoint of the optimisation purpose of the ideal man and nation.

4. Labour would be assigned according to capacity to work

Thus when resources (goods) are employed, utility is maximised by allocating each unit of a consumer good to those to whom it yields most utility (increase of life, health and culture) and who have the greatest (passive and objective) need of it—i.e., according to relative utility.

In the process of resource generation, costs are minimised when labour is assigned according to relative costs. Different individuals incur different decreases of culture, health and life when they perform identical labour. Such decreases represent costs to the state if the state manages care of the nation in accordance with the ideal of man and nation. If the state strives–when engaged in acquisition of resources–to minimise total costs, it must allocate each labour task sequentially to individuals to whom it causes least disutility, the least cost. This is because a given task can then be accomplished at minimum cost, and conversely a maximum of labour performance can be accomplished at a given cost. If some beasts of burden are stronger and others weaker they would be able to carry in total a smaller load if each were to carry the same load. Some would collapse under their burden while others would not be loaded fully. Let there be two individuals, and let us consider to which of them should be assigned a given task. Suppose that we would harm the first more than the second by assigning the task to him. We would then say that the second has a greater capacity to perform the task. If we therefore say that tasks are assigned according to relative cost it means exactly the same thing as when we say that tasks are assigned according to relative capacity. Hence it does not imply equal labour. Instead it implies unequal labour but a balanced development of the whole. This is the only way in which cost can be minimised in the process of acquiring resources. Different individuals are therefore not assigned equal labour tasks. The strong will work more and give more than the weak. The weak, on the other hand, will receive more assistance than the strong.

5. The bond of solidarity among citizens

There is therefore a (mandatory) bond between the strong and the weak, both in production and in consumption, with the result that balanced development of all is attained.

This recalls the bond among different objectives in economic organisations when obtaining satisfaction of wants, with limited resources, which results in an even satisfaction of all individuals striving to attain maximum satisfaction and proceeding in accordance with relative utilities. We have referred to this bond of purposes in the economy as material solidarity; it exists in every economic organisation (p. 00).

In the economy of a nation where all citizens are the object of care, we arrive at an analogous relationship between individuals. Care for individuals leads, as we have seen, to a bond among all of them, both strong and weak, and to a division of labour and consumption among them, such that the condition and development of all individuals with respect to health and culture should be even. Once again it is a matter of a bond of solidarism, but this time it is a bond among persons and hence we speak of solidarity of persons. This imparts to the entire economy whose purpose is care for the nation in the name of solidarist economy. (Because this approach to the exercise of care leads to state control over all goods, it is also referred to as communism, community of goods.) (See also p. 00 and ff. 00).

G. Polarity of the Individualist and Solidarist System

Thus there exist, in principle, two kinds of systems in the exercise of care to maintain and improve the life of the nation, according to whether each individual is the agent of care for himself, or whether all individuals are the object of care by the state as care-exercising agent. In the first case such care emanates from thousands of points, agents, in accordance with their subjective satisfaction as systemic purpose. In the second case it stems from a single point, the state, according to the objective ideal of the individual an the nation as systemic purpose. In the first case the individual is free with respect to both production and consumption and he is endowed with the control of goods (ownership). In the second case he is not free either in production or consumption. He is subordinated in every respect to the will of the state an is not endowed with control of goods. Only the state is endowed with this control.

In the first case every individual develops according to his potential. He is himself responsible for his destiny. In the second case it is the state (society) that assumes responsibility for the destiny and balanced development of all.

The effort of the individual to arrange the external world in accordance with his conception (his satisfaction) is an expression of his individual will to live and to be free. The effort of the state to manage the care for the nation according to an ideal of man and of the nation is an expression of the will of the nation to continue its life. In this way emerges the polarity of the individualist and solidarist economic system.

H. The Permanent Conflict of Individualism and Solidarism

There is permanent conflict between individualism and solidarism. Those who are strong and value freedom highly are adherents of individualism. The weak are adherents of solidarism. They perceive, above all, that the strong will be compelled to assist them. Both the strong and the weak are therefore egotists because they think only of their advantage. Man should think differently. An individual–not even the strongest individual–is capable of living without society and without the assistance of others. But he does not wish to be only an instrument of society; he wants to live his own life, to pursue his objectives, to be free as he sees fit. Society (the nation) lives–in a figurative sense–as a community of culture and mutual assistance and it assumes a real life of individuals. This cultural community should serve the life of individuals but it necessarily requires such life.

It follows that lasting prosperity of the individual and of the nation requires a balanced relationship of the two opposite poles and systemic foci of the nation's care to sustain and improve life, of individualism and solidarism. The care to sustain and improve life is a systemic mixture in all nations. Individuals exercise care for themselves, but the state intervenes in their behaviour by commands and prohibitions (the legal system), and it assumes a portion of the care (the public sector). We must examine for each separate activity, for each good, to what systemic order it belongs. Solidarist coming together of a nation strengthens its weight and power, provided that it occurs as a result of its will and in its interest. But pure solidarism that would suppress the individual totally (in communism), and which is in complete conflict with the interests and the desires of the citizens, would lead to a weakening of the nation.

J. Basic Economic Concepts

As we know, all economic organisations share a common form –their purposive structure. If their objective is maximisation (or optimisation) of an end, the purposive structure contains a number of correlative concepts and rules. Correlative concepts are those which express the relationships between ends and means. They include need, utility, usefulness, disutility, harmfulness, value, return, and cost. These concepts–which express purposive activity–are encountered in every economic organisation. We know of course that they accommodate any purposive content, that they are formal concepts, which enable us to understand not only economic organisations (purposive complexes in which occurs the care to preserve and improve life) but also all other purposive thinking (ordering in accordance with any objective whatever–defense, culture, health, etc.).

Only the specific content of an objective lends substantive content to these formal concepts. We say that the concepts are applied to a specific content. Therefore they are also applied to a specific purposive economic content, the purposive content that guides the economic organisation. Henceforth the correlative concepts (needs, utility, cost, etc.) become economic concepts, basic economic concepts. They acquire the substantive content of the systemic objective of the economic organisation.

Finally, we also know that society's care to sustain and improve life proceeds, in principle, from two purposive centers, according to whether individuals exercise care for themselves (individualism) or whether they are all the object of someone else's (the state's) care (solidarism). In the first case each economic organisation is governed by the subjective end of personal satisfaction. In the second case the state solidarist economy is governed by the paradigm of the ideal of man and nation–an objective end. Personal satisfaction of the individual and the ideal of man and nation (their qualities in harmonious configuration) are two objectives with distinct contents. Each of them orders (determines) society's care to preserve improve life in a different way. Children may want to play more, but father says: Finish. Go, do your homework or go to sleep! Free individuals would continue working and earning money longer than eight hours each day. But the government declares: Finish. Go and engage in recreational or educational activities!

Accordingly all basic economic concepts are divided (polarised) according to their content. Let us refer to the objective of personal satisfaction as individual purpose. (It cannot be communicated and is therefore subjective; it governs the individual's care for himself.) Let us further refer to the objective of the ideal of man and nation as social purpose. (It can be communicated an is therefore objective; it governs the state's care for society.) Basic economic concepts are then divided (according to their governing objectives) into individual and social. Both groups include the concepts of need, utility, usefulness, good, disutility, harmfulness, cost, return, and value. However, their contents are different. Individual utility is increase of personal satisfaction; individual disutility and cost are decreases of personal satisfaction, and analogous for all the others. Social utility is an increase of society's health and culture, social disutility and cost are decreases of its health and culture (whether society moves closer to or farther from the ideal). Individual needs derive from the purpose of individual satisfaction, social needs from the social ideal of a strong, healthy and cultured society. Accordingly there are also two kinds of value: A good such as tobacco may possess individual value but no social value because it is harmful to health.

E. THE STATE

A. The Concept of State

The concept of "state" includes the territory, the population, and the central sovereign authority (not subject to anybody) which governs both the territory and the population. When we speak of the state we sometimes mean its territory (a geographic concept), sometimes its population (a sociological concept), and sometimes its central authority (a political concept). When we say that the state promulgates laws for the population of the state territory we have in mind the central sovereign authority. When we say that Yugoslavia and Germany engage in trading goods, we have in mind population. When we say that after the First World War a part of Hungary was incorporated in Romania, we have in mind territory (people can emigrate, they can be exchanged but territory cannot be moved). But the full meaning of "state" includes all three aspects. We define the state as the central authority which governs the population of the state territory in sovereign manner.

B. Activities of the State
(Legal Order and Economy. State Policy)

The authority of the state can be expressed in two ways. First, it issues commands that state what the citizens must do and prohibitions that state what they must not do. State commands and prohibitions are legal norms which constitute, in the aggregate, the legal order.

The second form of state activity consists of the assumption of part of the care to preserve and improve society's life, of including it within the public economic sector. The state may order parents how they must educate their children. Alternatively it may itself set up schools. The law and the economy represent two branches, two arms of state activity. The situation is somewhat like that of a father who allows his children to play but tells them what they can and what they cannot do while playing. E.g., he may forbid them to play so hard as to get out of breath, to hurt each other, etc. He may order them to do their homework, to wash up, etc. This is analogous to the activity of the state in passing laws. But the father also provides food, clothing, etc., for his children, and that is analogous to the state's economic activity.

The state's law making and economic activities complement each other. When commands and injunctions are not enough, the state exercises care for its citizens directly within the public sector. Together government law making and economic activities–i.e., the totality of state activities–constitute government policy, which is directed by the unified (central) authority of the government and represents a unified purposive set.

From the vantage point of the government which promulgates legal norms and stands above the legal order, the norms that constitute that order are means (instruments) to attain the objectives that it pursues. From the viewpoint of the citizens subordinate to the legal order and are placed under it, they are duties. Citizens (and judges) are not concerned with the purpose of the norms but whether the norms are valid and binding. (Whether that is the case can be established by consulting the provisions of the constitution in which the state declares how its authority will be expressed.)

C. The Individualist State

What is the role of the state in an individualist system where everyone exercises care for himself? Here the state exercises no care for its citizens and operates no public sector. It does not promulgate legal norms to make citizens healthy and cultured, or to make the strongest assist weak, i.e, to strive for the solidarist ideal of society. Instead it promulgates legal norms that tend to make everyone better equipped to exercise care for himself, norms that prevent individuals, who pursue their own ends, from interfering each other which would restrict their freedom of movement. This is the function of traffic rules: You must drive on the right! Everybody is constrained–nobody is allowed to drive on the left; but this prevents collisions and driving is made easier. In addition to traffic rules in the literal sense, the individualist state also promulgates "traffic rules" in the figurative sense, for the purpose of regulating interpersonal relations. It delimits for everyone a sphere of control in which he is free to move (private ownership), where one is not permitted to disturb another (infringing on possession, theft, robbery). This sphere includes also the individual person (protection against bodily harm, against defamation). The state protects free agreements (contracts) between individuals. It enforces their observance and formulates model agreements (formulas) for the convenience of individuals (the law of obligations relating to purchases, leases, loans, commerce, etc.), agreement about joint business ventures (forms of business enterprises) etc. All these norms serve the subjective interests of individuals so that they may exercise care for themselves in ways that are better, easier and without conflict. This is private law. In upholding it the state performs the function of "traffic policeman."

D. The Solidarist State and the Mixed State .

In pure solidarism the large public sector absorbs the entire care for the nation's welfare–to preserve and improve its life. The entire legal system is designed to compel individuals to act in a way perceived as useful from the viewpoint of the ideal of society's life, health and culture–when working, consuming, in every respect. Solidarist legal norms are not therefore in the service of individual wants, of individual interests (subjective needs). They are rather in the service of what the state wishes for society as a whole, and possibly for the individuals too, what it regards–from the viewpoint of its objective–as useful for them, what it considers to be their passive, objective need. Such (solidarist) legal norms constitute public law.

Consider now a mixed system. Some part of care for society's welfare, including basic care, is carried on by private economic organisations where everyone exercises care for his own welfare, but another, supplemental part of care, is exercised by the state. The state performs the function of the individualist state vis-a-vis private economic organisations (through private law, through "traffic rules," not through its pubic sector). But it also performs the task (function) of the solidarist state. It performs it partly through solidarist public law, partly through its own solidarist public sector. The state intervenes, by solidarist law, in individualist exercise of care through "safety nets" to protect the weak (e.g., the workers–personal solidarity) and to protect health and culture (material solidarity). It also compels citizens to make contributions to the public sector.

Hence the legal code is also mixed. It includes individualist, private law ("traffic rules") and solidarist public law. Legal norms are thus centered and polarised in two distinct systemic focal points.

Government activity in these distinct cases can be represented by the following simplified schema:

•   GOVERNMENT POLICY

A. Legislative activity   B. Economic activity

I. Consequent individualism

There is only private law, "traffic rules" (they serve private interests)

There is none. The entire care for the nation takes place in private (individual) economic organisations' in accordance with subjective interests.

II. Consequent solidarism

There is only public law (it compells the citizens to live consistently in accordance with the ideal of the nation)

There is no economic organisation other than the public solidarist sector (the entire care for the life of the nation takes place there)

III. Mixed System

The legal code consists of private law and a supplement in public law (protection of the weak, protection of health and culture, obligation to make contributions to the public sector	The public solidarist sector provides only a part of the care for the nation's life, a supplement, otherwise everyone exercises care for himself in private economic organisations

E. What is the Origin of Central Authority in the State?

We have noted that the sum of government activity (both legislative and economic) constitutes what is referred to as government policy. Seen in this way, government policy represents the content of governing, as well as the content of the will to govern. We now ask the questions: Who governs? Who has the power to assert his will as state authority. This has been the cause of numerous major conflicts, bloody and otherwise, in the history of every country, and therefore because of this every country has experienced, in the course of their historical time, different forms of government.

Seeking to gain power in the state is politics but this should not be confused with government policy. This is practiced by those who desire to win power or stay in power (for example, dynasties, political parties, also some social classes, such as the working class). Politics is concerned with power, with the form of government. Therefore it is not directly concerned with how to govern, or with the content of government. For this reason we refer to it as formal politics. Government policy which establishes some type of care for society's life, i.e., the content of government authority, shall be referred to as content policy or material policy (material meaning content not matter in this context).

PART TWO
THE INDIVIDUALIST SYSTEM

A. THE ESSENCE OF THE EXCHANGE COMMUNITY

A. From Subsistence Economy to Exchange Economy

The individualist economic system is based on each individual exercising care for himself an being alone responsible for his welfare. When we say "everyone for himself" we include his wife and children, his household. There are as many economic organisations as there are households. Let us suppose, to start with, that each household lives, as if surrounded by a wall. Within this wall it would have to produce only for itself and consume only what it produced. It would be a completely autarkic economy. Everything within the wall (in a figurative sense) would represent its property: land, dwelling, tools, supplies. There were times, in the history of all nations, when this was the case. Each family lived by itself and there was no exchange. Indeed, everyone produced practically identical outputs. Only exotic products (spices) were brought in from distant regions. Foreign trade is thus older than domestic trade.

However, even when two economic organisations produce identical outputs there may arise occasions for trade based on differences of supply and valuation. One household may experience a bumper crop of potatoes but a failure of its wheat crop. Another may face the converse. It is very likely that they will trade some of their wheat and potatoes to even out their surpluses and shortages. Trade will benefit (be in the interest of) both participating economic organisations because each will derive more utility from its supply of the two products after trade than before trade. Each gives up something that yields less utility (importance, value) and obtains something that yields more utility.

As a consequence of the opportunities to trade, economies will make adjustments and produce in accordance with the advantages that they possess (that for which their land, labour force skills, etc. are better suited). They will trade these products for other products that they need and which are in turn produced by other economies that have made similar adjustments, in their own interest, to produce them. Division of labour thus parallels, goes hand in hand, with trade. The one is a condition of the other. Without the one the other would not exist.

Division of labour reduces cost of production (obtaining resources) and exchange increases utility (resulting from the employment of resources) of all producing and trading economies. Economies striving to maximise utility and minimise (subjective) cost will therefore continue to engage in division of labour (specialisation) and to increase the intensity of trade. This implies progress, greater welfare, and lower labour cost for all.

An economy may perhaps ultimately produce only one product and obtain all other products that it needs by trade.. At that point it can no longer manage without the other economies which acquire its product in exchange for theirs. It cannot exist by itself. Otherwise it would have to revert to its previous self-sufficiency, to produce again all goods that it needs, and give up, at the same time, the level of progress and welfare that it had reached through integration with all the other economies in the community of exchange. For the time being we are considering the spread and intensification of exchange on the territory of a state and we may refer to a national community of exchange.

Individualist exercise of care to preserve and improve society's life takes place in numerous individual economic organisations, each proceeding according to individual utility (personal satisfaction) and cost (disutility of labour). Each adjusts not only to nature and to immutable natural laws but also to existing opportunities to trade goods. Its integration within the community of exchange determines in part the composition of its production and its consumption. Its fate is also bound up with all the other economic organisations with respect to the quantity of goods that it can trade (and therefore produce) and with respect to the ratios at which it can trade. Each economic organisation is dependent on all the others, and all the others are partly dependent on it.

The interdependence of all economic organisations leads to the perception that the aggregate of all economies on the territory of a state constitutes a higher entity where all goods are produced, exchanged and consumed. Each individual economy constitutes a part of that entity. Each is distinct, each contributes something different to the common whole (hence it is not merely an identical subdivision of the whole). We have referred to this higher entity as the community of exchange. Sometimes it is also called the national economy. But is it a unified economy? There is no unified will (of an agent) and there is no unified purpose determining and ordering how goods are obtained (production) and employed (consumption). Production and consumption decisions are made by millions of individual centres (individual economies) according to subjective utilities and costs. Their interests lead to mutual contacts (exchange), mutual relations and groupings.

When a nation exercises care to preserve and improve life in this manner, it ceases to be an assembly, sum total, aggregate, of separate economies (like a flock of sheep), and becomes an organised society. We may call it an individualist society (as distinct from a solidarist society of a nation whose care to preserve and improve life is organised solidaristically).

B. The Origin of Money

For exchange to take place it is necessary for the partners to possess goods which they want and to find the exchange mutually advantageous. Even the first condition is difficult to realise under conditions of original barter exchange, exchange without money. An individual who has a sheep may need a suit of clothes; the individual who has a suit of clothes may not want a sheep–he may need a tool; the individual who has a tool may not want a suit of clothes. If by chance he should need a sheep, it would be sufficient that the three should come to know each other, get together and exchange the goods among themselves. But the series could be longer and more complex; barter exchange could be more difficult.

The next difficulty is no less important. If one individual has a sheep and wants a suit of clothes, while another has a suit of clothes and wants a sheep, exchange can take place–provided that they both find it to be in their advantage. But if the owner of the suit believes that it is not in his advantage to trade the whole suit for the sheep, then barter faces another difficulty: the suit is not a divisible good, its usefulness would be impaired if it were divided. To barter grain for legumes is easier because varying the weight of the two commodities traded can balance out the partners' judgements concerning the usefulness of the trade. Indivisibility of goods is thus another obstacle to barter trade.

The first of the above difficulties of barter would disappear if there was a commodity that everybody could use without limit because it could be exchanged for every other good. It would therefore have to be a commodity that was universally desired. But that is not enough. Bread, for example, is universally useful but not without limit. The second difficulty of barter would disappear if the commodity in question was freely divisible so that one could bring about, in the process of exchange, the balancing or complementing of usefulness.

Individuals would then accept such commodity in exchange, even if they had themselves no direct need of it, because they would know that they could obtain all that they needed in exchange for it. They would not regret it as a direct good but as an indirect and abstract one.

Such commodity would then always circulate without ever being used directly. To circulate, it must possess characteristics that make it easy for it to do so, it must be suited for circulation. Commodities suited for circulation are those that possess large relative utility compared to their volume and mass. For example, manufactured goods are better suited for circulation than raw materials because they possess more utility per unit of volume and mass and can be transported over greater distances. Commodities considered to be best suited for circulation are the precious metals.

Willingness to accept a commodity as medium of exchange depends ultimately on the belief that in the future one will be able to obtain for it as much of other goods as one can today, i.e., that its exchange value is stable.

Such commodity is money.

In the course of time nations have used different commodities as money, e.g., cattle (the Latin "pecunia" comes from "pecus," i.e., cattle–Homer estimates the value of the shield of Achilles as so and so many oxen), furs, chunks of compressed tea or butter (as Sven Hedin describes the "money" of the Tibetans), muscles and ribbons among the blacks, eventually metals, and as a final evolutionary step, precious metals. The latter possess all the requisite characteristics in the highest degree.

Precious metals can be universally used and the public desires them without limit; they can be perfectly divisible, without impairment of their usefulness; their relative usefulness, compared to their volume and mass, is high. They are therefore perfectly suited for circulation. Because of their usefulness as luxuries, they have relatively stable exchange value. Luxuries adjust more easily to available supply than necessities. In addition precious metals are not degradable and their entire past accumulated stock, dating back hundreds and thousands of years, is available for use. Compared to that stock their annual output is relatively small.

These are the reasons why precious metals have been accepted and used for exchange. And as long as they perform this function the public is not concerned with their direct, concrete usefulness derived from their material substance but with their indirect, abstract usefulness derives from their ability to effect exchanges. Precious metals have therefore become an indirect abstract commodity–money. Money is an indirect, abstract or universal good.

Precious metals were originally weighed at the time when exchange took place in the market place. Later on they were standardized as pieces of equal mass certified as to purity and weight. These were then merely counted in the market place. This was the origin of coins and of coinage. The latter was subsequently taken over by the state. More will be said about this below.

C. The Circular Economic Flow in the Money Economy

1. Exchange ratios and price ratios

After the introduction of money, barter exchange is divided into two parts, the sale and the purchase of a good for money. The goal is reached in a roundabout but more economical way. The amount of money paid for a good is its price. When two goods have a different price we say that they have a different exchange value. Price is therefore an expression of the latter. With barter exchange there is a quantitative ratio of exchange between goods, one that everyone has in mind, the exchange ratio. For instance five weight units of flour may trade for one weight unit of meat. The exchange ratio between flour and meat is 5:1. When money exchange is introduced, meat is once again five times more expensive than flour. It continues to be traded as before but in a roundabout way. But individuals now consider only one magnitude–price. They compare the relations of prices of different goods, the price ratios. Price ratios are the inverse of exchange ratios. If meat is five times as expensive as flour, one can obtain, for a given amount of meat, five times as much flour.

Let us suppose that before money is introduced, the ratio of exchange between gold, meat, and flour is 2/3 g, 1 kg, and 5 kg. 2/3 g of gold exchanges for 1 kg of meat or for 5 kg of flour. If one-third of a gram of gold is chosen to be the unit of money, 1 kg of meat will sell for two units of money and 1 kg of flour will sell for two-fifths of a unit of money. Prices are derived from exchange ratios that already exist before money is introduced.

We have seen (p. 00) that price ratios correspond to ratios of marginal utilities of the buyers of various goods. These marginal utilities are directly related to prices and are therefore inversely related to the quantities of goods exchanged because price ratios are the inverse of exchange ratios.

2. Households and enterprises

Money dissolved the primary economic organisations, households, within which took place all of economic life–production, distribution and consumption. This was the period of so-called closed (self-sufficient) household economies.

Following the introduction of money and the general spread of exchange a fundamental change began. Households were eventually left only the function the function of spending money income on household consumption. Income (regular periodic money revenue which finances household consumption expenditures) comes to the household from outside. It represents the money earnings of the head of the household (of the family) or of other family members who help to earn the income.

All earning of money takes place in other (partial) economic organisations, business enterprises. Each enterprise is engaged in production, transport, etc., of some product for sale to other enterprises or to households. An enterprise may extract ore for iron producers, another may smelt it to produce iron, another may produce iron tools or utensils, etc.; one enterprise may grow grain, another may grind it into flour, another may bake bread for the households; some enterprises operate as intermediaries between purchasers and sellers of goods (commerce), other arrange transport, etc. To accomplish these purposes, a number of individuals usually associate in enterprises (we shall see later who they are and how they do it). They form working teams which serve households and other enterprises (via production, commerce, transport) selling to them goods or services (physicians, bakers, etc.).

The price of goods sold constitutes the revenue of the enterprise, the price of its output (or service). In order to produce, the enterprise must obtain from other enterprises material inputs, including goods that depreciate such as machines, tools, motors, and other fixed equipment (so-called investment goods) as well as goods that are used up in the production process (raw materials such as ores, fibers, grain, and auxiliary materials, such as fuel, lighting materials, lubricants). These goods are thus either totally consumed in the process of production (goods used up in production) or depreciated (investment goods).

3. The objective return of enterprises

The value of its output (e.g., in a year) is the working teamed income and the value of goods used (including allowances for the depreciation of investment goods) is its cost. The difference between the cost of goods that thus flow into the enterprise and are used in the process of production, and the value of goods (produced and sold) that leave the enterprise represents the joint money return of the enterprise as a working team. This can be shown schematically (see p. 00).

The objective return of the enterprise as a working team is divided among its participants (as we shall see later, this includes the entrepreneur, the workers, the creditors). This goes to their households as household income. This is no source of income other than such returns of enterprises as working teams. (Unless one considers derived incomes–those formed by dividing the primary incomes originating in enterprise–such as maintenance, alimony, etc., which are distinct from the direct incomes obtained directly from the joint returns of enterprises.)

Because the return of enterprises as working teams is created by increasing the value of goods (lumber is made into furniture, commerce and transport brings goods closer to the consumer) there are no incomes other than those generated by increasing the value of goods, by national production. The annual value of the national product, the returns of all enterprises as working teams (the return to society's labour) and the incomes of all households (national income) represent identical money (economic) series.

Price of agricultural produce and product

The price of goods sacrificed to the production (consumption of raw materials), auxiliary material and gradual consumption (amortization) of investment.	The objective yield of the enterprise as one working group.

4. Schema of the circular flow of exchange

The economy thus represents a circular flow as shown in the diagram on p. 71.

D. The Real Economic Base and the System of Economic Series

1. Introductory concepts

The existence of a money using economy is responsible for the fact that with every good is associated a numerical expression of its price, with every business enterprise a numerical expression of its return, and with every household a numerical expression of its income. How does this fit in with the circular flow of economic life (cf. diagram on p. 71)? There are three main series (levels) of economic magnitudes: The diagram shows the price series in the middle, the series of returns on one side, and the series of incomes on the other side.

Together these three series form a system, because they are interconnected, so that a general change in one carries, necessarily and automatically, over to the other two. The sum total of money incomes equals the sum total of money returns and this in turn equals the sum total of prices (excluding prices of intermediate items).[1] We shall refer to these totals as economic series. The basic economic series are returns, prices, and incomes. There are other series, such as wages, etc., which shall be discussed below.

It is precisely because all economic series are interconnected and closely related, that changes in one series must carry over, in wave-like fashion, to the others–i.e., gradually and with difficulty. That is why the system of economic series exhibits considerable stability.

---

[1]   Intermediate goods are goods bought and paid for by enterprises; in calculating returns they appear as cost items.

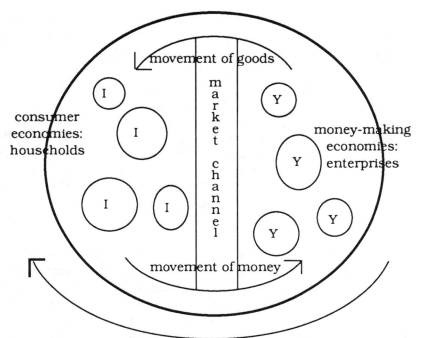

The yield (Y) of enterprises being transferred into the households as their income (I)

That which stands behind the system of economic series (production, consumption, etc.) represents the real economic base (substrate).

2. The origin of economic series

The money economy originated in barter exchange. Before there was money, there was exchange and there were exchange ratios, i.e., quantitative ratios at which goods were exchanged. When money was introduced, exchange ratios became prices and price ratios.

Let us suppose that in an exchange community are produced goods s_1, s_2, s_3 ... s_n in quantities v_1, v_2, v_3 ... v_n. Let the exchange ratios between these goods be: $q_1 : q_2 : q_3 : .... : q_n$.

Suppose that we choose as numeraire q_1 of good s_1. Then the value of output of good s_1 is v_1 / q_1, i.e., as many units of money as the total output of v_1 of good s_1 amounts to of units q_1 which was selected as numeraire. The value of a unit of weight, e.g., of a kilogram of good s_1 is so many units of money as the quantity of good q_1 chosen as numeraire is contained in one kilogram. For example, if we choose as numeraire 1/3 gram of gold then the price of a kilogram of gold is 3000 units of money that can be made from a kilogram of gold. As long as the money unit is given and as long as it is defined in this way, the price of a kilogram of gold cannot be different. We say that the price of the money commodity is fixed.

If the exchange ratio between goods s_1 and s_2 is q_1 : q_2, and if we choose quantity q_1 of good s_1 as the unit of money, then we can always buy with a unit of money quantity q_2 of good s_2, and the total output v_2, of good s_2, will have a value of as many units of money as there are units q_2 in the total output v_2, i.e., v_2 / q_2. For example, if the exchange ratio between gold and meat is 1/3 gram of gold = 500 grams of meat and if 1/3 gram of gold is chosen as the money unit, we can buy 500 grams of meat with one money unit and the total value of meat output will equal so many money units as there are multiples of 500 grams in that total.

An analogous statement can be made about every other good, so that the monetary value of aggregate production becomes:

$$v_1/q_1 + v_2/q_2 + v_3/q_3 + \ldots + v_n/q_n$$

which is the nominal value of aggregate output when intermediate transactions are excluded (grain sold by the farmer to the flour mill and grain bought by the flour mill from the farmer can only be counted once, i.e., at the last stage where enterprises sell to consumers). Economic series are therefore derived from the value of production for sale, from exchange ratios, and from the fact that some quantity of one commodity was chosen to be the money unit.

When the money unit is thus based on one of the commodities, an economic series can only change when there is a change in the volume of production, or in the exchange ratio between the money commodity (gold) and other goods.

We have already noted that the exchange ratio of precious metals to other goods tends to be relatively stable. This is so because the supply of precious metals changes only very gradually, since it includes all previous production, except that part which has been destroyed by use. Also, the prices of necessities (such as bread) rise sharply in times of shortages because the public does not wish to curtail consumption and conversely for luxuries. Precious metals are used mostly as luxuries, a use–as already noted–which is much more elastic. Demand for precious metals adjusts more easily to available supply.

But the exchange ratio of the money commodity is made more stable by its being chosen as numeraire. Changes in the exchange ratio of bread mean that bread is more expensive or less expensive. This cannot be the case with gold, when gold is the money commodity, because its price is fixed. The exchange ratio can only be expressed in that the prices of all other goods either rise or fall, in that the whole price level rises or falls. The general price level cannot fluctuate daily and therefore minor daily changes in the exchange ratio of the money commodity are not obvious. But the exchange ratio of the money commodity is therefore not completely stable.

E. The Money Unit

We know what is the essence of the commodity money. It is an indirect abstract good. It is a good that is substitutable like grain, alcohol, etc., whose units are defined in terms of weight or volume (kilogram, litre, etc.). Accordingly the commodity chosen to be money (ultimately this meant gold) must also be expressed in terms of such physical units, especially units of weight. The money commodity is a certain weight of the precious metal. As their names indicate, at one time Marks,

Pounds Sterling, Talents, were certain weights. The money unit is therefore initially only a certain unit of weight of the money commodity (the technical content of the money unit).

However, when money came to be generally used the public ceased to think of the money unit (the Crown, the Franc, the Dollar, etc.) as some weight of the precious metal. As a rule, when buying a house for 100,000 no one thought of the weight of gold he was giving for the house. The public was still less aware of this when making minor daily purchases. Nevertheless, when the public uses some money unit as unit of account, it clearly uses one that is different from the unit of weight of the precious metal. What is this unit?

This is explained by the fact that when individuals use money, they are not concerned with what it is made from, but with what they can buy with it, i.e., not its direct but its indirect usefulness. Nor are they interested in what they can buy with the precious metal that is the money unit some quantity of other goods, but simply with what the quantity is. But money can buy all goods that are bought and sold. The question is what does the money unit represent–what goods, how much of them, and what quantitative proportions, in other words, what is its economic content (its technical content is the weight of the precious metal of which it is made).

Who is concerned with the economic content of the money unit? Everyone who uses it, to buy, sell, save, make deposits of money, etc., i.e., every individual who participates in economic activity. Such economic man is not concerned with every potential indirect use of money but only with uses that are important to him, i.e., with the usefulness of the goods that he may buy. For example, a table has different uses (as furniture, as fuel) and its owner decides how he will use it, whether as furniture or as fuel. But the possessor of money makes decisions not only about the uses of the goods that he can buy, but also how much and in what proportions to buy them. He simply sees in his money the uses of the goods that he would buy in accordance with relative utility. And this says it all–about what is in his mind behind the veil of money, about goods and their proportions. This internal image in the mind of economic man is only revealed ex post, as his actual expenditures, his consumption, his living standard, the counterpart of the money spent on that consumption. The money unit is then a fraction of that consumption, a living standard in miniature, which differs from individual to individual depending on their wants and their incomes. It is this unit that the individual takes into account when he uses money to make purchases and sales.

In addition to the economic man, some notion of the content of the money unit is formulated by economic science and by policy makers–especially when they consider changes in that content. They are not concerned of course with goods that they need themselves, but with all goods in the market. And so one can scientifically construct a series of quantities of goods that can be bought with money. Taken together, of course, these quantities would be bought for n money units because there are n goods. The money unit would therefore be the following fraction:

$$\frac{s_1 q_1 + s_2 q_2 + s_3 q_3 + \ldots + s_n q_n}{n}$$

However, if we substituted into this expression magnitudes corresponding to two different periods (e.g., before and after the First World War) and calculated the change in the content of the money unit, we would find that the formula contained some errors. First, it would contain many instances of double counting of the same items, the value of flour and the value of grain already included in the value of flour, the value of shoes an the value of hides and the value of cattle, etc. Changes in the expression would therefore be most affected by those goods that have gone through the longest sequence of interfirm transactions from primary production to the consumer. If we wish to avoid this, as we must, we must include in this series only goods in the last stage of production and consumption and thus exclude goods which come to the market and then, after some change or without any change come to the market again, i.e., goods bought to be processed further, not for consumption, but goods bought by enterprises, not households. The series must include only consumer goods bought by households.

This distinction cannot be made in the market and it would be necessary to undertake research of household expenditures in order to construct the series. However, even when the series is thus corrected, we make another mistake when we include the quantity of each consumer good that can be bought with a unit of money. In doing so we assign the same importance for change in the content of the money unit, to saffron as to meat, although everyone would agree that if the price of saffron rose a thousand-fold it would not be as important as if the price of meat rose by one percent. The series must therefore include consumer goods in such quantitative proportions as they are bought, sold, and produced. Obviously, this includes also services, such as the service of barbers.

If consumption of good s_1 is k_1 (consumption), consumption of good s_2 is k_2, and consumption of good s_n is k_n, then aggregate national consumption is

$$k_1 s_1 + k_2 s_2 + k_3 s_3 + \dots + k_n s_n.$$

The value of this aggregate consumption is equal to the aggregate consumption expenditure of national income. The money unit is the following fraction of that aggregate expenditure

$$\frac{k1 \; s1 + k2 \; s2 + \dots + knsn}{D}$$

where D is national income. The numerator is real national consumption designated as K. For the economist an the statesman the money unit is defined as the fraction K/D. When we reduce both numerator and denominator in the same proportion the value of the fraction does not change. When we divide both numerator and denominator by the number of families r, we get the result that the money unit equal

$$\frac{\dfrac{K}{r}}{\dfrac{D}{r}}$$

i.e., average consumption per unit of average income. In other words, for the economist as well as the policy maker the money unit represents a certain standard of living in miniature, and (as distinct from the case of the participant in economic life) this is an average living standard expressed as the production or consumption of all consumer goods divided by the national income. National income is a net cast over production and consumption of all consumer goods. What we see through a loop of this net is the money unit.

F. Inflation, Deflation, High Prices, Low Prices

1. Inflation–deflation

Production in enterprises, exchange in markets, and consumption by households from the physical base (real substructure) of the economy . Above this base extends a superstructure of nominal magnitudes, the system of economic series consisting of the series of objective returns as the counterpart of production in business enterprises, the series of prices as counterpart of market exchanges, and the series of incomes as the counterpart of household consumption. We know that these series are interrelated and therefore constitute a system. Prices determine returns of enterprises (as working teams), these determine incomes of households, the aggregate of these (national income) is used to buy in the market the aggregate output, national product. The totals of returns, prices, and incomes therefore constitute the same magnitude, the aggregate measure of economic activity. The ratio of the nominal measure of aggregate economic activity to its real substructure, the real national product, which corresponds to real national consumption (saving and using up inventories is discussed below) is an expression of the value of the money unit; it is real national product (real national consumption) divided by the nominal aggregate measure of economic activity.

It may happen that the real economic substructure is unchanged, that production and consumption are unchanged, but that the whole process begins to proceed at higher levels of prices, returns and incomes. The purchasing power of the money unit is reduced proportionately. A process of swelling of the system of aggregate measures of economic activity is under way. This is inflation. The opposite process, in which the system of aggregate economic measures is shrinking while the real economic substructure is unchanged and the purchasing power of the money unit therefore rises, is the process of deflation. We shall see below how (in what way) the swelling and the contraction of the system of aggregate economic measures take place, and how else these changes affect the operation of the economy.

2. High prices–low prices

We are still concerned with changes in aggregate nominal measures rather than with the economic substructure of production and consumption. If the substructure (production and consumption) has not changed and only the system of nominal aggregate series did (inflation or deflation) then the swelling or shrinking of aggregate economic measures in all three forms is necessarily equal and simultaneous. The overall (as well as average) contraction of prices will be the same as the overall (and average) shrinking of enterprise returns and household incomes. When the real economic sub-structure, production and consumption, changes this will show up quite differently in the aggregate economic measures.

If production declines (and therefore consumption does too) households must experience lower living standards compared to those they enjoyed before; with incomes that have not changed they can buy less than before. This will occur, with unchanged incomes, if prices per unit rise. If more money is paid for less goods, there may in fact be no change in enterprise returns (less is sold but at higher prices, as much money may be made as before) and therefore no change in money incomes, but the level of prices will depart from the level of incomes and returns. This means genuine high prices due to lower productivity. People wish to avoid the consequences (lower consumption) and attempt to raise their incomes (wages, salaries). But this will not help–if all incomes rise, prices will not remain unchanged but will rise again.

The decline of consumption due to lower production can only be corrected by increased production. If some group, e.g., white collar workers, would then succeed to have legislation passed according to which their income (salaries) would automatically escalate to match rising prices, the burden of the decline of consumption would be borne by the rest of the population who would bear not only their share but also the share of the white collar workers who would be exempt from the effect of the general decline.

High prices are caused by a general decline of productivity which does not lead, unlike inflation, to a swelling of aggregate nominal measures of all three series–incomes, prices, returns–but only to a shift of the price level away from the level of ret urns and incomes. A genuine decline of prices is then the result of increased productivity which causes prices to move in the opposite direction.

B. CONTROL OF GOODS

A. Consumer Goods and Producer Goods

When each individual exercises care to preserve and improve his life (or the life of his family) he is the agent of the economic organisation operated for that purpose and he must also have control of all goods required for that purpose, be they movable or immovable, used repeatedly, or used up at once.

Following the appearance of money there is separation of consuming economic organisations (households) from producing economic organisations (enterprises). Goods used in the two types of organisations become separated as well, and so does the control of goods. They belong to one type of economic organisation or the other. Households need goods and control over goods (shelter, household equipment, stocks of clothing, food, etc.). Enterprises also require goods (buildings, engines and motors, raw materials and auxiliary materials). Goods used by consuming economic organisations (households) are consumer goods. Goods used by enterprises are producer goods. They are often identical but nevertheless they are one or the other, depending on the type of economic organisation where they are used (for example, a sewing machine in a tailor shop versus a sewing machine in the home; coal or kitchen equipment in a restaurant as against a household). What is decisive is actual use. A sewing machine is used to make clothing both in a tailor shop and at home, but in the enterprise it is used to make money. In the enterprise clothing and underwear for others is produced to make money. In the home it is made for members of the household, not for profit.

Both consumer goods and producer goods yield services to their economic organisations either by existing or by changing. This–as we can see–is the distinction between goods used repeatedly and goods used up in a single use. Durable household goods that are used repeatedly include dwellings, household equipment, paintings, carpets, stocks of clothing, books,

musical instruments, personal automobiles (for pleasure), etc.
Non-durable household goods used up in a single use include
food, beverages, victuals, tooth paste, etc. Goods that are used
repeatedly in enterprise include business structures, tools,
machines, motors, railroads, wagons, etc. Goods used up in a
single use by enterprises include raw materials (ores, wool,
cotton, ceramic clay, etc.) and auxiliary materials (lighting
materials, fuels, lubricants). Finally, the products themselves
are producer goods, as long as they have not been sold. Goods
used repeatedly are investment goods–either household investment (durable) goods or enterprise investment goods. In addition to durable goods used repeatedly there are also goods that
do not wear out (land).

The types of goods can be represented schematically as
follows:

	Goods	
	I. Consumer goods	II. money making goods
a) goods of gradual consumption (investment goods) non-consumable (real estates)	dwelling-facilities, apartment-equipment, clothing, personal cars, books, decorative gardens, playing-fields, etc. I. a)	buildings, machines, engines, motors, vehicles, real estate under cultivation and building-sites II. a)
b) consumption goods (goods capable of consumption)	victuals, foods stuffs, beverages, etc. I. b)	raw-materials, auxiliary material II. b)

In addition to this there is money which can be held by households (e.g., income that has not been spent) or by business enterprises (e.g., money received as sales revenue). The distinction between goods that are used up and goods that are used repeatedly does not fit this case. Money can buy either type of good. However, money in the household is a consumer good and money in the business enterprise is a producer good.

B. Control of Goods

To be able to use goods freely, economic organisations must have control over them. They have complete control when the goods belong to them, when they are their property (property of farm operators, heads of households, owners of businesses). However, a farm operator may also arrange to control goods by renting them from another person who owns them. And so there come into being various relationships–rentals, leases, loans, or usufructi (when a farm operator is entitled to use a good belonging to another person only in some particular respect, e.g., to draw water from someone else's well).

People are not interested in owning a good if there is plenty of it for everyone. However, if the good becomes scarce they will soon come to fight to acquire it, and it becomes necessary to establish legal control over such goods. Nomads did not own land but societies that have established permanent settlements find it necessary to establish rules of control of land in order to prevent violence. This is how property law, which recognises the rights of individual owners and protects them against violation, comes into being. It constitutes the "traffic rules" with respect to property relationships among owners. As was noted, it establishes and enforces types of contracts and property relationships.

In the individualist economy all goods may be held, in principle, buy individual owners as their private property. Land (fields, forests, meadows), mines, streams, as well as man-made goods, are privately owned. It may then happen that there are many individuals who own no land, and because they cannot live without having access to land, they are dependent on those who own it. (This is one reason for the so-called workers' question.)

C. Capital

A businessman speaks of capital when he refers not only to goods used in his business, but also stocks of household goods. E.g., when he has a stock of food he thinks of it as capital. By the same token he thinks of his collection of paintings or ceramics as his capital.

However, when we consider society as a whole and say that it has much or little capital, we have in mind goods used by enterprises to facilitate productive activity in manufacturing and transport. This applies to physical goods (direct and concrete) as well as money (indirect and abstract). In this sense money in a business enterprise is capital whereas money used for consumption in a household is not.

However, just as land can be leased and houses rented, money too can be lent and the only concern of the lender is that the borrower should pay back the sum that he has borrowed whether or not he returns the same coins. Compensation for the use of borrowed money is interest. It is a proportion of the amount lent (per cent) an the amount of interest is a function of the duration of the loan. All who wish to lend and all who wish to borrow constitute collectively the money market. We may picture it as a place where an intermediary receives money as a deposit and lends it out. This intermediary activity constitutes special business activity of financial and credit institutions.)

Where do deposits in the money market come from? Mostly from households which do not consume all of their income but save part of it. Who borrows the money? Mostly business enterprises to buy capital equipment (investment), and to expend their activities, production, etc. (operating purposes). Businesses seek investment credit (for capital equipment) and credit for operating purposes. With the funds that they borrow they buy machinery, raw materials, develop new products, etc.

Money that is lent and borrowed constitutes capital both for the creditor and the debtor.

Borrowed funds are put to work in business enterprises and money capital is transformed into real capital–goods that businesses buy or goods that they produce. Concrete assets in business enterprises are therefore a counterpart of money savings and real national savings are a counterpart of national money savings. Expanded business activity, made possible by the savings of households, means that production and social welfare grow. If the nation consumed its entire annual output there would be no economic growth.

Of course it happens also that funds come to the money market from business enterprises when they pay back outstanding loans, or when they curtail their operations and temporarily deposit their capital funds. Furthermore it also happens that money is borrowed by consuming economic organisations (for emergencies such as death, illness, etc.). As noted, when funds come to the money market from business enterprises, new capital is not formed, but real capital of business enterprises (real goods such as machinery or products) is once again transformed into money capital. New money capital comes only from household savings.

When households borrow money capital for consumption, no savings takes place in the aggregate. Consumption shifts from one household to another and the money capital formed by one household is consumed by another. No assets are created which would support future production and welfare (which is what happens when money is borrowed by business enterprises). However, savers are not concerned who borrows their savings and for what purpose. Their money earns interest an they always view their savings as capital. Money capital that is lent out is also called financial capital or credit capital.

The term capital has therefore several different meanings:

1. All stocks of physical goods and of money in households or in business enterprises.

2. All assets (including money) employed in business enterprises.

3. All assets that bring returns, either in the form of rent, lease, or interest; when it is money that returns interest on a loan, the capital is called financial or credit capital.

4. Money capital–income that was not consumed and not transformed into physical assets–is free money capital supplied in the money market. When such capital is in plentiful supply we say that the money market is easy; when it is in short supply we say that the money market is tight.

We shall have more to say about this when we discuss the capital market.

When we say that a nation is capital-strong or capital-weak we have in mind either the stock of physical assets that facilitate productive activity–investment goods, machinery, motors, railroads, etc. (as in 4) or else the formation of new money capital. The one is related to the other, as we have seen (under 2).

When we speak of capital in contrast to labour, e.g., that the return to capital limits the compensation of labour, we mean by capital all assets that generate returns.

D. Capitalism

Capitalism (capitalist economic system, capitalist system of production, etc.) is a system of business enterprise whose essence is production of goods for household consumption carried on by business enterprises, each striving to make money. The choices of goods produced (and their quantities) are determined by the profit making drive of businesses and businessmen, given consumer demand and prices. As long as this system exists business enterprises must have control of the assets which they employ. But individual control of assets implies that their owners do not allow others to use them, unless they receive compensation in the form of interest or rent. And when they employ assets in their own enterprises they require such compensation for themselves–as prior claim on the objective return of the enterprise. Without it they would not engage in business activity, since they have the opportunity to receive interest or rent. Labour regards itself as deprived of this compensation received by capital.

E. About Land in Particular (Ground Rent)

Land serves economic purposes by providing (a) surface areas (construction sites, playgrounds, roads), (b) its capacity to bear (arable land, meadow land, forest land, rivers, ponds), or (c) its underground wealth (ores, mineral waters, coal, etc.). When land is permanently settled and there is no surplus land it must be determined how it is to be controlled. In the capitalist system land too is privately owned.

Different kinds of land do not serve various purposes equally well. As (a) surface area land can be more or less advantageously located (this applies in particular to construc-tion sites close to city centres as against those located on the outskirts)/ (b) land serving through its capacity to bear can be more or less fertile, and can be located closer or farther away from markets; and (c) land that yields underground wealth can be endowed more or less generously with natural resources.

What is involved in all the cases from (a) to (c) is the relationship between the price of a product and the cost of producing it. (a) The cost of constructing an apartment house, (the cost of residential housing) is the same whether it is built close to the city centre or farther away from it. But prices of apartments and apartment buildings differ, depending on how favourable is their location. (b) Products that depend on the fertility of soil (for example grain) and (c) products derived from the underground wealth (ores, crude oil) sell at identical prices, whether they are produced at lower cost (on more fertile soil, from richer sources) or at higher cost (on less fertile land, from poorer sources). Whether the product (building) on different parcels of land is produced at the same cost and sells at different prices, case (a)–where land serves only as surface area and location, or whether the products sell at identical prices, though produced at different costs, case (b) where land renders it service by its fertility, and case (c) where it serves by its underground wealth, all have in common that on different parcels of land there is a different relationship between price and cost,* i.e., a different return to the owner.

If identical parcels of land yield different returns, when employed in one or another way, we credit the lager return to the special nature of the land parcel, to advantages of its location, to its fertility, to its mineral wealth. The difference of the return on land that yields the least return and the return on every other parcel of land is known as ground rent. Ground rent si therefore of a differential nature. It is due to the advantages of different locations, different fertilities of soil, or different endowments with mineral resources.

An individual who owns land that yields rent will not permit others to use it, unless he is compensated for the rent. Such compensation is the rent or lease payment (in the case of housing the rent payment represents not only ground rent but also interest and amortisation of construction costs). Land is then also demanded by financial capitalists (savers) merely for the purpose of return to them, in the form of lease or rent payments, an interest on the investment that they have made when they bought the land. They know that if they deposit money in a savings account that pays four per cent interest they will receive 1000 crowns interest if they deposit 25,000 crowns. If the rent of a parcel of land is 1000 crowns and the bank pays four percent interest on deposits, then the value of the land is 25,000 crowns. With rent unchanged but with an interest rate of two per cent, the land would have a value of 50,000 crowns, and with unchanged rent and an interest rate of 5 per cent the land would have a value of 20,000 crowns. The value of land represents capitalisation of rent in line with the general rate of interest (to be discussed later).

---

* By cost we mean here everything that the landowner must spend to obtain the product. Cf. p. 00.

C. ECONOMIC ACTIVITY

A. Economy and Technology

An economic organisation may either be at rest (be stationary) or it may be active. Economic activity consists in continuously obtaining and employing resources. This holds true for consuming economic organisations (households) and producing organisations (enterprises).

Economic activities of consuming economic organisations are guided by the head of the family in accordance with the ordering purpose of his satisfaction. Economic activities of business enterprises are managed by the businessman who strives to achieve his objective–profit.

However, other activities, mental and physical, must be distinguished from the guiding and ordering (ideational) activity of the individual who directs the economic organisation. Those activities took place within the framework of the overall system set up for the organisation by the individual who guides it, and they are always directed toward definite special objectives dictated by the central purpose. The businessman decides what goods the enterprise should produce and in what quantities, what investment projects should be undertaken and on what scale, etc. (all this with an eye to maximising profit). That is economic activity proper. Individuals (engineers, workers) charged with producing one of the products (in accordance with a plan) strive to produce it at least cost and in the best quality within the framework of the plan. They follow a particular objective determined by that plan and their activity is technical. Therefore there is economic activity of the individual who guides the organisation according to plan an there is technical activity which strives to achieve economically particular special tasks derived from the plan. When the person who is in charge of economic activity (the entrepreneur, the commercial director) is different from the persons who carry on technical activity (technical director, engineer, office workers, manual workers) then it is economic activity that is naturally superordinate to technical activity (the technical director is subordinate to the commercial director).

This is also how it is in a household, where–in addition to management activity–there is also much technical activity (cooking, sewing, cleaning, etc.). In a small economic organisation the head of a household or a small businessman can take care of both activities himself (a widow may take care of the whole household by herself; a small tradesman may take care of the commercial, economic, and technical aspects of his business without any assistance. But in a large business these activities are divided among a number of individuals. However, the guidance (management) of the organisation can and must be the sole responsibility of a single authority.

An economic organisation thus includes many technical activities but the type and extent of such activities is a function of its central objective. When viewed in isolation, outside the whole of which it is a part, each such activity is technical, but when viewed as a link of the economic whole, by which it is ruled, it becomes economic. The question of what type of bridge is least costly, given a maximum carrying capacity, is technical. The question of what type of bridge will be chosen by an economic organisation, e.g., a province (which must also consider other ends) is an economic question, a question of the provincial economy.

B. Classification of Activities and Workers

In what follows we shall be mostly concerned with activities of business enterprises. Here we have economic (business) activity and technical activity. Economic activity includes, first of all, selecting the field of productive activity, i.e., what service, what new or better product, or what addition to existing production should be undertaken. Production includes trade, transport and other services. The businessman must secure the requisite capital (either equity capital or borrowed funds), equip the plant where the activity is carried on, acquire means of production an secure the services of coworkers, negotiate agreements with other capitalists and with workers, and finally organise all activities including sales of the product or service in such a way as to be able to cover, in the first instance, the cost of goods used up in the process of production (raw materials and auxiliary materials) and the depreciation cost of goods that wear out over time, investment goods. This is how is derived the objective return of the business enterprise as a working team. From the objective return are then paid interest on borrowed capital and wages of hired labour. The residual is the businessman's (personal) entrepreneurial return which is distinct from the return to the enterprise as a working team. For the businessman it is the stimulus and incentive for all entrepreneurial activity.

The businessman must continuously monitor changes of prices, interest rates, and wage rates to make certain that they do not swallow up the entire objective return or interfere with production activities. He must seek the best possible organisation of activity and of physical capital. He must shift, when circumstances dictate, from one product to another or from one location to another. He must assess the evolution of the time period for which the productive process continues and the changes that determine its return. He must pay attention to developments abroad in countries where he exports and from whence he imports (raw materials). He must keep abreast of various domestic legislation (laws for the protection of workers, tax laws, etc.). He must be conversant with accounting which enables him to follow the behaviour of monetary values in all segments of the business (investments, raw and auxiliary materials, semi-fabricates, inventories, claims and liabilities. He must also possess the requisite language skills, so that he may communicate with his coworkers, customers, and others. The business enterprise is like a clock. Changes in the constituents that make up its return (interest, wages, prices) may destroy its return and thus bring to a halt the operation of the business just as the operation of a clock can be brought to a halt. The result is then loss of livelihood of all hired employees.

There would be no business enterprise without entrepreneurs. It is necessary to bring up young people for the tasks of entrepreneurship, to nurture in them the desire and love for this leadership role in the economy. (More on this topic later).

The remaining business activities are technical activities. When we consider all activities in all enterprises we note that they represent an enormous number of different activities and productive processes, mechanical and chemical, transport, operation of machines and motors, work without machines, etc. These activities are divided among enterprises. Activities are sometimes classified according to kinds of goods (clothing, footwear, food, toys), sometimes according to materials of which the products are made (leather goods, wood products, iron and steel products), and sometimes according to production processes (chemical industry) etc. We shall see below what is the significance of this division of labour. Productive activity also assumes different forms within the enterprise and is divided in turn among different individuals and groups of individuals. (E.g., in a bakery flour is prepared and so are ovens, dough is made from flour, loaves of bread are made from flour, then follows baking, cleaning up, transport, etc.) Even separate activities involve several movements. We realise this when we try to replace human labour with machinery. E.g., a spinning machine performs all the basic movements–rotation, pulling–as a spinner does at the spinning wheel.

Ultimately there is thus also division of labour among individuals. Everyone trains fro a some type of work and occupation, for some kind of technical activity, operating a machine, etc. Different kinds of labour divided in this manner require from the workers different physical and mental performance and therefore also different combinations of natural abilities (alertness, physical strength, etc.) as well as qualities acquired by education and training. Hence the closer the performance of a particular task fits the combination of the workers' qualities, the less strenuous is the work for the worker and the more does he produce with the same effort. Therefore he can also be paid better. Researchers conduct investigations aimed at discovering combinations of workers' capabilities for technical work (psychotechnics). According to these combinations of workers' capabilities required by the production processes, labour is divided into work that is predominantly mental, which is considered to be of a higher type (white-collar work) and predominantly physical (manual) work. Physical work is either skilled work that requires training or unskilled (manual) work.

C. The Work System

In every economic order men obtain the goods required for preservation and improvement of life only by their labour. When all of society is the object of care, every individual–as we have seen–is obliged to work and he cannot choose what kind of work he will do. Work is assigned to him. When each individual exercises care for himself there is no obligation to work. No one is compelled to work by law. However, he is forced to work by his biological needs, unless he owns property that enables him to live without work. No individual is forced to do a particular kind of work. He may choose what occupation to prepare for and he may also choose a particular job provided there are enough job opportunities. In this sense labour is free.

An individual who owns land or an established business (craft shop, store, etc.) can be active in his own business, he is independent. Those who do not own such assets must approach the owners of land or businesses and offer their labour for wages. There work is thus not independent, it is work for hire (work for white collar and blue collar workers). The greater the concentration of ownership of land and business capital among few individuals, the greater is the proportion of society that makes a living by hiring itself out.

Independent businessmen earn sometimes more and sometimes less operating their own business, depending on the return that they eventually earn. Workers who are not independent receive their wages regardless of what the business return is, even when the businessman suffers losses. Of course, a business that suffers losses cannot pay wages forever. The return of the business is derived from the price of the product and so is the price of labour. The price of a product is not derived simply from the fact that so and so much labour was expended in producing it. But it pays to employ so and so much labour to produce a product if its value is such as to make it profitable.

D. The Structure of Individual Economic Organisations

There are two kinds of economic organisations: 1. households which are consuming organisations that spend household income on consumption, and 2. business enterprises where all useful goods are produced and at the same time money is made, which then flows to households as income. Let us take a closer look at the internal make up (structure) of both.

A household may consist of a single individual (a widow, a bachelor) or several individuals (a family, a convent) who wish to live in a consuming community, i.e., to spend a joint income on common needs. The income community may also be a partial one (a young adult may be earning a wage, hand it to the head of the household and live like the rest of the household, or he may keep part of the wages he earns to pay, for example, for his clothes and entertainment). Income may be consumed or a part of it is saved, accumulated as capital. Of course, households may borrow and consume more than their income. In addition to economic activity, i.e., making decisions about how consumption expenditures should be allocated, households also engage in a great deal of technical activities (cooking, sewing, cleaning). Technical activities are performed either by members of the household themselves or else by hired help (household servants) who may be paid in kind (room and board) and in money (to buy clothing and other needs).

The essential factor of business enterprise (an economic organisation engaged in production) is the businessman (more than one entrepreneur may join to form a company for the purpose of producing–this is discussed below in more detail).

Businessmen may be active on their own or they may hire others for wages and salaries. They may use their own capital or the capital of others that they have rented, leased, or borrowed at interest. They render services to other (consuming and producing) economic organisations. They offer and sell their products or services (e.g., medical services). They are motivated by the desire to make money.

Business enterprises are working teams. As we saw, they make money by adding value to goods (producing iron from iron ore, iron tools from iron, tables from wood, horse collars from hide, flour from grain) or by rendering services (legal, technical, intermediary–commerce, industry, etc.). In the process of producing goods and services some goods are consumed (raw materials and auxiliary materials such as energy for light and heat, and fuel for engines), while other goods depreciate gradually (investment goods such as machinery and structures). The working team therefore makes a basic calculation: Revenue from goods and services sold versus the cost of goods used up (including depreciation of investment goods).* The difference is the return of the business enterprise which depends on prices of outputs and prices of goods that are used up and goods that are depreciated. Returns therefore depend on prices of goods.

From the returns of business enterprises as a working team (i.e., returns of joint activity) the businessman pays compensation to outside capital (rents, lease payments, interest) and wages to hired labour. What is left is his personal return, the return of the entrepreneur. If he uses his own capital, then his personal return represents both compensation of entrepreneurial activity and entrepreneur's capital.

When the businessman's return is compared with the composition of hired labour and outside capital and it turns out there is a difference in his favour, we speak of a special entrepreneurial profit; if the difference is in the opposite direc-

---

* If a machine lasts ten years then annual depreciation is one-tenth of its price.

tion, he has reason to become concerned about losses. The business may thus yield to him a personal return, but if the return does not exceed the compensation of hired labour and of the current interest return to capital there is no entrepreneurial profit. Entrepreneurial profit is an incentive for independent entrepreneurial activity. If the entrepreneur's labour in his own business does not yield to him as much as he could earn working for wages, or if using his own capital he does not make as much as he would if he loaned it out at interest, he would have no incentive to engage in entrepreneurial activity, unless he valued his independence very highly. Of course, he could go on earning a lower return (though not at a outright loss which would result in diminution of his capital). His fate hinges on the prices of goods, interest on borrowed money, and the wages of labour. Entrepreneurs represent economic leadership.

It is also shown in the following schema:

Value of agricultural produce and product (services)		
I. Value of goods sacrificed to the production	II. Yield of enterprise as a working-group from which is paid:	a) compensation of outside capital (rental, lease payment, interest
		b) compensation of hired labour (wages, salaries)
		c) the residual is the personal return of the entrepreneur
		a) goods that are consumable (raw materials, auxiliary material)
		b) goods that wear out: depreciation of investment goods

E. THE INTERECONOMIC ORDER

I. FREE COMPETITION

A. Introduction. Three Types of Markets and Three Equilibrium Points

There are very many consuming and producing economic organisations (households and business enterprises). They all differ with respect to consumption and production of goods, formation and employment of capital, supply and employment of labour (hired labour, etc.). Individual economic organisations confront other economic organisations (exchange, buying and selling, lending money, selling labour services). They are concerned with other organisations that confront them in supplying or demanding the same product or service–with their competitors.

Competition thus consists of the fact that many individuals and businesses demand or supply the same thing and are engaged in struggle with one another. Therefore, for competition to exist 1. the object of competition must be homogeneous, 2. there must be a large number of (competing) individuals and businesses, and 3. they must be engaged in struggle (compete) with one another. This means that many individuals and businesses buy or sell the same good, supply or demand the same kind of financial capital, or the same kind of labour. The struggle consists in suppliers offering lower prices to sell more of what they supply and demanders offering higher prices to get what they demand.

Concern about competitors leads to centralisation of competition in time and place–the market. Those who demand or supply the same thing met on particular days and hours in a particular place and make a market. The market is both a place and an activity.

We can distinguish three main kinds of markets, according to what are the main objects of competition: the market for goods (and services that goods yield, for example housing services), the capital market, and the labour market. In the goods market are sold goods (or the services which goods yield–e.g., renting of apartments); loans of financial capital are demanded and supplied in the market for financial capital, and labour for hire is supplied and demanded in the labour market.

In every market competition leads to uniform market prices. We mean prices broadly defined, including prices of goods (prices in a narrow sense), the price of capital (interest rate), and the price of labour (the wage rate). We shall explain for each market separately how prices reach a stable level and become uniform, but we can point out immediately that prices (broadly defined) have a feedback impact upon economic organisations which codetermine prices via supply and demand.

Market prices of goods are an inducement to producers, they stimulate supply and depress the desire to acquire goods which is the basis of demand. Ultimately price establishes balance between production and consumption in the goods market, between demand and supply of capital in the capital market, and between demand and supply of labour in the labour market. Supply, demand, and price are mutually related. Supply and demand are constituents of prices broadly defined (that includes interest rates and wage rates). Prices keep the balance between them.

The entire equilibrium order of economic organisations in the capitalist system rests upon these three scales (markets) and their points of equilibrium (on prices broadly defined). Everyone produces and demands something different and in different quantities. It would seem that thee would be total anarchy because there is no central authority, no central plan. And yet, in the end no more is produced than is purchased and everyone can easily buy in the store all that he needs and all that he wants to buy. There is an equilibrium order and it is kept precisely by those scales and those equilibrium points.

2. THE GOODS MARKET. PRICE IN A NARROW SENSE

To start with we must exclude goods acquired only because of the returns that they yield, such as parcels of land that yield rent and whose price is the capitalised value of their return, which is a function of the prevailing rate of interest. These are goods acquired for the purpose of earning returns. For the rest we must distinguish goods bought by households to be consumed in accordance with subjective utility–consumer goods–and goods bought by business enterprises as productive equipment to operate the business–capital goods. Ultimately even capital goods indirectly serve consumption because they are used to produce consumer goods, so that prices of consumer goods are the basis–via the profit drive of business–of the prices of capital goods. Business enterprises buy capital goods in accordance with their profit motivation, but this depends ultimately on the prices of consumer goods. The constituents of the prices of consumer goods and of capital goods are therefore not the same but the following holds for both kinds of goods:

1. The conventional explanation of price as determined by supply and demand is not adequate, because neither supply (production for the market) nor demand (purchases) can exist without price. Ceteris paribus a higher price elicits more production (supply) and depresses the urge to buy goods (demand). A lower price has the opposite effect. To every price corresponds some production and some consumption (supply and demand). Supply and demand are thus jointly determined by price. (Suppose that a housewife goes to buy a kilo of butter, knowing that yesterday's price was 20 crowns. She would buy more if the price were only half that. A higher price would give butter producers an incentive to produce and offer to sell more butter than a lower one.) This follows from the law of relative utility, which households follow in buying goods. Relative utility declines as price rises. It also follows from the law of relative producers' cost. Price settles at the point of balance between supply and demand.

2. The conventional explanation of price as determined by cost of production is not adequate. A good produced by different enterprises and sold at the same price may have been produced at different costs (e.g., wheat of the same quality produced at a higher cost on less fertile and land wheat produced at proportionately lower cost on more fertile lands sells for the same price). We say that price is determined by the highest cost, the cost of that output which was just required to supply the market. But how was this quantity determined? By price because to each price corresponds some quantity of goods that the public wishes to buy and which is therefore required to "supply the market." At the same time price determines what cost may still be incurred and hence the volume of output as well.

3. The price of a single good in isolation cannot be explained because prices of all goods are interrelated in the minds of producers and consumers. Consumers' decision how much of each good depends as much on the desirability of the good as on its price. Both determine relative utility of goods. If the price of a good rises, less will be bought and the public will switch to another, relatively more useful, good. Producers decide how much of what to produce. Their decision is based on the cost of production and the price of each good, because production is motivated by the profit drive (in the production of what good can money be make at relatively least cost). Where the production of one good stops, the production of another begins. In the aggregate price constitute a continuous set.

4. The equilibrium function of price. For economic life to proceed without disturbance and at a steady pace presupposes all-around balance, first and foremost between real production and consumption. The task of prices is to maintain such balance. The price of a particular good must be sufficiently high to keep balance between its production and consumption, to elicit a sufficiently large volume of output for those who wish to pay and can afford to pay that price. Prices of different goods must be mutually related in such gradation that production

and consumption remain steady. An artificial departure (lowering) of the price received by the producer of a particular good (for example, because a tax is imposed) will lead to a shift of production away from the lower-priced good to other goods that thus become higher-priced, whereas consumption will shift in the opposite direction. Balance and steadiness of economic life will be disturbed. When a price ceiling is imposed on flour consumers will want to buy more, at the lower price, but producers will not want to produce and sell as much as before. They will prefer switching to produce meat and using grain as feed. A rise or fall of a price is an indication that equilibrium has been disturbed. The price changes in order that equilibrium be restored.

What we are discussing here is the regulatory function of price with respect to production and consumption. To each price corresponds a particular level of production and consumption. Prices settle at the point where they maintain balance between production and consumption and a steady pace of the production and consumption of various goods.

C. The Capital Market

The capital market consists of sums of money supplied as new credit, and demanded by borrowers. In greater detail we may say:

a) Money capital is supplied by:

1. consuming economic organisations (households) that save part of their income and either supply it in the form of deposits, or by organisations that repay, from their savings, previously incurred debts that went to finance consumption expenditures. This represents a transfer from income to money capital.

2. producing economic organisations (business enterprises) that require less money capital for future operations because they intend to reduce the volume of production and have the cash from previously obtained revenues. If they have outstanding loans they repay them. This represents a shift from real

capital (real assets are being reduced) to money capital. (We speak of the reproduction of capital.)

b) Money capital is demanded by:

1. Consuming economic organisations that wish to increase their consumption expenditures by augmenting their income by the amount of the loan. This is a shift from capital to income.

2. Producing economic organisations that require money capital to finance capital investment (to acquire productive assets), to buy raw and auxiliary materials (fuel, light, etc.), to pay wages during the time that elapses before the output is completed, to make rent an lease payments during such time, etc. Additional financial capital is demanded when equipment is required for a new enterprise or when an existing enterprise is being expanded. What is involved is a shift from financial capital to physical capital. This can be represented schematically as follows:

Economic organisation	Financial capital	
consuming	shift from income to capital	shift from capital to income
producing (enterprise)	shift from physical capital to financial capital	shift from financial capital to physical capital

A person who allows another to use his financial capital gives up its present use and demands compensation for the utility that he foregoes. An individual who obtains from another the use of his capital derives utility from it and is willing to pay a compensation for it. The compensation is interest which is expressed as a percentage of the capital per unit of time, e.g., per year.

Money is supplied and demanded in the money market.* This leads to equilisation of interest rates except that different rates will apply to different kinds of loans (short-term loans, long-term loans, loans secured by movable assets, by real estate (mortgage loans), unsecured loans, personal loans, etc.). How are interest rates determined? Supposedly by supply and demand. However, supply and demand of financial capital depend in turn on interest rates, just as supply and demand of goods depend on the prices of goods. How does the rate of interest affect supply and demand in the capital market?

A saver who is offered interest at the rate of ten percent will save more and supply a larger portion of his income than one who is offered only one percent. Businessmen are more likely to borrow funds for their enterprises at lower interest rates than higher interest rates because interest swallows revenue and lowers entrepreneurial profit. High interest rates depress business activity, they depress demand for new capital and shift financial capital away from enterprises and back into the capital market. Low interest rates have the opposite effect. Interest rates thus impact on both demand and supply.

Those who compete for scarce capital and those who compete in supplying it do so via the rate of interest. This means that interest rates keep the balance in the capital market. A looser capital market means a tendency for supply to exceed demand and leads to lower interest rates while a tighter capital market signifies a tendency for demand to exceed supply and leads to higher interest rates.

Prices of goods and rates of interest are related. In general, prices of productive assets (land, buildings) represent capitalisation of their returns according to the rate of interest. The

---

* This service is provided by financial institutions where the public deposits money and from whom people borrow. Financial institutions are discussed below.

prices of capital goods that business enterprises buy are related to interest rates because high interest rates dampen business activity and the desire to acquire those assets. Low interest rates have the opposite impact. High prices of the goods that business enterprises buy dampen the incentives of businessmen because they lower their entrepreneurial profits and therefore also their demand for additional business capital. Low prices have the opposite effect.

Prices of consumer goods on which household incomes are spent are also related to the rate interest. On the one hand high prices of consumer goods make it more difficult for households to save. On the other hand, high prices provide an incentive for business to seek expansion of production and capital. Low prices have the opposite effect. High interest rates stimulate saving, depress consumption expenditures and the prices of consumer goods; low interest rates have the opposite effect.

D. The LABOUR MARKET

The labour market is a market where labour is hired, a market where it is demanded and supplied. It is constituted as follows:

a)   Labour is supplied by:

1.   Consuming economic organisations–households, families, consuming economic organisations that include several persons. Members of families seek outside work opportunities when they lack other sources of income, or when they wish to add to their income.

2.   Producing economic organisations–enterprises which release manpower when they reduce their activity. Subsequently, of course, such enterprises, no longer supply labour. Their former employees become separated from them. This constituent of the labour supply occurs through the release of labour by enterprises (in much the same way that financial capital returns to the market when business activity is reduced).

b)   Labour is demanded by:

1.   Consuming economic organisations. They require hired labour to help with household work (cooking, sewing, cleaning, etc.).

2.   Producing economic organisations. They require both white and blue collar workers to operate the enterprises. The demand depends on the level, of business activity, whether it is rising or falling. Depending on the nature of enterprise activity and the variety of labour skills, various kinds of labour are supplied and demanded in the labour market.

Those who hire themselves out, give up some of their personal freedom. They become bound by the hours that they must work, the environment where they must work, etc. They incur simultaneously the burden of the labour that they perform and they sacrifice the direct benefits of their labour which they could get if they worked for themselves. They demand compensation for this. Those who hire someone else's labour obtain benefits such as the goods that are produced, or the saving of their own labour and effort, and they are willing to pay for it a compensation–a salary or a wage (salary si compensation for labour that is primarily mental, while wage refers to compensation for labour that is primarily manual).

It is frequently asserted that demand for and supply of labour determines the wage rate. However, the wage rate co-determines supply and demand for labour as its constituents. High wages rates encourage members of households who have not worked for wages to enter the labour force and try to earn wages. On the other hand, they discourage households from seeking hired help to do household work and business enterprises from expanding their operations, because high wage rates reduce entrepreneurial returns and may even turn them into losses. Low wage rates work in the opposite direction.

The concentration of supply and demand for labour in the labour market leads to competition and equalisation of wage rates (of course, wage rates paid for the same kind of work). Different wage rates will be paid for different kinds of work, just as different prices are paid for different products. The question is what will be the level of the wage rates (either the average or those paid for different kinds of labour). The wage rate settles at the point of balance between the supply and demand of labour. If this is to the case then excess demand will push the wage rates up and excess supply will pull it down.

Because employment of hired help in the household sector involves only a few kinds of labour and a comparatively small number of workers (relative to the total), the main point of interest becomes the employment of labour in the business sector. Here a higher (lower) level of employment implies a higher (lower) level of production an therefore also a higher (lower) need for financial capital. The wage rate as the price of labour in the labour market is therefore connected with prices of goods in the product market and their price of financial capital in the capital market.

The relationship can be described approximately as follows: High prices of consumer goods tend to bring about expansion of business activity, higher demand for labour, higher employment and higher wage rates. Business enterprises can afford to pay higher wage rates when their returns as working teams are rising. Low prices have the opposite effect. (As before, when we contrast high and low prices we mean prices that are rising or falling.) High prices tend to bring about higher levels of business activity and higher wage rates. This lead to more capital being required, to pressures in the capital market, and to higher interest rates. However, as we saw, higher interest rates exercise upward pressure on prices. They exercise upward pressure on wage rates, not only via prices but also via the returns to enterprises as working teams. They absorb a higher share of enterprise returns as priority claims, because–unless capital receives its interest "nourishment"–it quickly escapes elsewhere. It is liquid and can be used anywhere (unlike labour which tends to be specialised and hence non-substitutable: A metal worker cannot be substituted for a textile worker).

E. THE INTERRELATIONSHIP OF THE THREE MARKETS

THE IMPORTANCE OF COMPETITION

The interrelationship of the three markets is quite obvious. Balance in each market is kept through prices (broadly defined) of goods, capital, and labour. This captures fully the content of the equilibrium order among economic organisations in the individualist-capitalist system. Equilibrium therefore rests on three balances and three equilibrium points. But the three markets are interdependent. As a result changes in one market–rising or falling prices (broadly defined) bring about changes in the other markets. For this reason there cannot be equilibrium in one market unless there is equilibrium in all the others. A disturbance in one causes disturbances in the others. However, this also works in reverse–toward restoration of general equilibrium. Equilibrium among economic organisations is part of the individualist-capitalist order. Disequilibrium represents malfunctioning of the order, a crisis in the economic sense.

In addition to maintaining–via prices–the equilibrium order among economic organisations, competition also performs other functions–as does every struggle. Everyone exerts himself because the better product wins the struggle and this means economic progress. It is for this reason that competition also plays a role in sports. But it means that the weak are the losers, and this is also true of economic struggle. Weak business enterprises lose out to strong ones. The poorest workers (manual or mental) cannot succeed in the struggle with better ones.

II.   OUTSIDE   FREE   COMPEITION

A. INTRODUCTION

When prices (broadly defined) are not determined competitively they may be fixed by agreement between participating economic organisations on either side of the market, in which case they are autonomous (the participants fix the prices themselves). Or else they may be fixed by higher authorities, by government command, in which case they are heteronomous (imposed on the participants by outside command.)

When participants agree about prices (broadly defined) this is known as syndicalisation (or cartels). When the government does not allow prices to be formed either by competition or by syndicalist agreement and manages them itself, they become managed prices, and the associated economic organisation is a managed as well.

If it is to make sense for prices to be fixed by agreement of the participating parties rather than by freely competitive markets, or for the government to control (impose) prices to replace free competition or the syndicates, then price displacement must always be involved. Because the operation of free competitive markets results in equilibrium prices, displacement of prices implies displacement from equilibrium as well. However, because there must be equilibrium, it becomes necessary to restore it in the same way that prices were displaced (syndicalisation, controls).

B. SYNDICALISM

When economic organisations that are engaged in competitive struggle on either the demand or supply side of a market (for goods, for capital, for labour) agree not to compete, but instead come to an agreement about price (broadly defined–the price of goods, the rate of interest, the wage rate) we speak of syndicalisation. E.g., firms on the supply side of the goods markets (suppliers, producers) may come to an agreement not to compete, to charge the same price, and to impose that price to those on the other side of the market (buyers, consumers). If such an agreement is to last there is a need for a permanent agreement and association between the economic organisations that have entered into such agreement. Such associations are called syndicates. (In the case of producers of goods and the suppliers of capital we speak of cartels–cartels of sugar refiners, cartels of banks.)

There are three basic types of markets and prices (goods, capital, labour) and each market has a supply side and a demand side. Consequently there are six conceptually possible types of syndicates:

I.   The goods market:
   a) Supply (producers, sellers).
        Cartels of sugar refiners, cement makers, steel makers, beet growers.
   b) Demand (consumers, buyers).
        The cartel of sugar refiners agrees on the price that it will pay to growers of sugar beets. (As we shall see, consumers' syndicates are impractical.)
II.   The capital market:
   a) Supply.
        Cartel of banks.
   b) Demand.
        This would be a debtors' cartel (As we shall see, debtors' cartels are impractical.)
III. The labour market:
   a) Supply.
        Syndicates of employees (labour unions).
   b) Demand.
        Syndicates of employers.

There are many kinds of goods and of labour. The object of a syndicate can only be a good or labour of the same kind. This follows from the fact that sugar producers do not compete against cement producers, nor do workers in one trade compete against those in another trade (hence "trade" unions). If a permanent association of economic organisations is to replace competition, the organisations must have a major (vital) interest in reaching agreement and the price in question must be of fundamental importance to them (the price of sugar for sugar refiners or the wage rate for workers). It must be a permanent vital factor responsible for their success or failure. That is why there are no syndicates of debtors–because indebtedness is variable. If an agreement is to be reached it must be practically possible. There are millions of farmers–how could they negotiate an agreement! It was also for this reason that it was difficult for a syndicate to be formed in the textile industry with its many scattered producers. For the same reason a consumers' syndicate is not possible because consumers are numerous and the goods involved are innumerable.

Syndicates on one side of the market may be opposed by analogous syndicates on the other side of the market (a sugar refiners' cartel opposed to a cartel of sugar beet growers; a syndicate of employers opposed to a syndicate of employees). In such a case one syndicate cannot dictate its price to the other and they must reach an agreement.

Let us look closer at producers' cartels. The cartel displaces the competitive equilibrium price, raising it above the equilibrium level in order to increase the returns of the associated enterprises.

However, the higher price is no longer an equilibrium price because at such price and with such return enterprises would produce more than could be sold. Inventories would accumulate and the enterprises would tend to violate the cartel agreement in order to liquidate their inventories. If there is to be balance the cartel must regulate production and it mus t assign output quotas (determine the overall volume of output) and reapportion (redistribute) output among the associated enterprises. Sometimes the cartel shuts down an enterprise that was assigned a production quota because it produces uneconomically and transfers the quota to other enterprises. Enterprises which own a quota derive an assured return from the output quota assigned to them. If they let some other enterprise use their quota they also pass on to them their advantage with respect to returns. They do not do so for free, they sell the quota, and the quota therefore has commercial value. An enterprise that is shut down receives compensation for its quota.

C. THE REGULATED ECONOMY

Competition equilibrium prices can also be displaced by government authority (heteronomously). The government performs this function when it pursues its solidarist objectives. E.g., when competing economic organisations are unable to help themselves because they are too numerous (farmers, workers), when too many goods are involved (consumers), when the price does not represent a permanent base of their vital interest (debtors), or when the government does not wish–in view of its policy of promoting the life, health, and culture of the nation–for prices to be the regulator of production and consumption, when it desires a different kind of regulation. Conceptually the government may administratively displace prices (broadly defined) in each of the three basic markets either up or down. Hence the following possibilities:

    I.   The goods market.
        a) Prices raised above competitive equilibrium
            (to benefit scattered producers, e.g, farmers)
        b) Prices lowered below competitive equilibrium
            (to benefit consumers at times of war-time
                shortages of food or raw materials, etc.).
    II.   The capital market.
        a) Interest rates raised above competitive
            equilibrium
            (not a practical alternative–it is accomplished
                by cartels of financial institutions).
        b) Interest rates lowered below competitive
            equilibrium
            (to benefit debtors).

III. The labour market.
  a) Wages rates raised above competitive equilibrium
     (to benefit numerous workers)
  b) Wages rates lowered below competitive
     equilibrium
     (not a practical alternative–does not correspond
        to the solidarist purpose of the government).

If the government displaces prices from their competitive level it must also assure–if necessary–that another equilibrium be established. E.g., when the government reduces prices of animal fats during the First World War because of shortages, and because rising prices would have depressed consumption of the poor to the point where supply would have been sufficient to satisfy only the demand of the rich (something that the government would not allow) the government was forced to ration consumption of animal fats and to increase their supply by imposing obligatory deliveries by farmers. When increased wage rates cause unemployment the government must care for the unemployed. The regulated economy is part of the solidarist system which is discussed in more detail below.

F. ORGANISATION OF ECONOMIC ACTIVITY

I. Introduction

Organisation is any rational, hence purposive, arrangement of anything. The organisation of labour is purposive arrangement of labour corresponding to the principle of optimum economic effect. Organisation of money is the arrangement of monetary matters that best promotes the purpose of money. At times organisation involves dividing (e.g., division of labour), at other times recombining (again, of labour), and at still other times association, e.g., association of individuals seeking to promote better achievement of their objectives by means of political, cultural, religious, etc., "organisation."

Here we discuss the organisation, (purposive arrangement) of economic activity. It includes:

1. technical organisation, i.e., the organisation of labour and of physical capital (machinery, engines, etc.);
2. organisation of economic units, i.e., the organisation of consuming economic organisations–households–and producing economic organisations–enterprises;
3. organisation of mutual relations between economic units, including monetary organisation which facilitates the relations between economic organisations and the organisation of the markets for goods, capital, and labour.

Organisation may start from below, from agreements and customs among individuals, or–at a later time–from above, from the initiative of government which assists such organisation by establishing certain institutions (e.g., types of business enterprises), by unification and generalisation (weights and measures), or finally, by purposive arrangement (e.g., money and monetary institutions)–all for the benefit of individual economic organisations and in the interest of improving relations among them.

II. Technical organisation

A. Labour

When we visit a factory we see machines, engines, processed materials, mechanical and chemical processes, human labour, the work of motors and of draft animals. We see only technical things, rather than anything economic. The economic aspect is the invisible arrangement of all this which determines how must of what is produced, etc. What we observe in the factory is the plant. The plant becomes an enterprise only through the economic arrangement of technical activity. The technical content of the enterprise is labour and physical capital (goods, raw materials, machines, engines, etc.) their transformation and activities. When we speak of technical organisation we have in the mind the organisation of labour and capital.

When we speak of the classification of labour and of workers, we had in mind division of labour among enterprises an within enterprises and among individuals. Division of labour occurs because it increases labour productivity, because the simplification of work facilitates mechanisation. A thousand individuals living side by side without division of labour have a much lower standard of living than a thousand individuals whose labour is divided and purposively recombined.

When economic organisation was identical with the household that consumed all that it produced and produced all that it required (a closed, in nature economic organisation) labour was divided among family members, men and women, adults and children. There were instances of special dexterity and inclination which led in turn to a more professional division of labour.

All subsequent development–from closed households to economic organisations verging on a world economy–occurred, through ever wider extension of the division of labour. Productive activities became separated, one after another, from production within the closed economic organisation of the household, and they become independent. In addition to the economic organisation of the family enterprises came into being. Division of labour was taking place not only within enterprises but also among enterprises.

As time went on production carried on in one enterprise was divided still further and new parallel branches of production came into existence (e.g., in metal working: the activity of locksmiths, smiths, tin smiths; in wood working: the activity of various kinds of carpenters, wheelrights, box makers, etc.). Invention led to establishment of new enterprises that joined existing ones (e.g., the production of sewing machines) and took over part of the productive activity of existing enterprises, in this case the activities of tailor shops.

Clearly, a very intensive separation, division, and recombining of labour also takes places, within enterprises,–especially when they grow and have more employees.

All these phenomena are in constant motion as they evolve along the path of least resistance, i.e., in the direction of maximum economic effect. Division of labour, even within enterprises, is so pronounced that different categories of workers with different employment conditions are classified in accordance with it.

By division of labour we mean on one hand the development that was just outlined, i.e., the fact that the sum total of the nation's economic activity becomes continuously more specialised and that separate productive activities are carried on by different enterprises and different individuals. On the other hand we mean the outcome of this development, i.e., the state in which each individual who is part of the economic organism belongs to some occupation and the entire population is to some degree divided according to occupational structure.

However, the mechanisation of labour which requires less attention on the part of the worker, but also stimulates less interest, affects the worker's psychological state unfavourably. It occupies his mental powers onesidedly and his other powers are therefore weakened. It dulls his spirit and takes away the joy from his work. There is no joy of work for someone who spends a lifetime sewing button holes, turning out one type of gear for a watch, machining one kind of thread in a steel pipe, etc.

Division of labour and its consequence, exchange, lead to interdependence of economic organisations and they unite the economic organisations of a given country in one big whole, the economic "organism." Eventually the division of labour brings together the entire world with all the consequences that follow from this organisation of economic life.

Whereas the division of labour leads to unification of formerly isolated enterprises into a single big economic organism, it divides at the same time the population into distinct groups according to different occupations. Movement between these groups becomes always more difficult and as a result the groups become more flexible and create the basis for the formation of social classes or estates. More will be said about this below.

The inflexible occupational grouping of the population makes it naturally more difficult for an individual included in one group to transfer to another. An excess supply of clothing workers is naturally of no use when there is excess demand for metal workers or textile workers. Employment conditions in different branches of production therefore develop quite independently and the workers organise according to trades.

Division of labour among individuals and among enterprises therefore leads to the following grouping of occupations:

I.   Material production, which can be classified into
   a) primary production which produces raw materials
      and includes agriculture, forestry, fisheries, hunting,
      mining, and perhaps also smelting of metals
   b) industrial production which processes raw materials
      mechanically or chemically an is further classified
      according to products, type of processing of raw
      materials, or production processes.
II. Trade and finance; this involves mediation between
     producers and consumers, between lenders and
     borrowers, between employers and employees.
III. Transport; including transport of persons and freight,
     and communications.
IV. Services; which do not involve production of goods but
     such work as that of teachers, physicians, barbers, etc.
     Also included is the work of persons employed in
     government administration (by public bodies, to be
     discussed below).

When we visit a factory we observe machines, engines, processed materials, mechanical and chemical processes, human labour, the work of motors and of draft animals. We observe only technology, rather than anything economic. The economic aspect consists in the invisible arrangement of all this which determines how much of what is produced, etc. What we observe in the factory is the plant. The plant becomes an enterprise only through the economic arrangement of technical labour/work/effort/activity/. The technical content of the enterprise is given by labour and physical cap;ital (goods, raw materials, machines, engines, etc.) and their transformations and activities. When we speak of technical organisation we have in mind the organisation of labour and capital.

When we speak of the classification of labour and of workers, we had in mind division of labour among enterprises and within enterprises and among individuals. Division of labour occurs because it increases the productivity of labour, because the simplification of work leads more easily to mechanisation. A thousand individuals who live side by side without division of labour live much worse than a thousand individuals whose labour is divided and purposively brought together/assembled/seclenena.

When the economic organisation was identical with the household that consumed all that it produced and produced all that it required (a closed, in natural economic organisation) labour was divided among family members, among men and women, among adults and children. There were instances of special dexterity and inclination which led in turn to more expert-like division of labour.

All subsequent development—from closed household economic organisations to an economy tending toward a world economy—occurred, under the influence of the division of labour being extended to ever larger areas. From production within the closed economic organisation of a household productive activities became separated, one after another, and they became independent. In addition to the family economic organisation enterprise came into being. The division of labour was taking place not only within enterprises but also among enterprises.

As time went on production that was carried on by one enterprise came to be further divided and new parallel branches of production came into existence (e.g., in metal working: the activity of locksmiths, smiths, tin smiths; in wood working: the activity of carpenters of different types , wheel wrights, box makers, etc.). Inventions led to the establishment of new enterprises that joined existing ones (e.g., the production of sewing machines) and took over a part of productive activity from existing enterprises. In this case the activities of tailor shops.

Clearly, there also takes place, within enterprises, a very intensive separation, division, and recombining of labour–especially when they grew and have more employees.

This entire phenomenon is in constant motion and development along a path of least resistance, i.e., in the direction of maximum economic effect. The division of labour even within enterprises is so sharp that in accordance with it are classified different categories of workers whose employment conditions are different.

By division of labour we mean on one hand the development that was just outlined, i.e., the fact that the total of economic activity in the nation becomes continuously more specialised and that separate productive activities are carried don by different enterprises and different individuals. On the other hand we mean the outcome of this development, i.e., the condition in which each individual included in the economic organisation belongs to some occupation an the entire population exhibits a certain degree of division in its occupational structure.

However, this mechanisation of labour which demands less attention but stimulates also less interest, is unfavourable for the worker's psychological state. It occupies his mental powers onesidedly (and his other powers therefore weaken). It dulls his spirit and takes away the joy from his work. There can be no question of joy of work for someone who spends a lifetime sewing button holes, turning out one type of gear for a watch, machining one kind of thread/zavit/in a steel pipe etc.

The division of labour and its consequence, exchange, leads to interdependence of economic organisations and unites the economic organisations of a given country into one big whole, an economic "organism." And finally it brings together the entire world with all the consequences that follow from this organisation of economic life.

Whereas the division of labour leads on one hand to unification of formerly isolated enterprises into a single big economic organism, it divides at the same time the population into distinct groups according to different occupations. Movement between these groups becomes always more difficult and as a result the groups become more inflexible and generate the basis of the formation of social classes or estates. More will be said about them later.

The inflexible grouping of the population according to occupation makes it naturally more difficult for an individual included within one group to transfer to another. An excess supply of clothing workers is naturally of no use of ran excess demand for metal workers or textile workers. Employment conditions /pracovni pomery/ in different production branches develop therefore quite independently and the workers organise according to trades.

B. Capital

Purposive arrangement of economic activity includes also physical aids of human labour, physical capital, which can be either active (machinery, engines) or passive (processed materials and auxiliary materials).

The progress from primitive tools emulating human limbs (hammer, fork, etc.) to modern machines and engines that make use of natural energy, forces, radiation, etc., has been marvelous. From spindle to spinning machine from wheelbarrow to locomotive, automobile, and aeroplane, from messenger and light signal to radio-telephone and television is the long way of miraculous development, which still continues at breathtaking speed. Man has harnessed to his service all of Nature's energies and made them into his helpers in the struggle with Nature for scarce resources.

C. Rationalisation

The complex of all measures that make up the technical organisation of labour and capital is called rationalisation. It is the realisation of the principle of maximum efficiency by lowering outlays of labour and material inputs for better utilisation. Systematic efforts to achieve this objective by scientific management of production is the task of specialised institutions.

III. ECONOMIC ORGANISATIONS
(FORMS OF BUSINESS ENTERPRISE)

Economic organisation is the organisation of producing or consuming units. Single individuals can have their own consuming units. Individuals who are members of the same household are usually members of a family. A relationship of mutual closeness and solidarity exists within the family which makes possible community of goods and consumption. There are as many consuming economic organisations as there are families and vice versa. (Outside the family circle individuals associate for consumption purposes only exceptionally, e.g., in monasteries for religious reasons.) This is a very ancient and stable situation. Individuals may also join in partial technical associations to save on living expenses, e.g., by sharing an apartment or jointly preparing meals. But each individual pays his share (none pays anything to another).

On the other hand the organisation of business exhibits a rich and varied development. Individuals may operate their own business which is they known as individual proprietorship. On the other hand several individuals may associate to carry on business activity and collective enterprises thus come into being. The individual business enterprise may employ several persons hired by the proprietor for wages or salaries, and the management of a collective enterprise may include two or more individuals. Management is then joined by other co-workers who work for wages and salaries.

Why do individuals associate to carry on joint business activity? Very likely in order to achieve greater success. At times one individual may have the money an another the talent, at times the main reason for the association is to get more capital than they own themselves (borrowing is expensive). The more capital is needed the more associates are usually required to raise it. Success of the business depends, among other things, mostly on three factors: flexibility in decision making, motivation and responsibility, and capital.

Flexibility and adaptability is a function of management control of the assets and labour employed in the business. An individual manager can make decisions quickly. When the business is managed by several individuals they must reach a concensus and that takes longer.

An individual proprietor does not receive specified compensation from his business an he is therefore motivated by interest in the success of the enterprises (business return). His own existence depends on the success of the business and he is strongly motivated by it. His liability for the enterprise extends to all his assets. When there are several entrepreneurs who do not risk all their wealth (indeed their living) but only a specific amount of capital invested in a joint enterprise (and who are not responsible for any more than that) then their interest in the success of the business is weaker, it is no longer vital. Whether capitalisation is larger or smaller determines whether one can carry on more or less business activity (how much capital one owns also determines credit worthiness). As a rule an individual businessman usually does not have enough capital, whereas several associated entrepreneurs do.

When a business is operated by more than one person this increases neither flexibility nor motivation, it only increases capitalisation. Evolution of business organisation indicates clearly that the number of joint managers increases in order to increase capitalisation of the enterprise. It shows how decision making (flexibility) and responsibility (liability, motivation), change.

Closest to an individual proprietorship is the partnership [public company]. It is called public because the names of the partners usually appear in the name of the form, e.g., Belsky and Jezek. Each can make decisions as if he were alone and each is liable for the liabilities of the business with all his personal assets. Such a relationship of trust is possible only when the number of partners is small. The partnership is a flexible form of business. The partners have a major interest in the success of the business (they are liable with all their assets). But it is not adequate for major undertakings because it capitalisation is inadequate since the number of partners is small.

When the partners are joined by additional participants who invest their capital not at interest but for profit (or loss), and when these do not have the power to make decisions, and are liable only for the capital they have invested (which they may lose) the resulting form of business is the [komanditni spolecnost]. The firm is managed by the public partners who have full decision making power and are liable with all their assets. They are now called [komplementari]. The silent partners [podilnici] who are called [komandiste] have the right to oversee the business and they share in profits and losses. In this case the name of the firm includes the names of the public partners [komplementari] and the words "and company" are added which indicates that there are also silent partners [komandiste].

In the case of a limited liability company (Ltd) there is no individual liable with all his assets, liability extends only to the share of capital that individuals have invested. Management decisions are made by executives chosen by shareholders. The shareholders still have a personal relationship vis-a-vis the company because their number is small. This form of business enterprise involves no full assets liability and is suitable for smaller enterprises.

In the case of joint stock corporations (anonymous company) the company's capital stock is divided into shares. E.g.,

10,000,000 crowns may be divided into 10,000 shares of 1,000 crowns each. Those who buy shares receive share certificates representing 1/10,000th part of the business. Shareholders can sell their shares at any time and shareholders' identities are therefore not known. The business is managed by a board of directors elected by shareholders at a shareholders' meeting which also elects a board of control The board of directors manages the corporation and the board of control performs the oversight function. When a shareholder holds the majority of the corporation's shares he has control of the enterprise. Shareholders do not receive interest but a share of the corporation's profits (dividends). Corporate shares are therefore securities that bring a return and their market price represents capitalisation of the expected return. Estimates of the expected return are made an the price of the shares fluctuates. There is speculation that the prices of shares will rise or fall. Shareholders have no liability other than the investment in their shares which is the maximum that they can lose. This makes it possible for a large number of capitalists to participate in large scale enterprises. In addition to expected returns they are motivated to buy shares because they can sell them at any time their capital is therefore liquid. The corporation is managed by a whole collective (shareholders' meeting, board of directors). This means that management is not ever flexible unless decision making is delegated to a chief executive officer who receives a salary (and perhaps also a share of profits known as [tantiema]. Also the shareholders' concern with the affairs of the enterprise is not very great (they may know nothing about the business). On the other hand, the corporation makes possible a large concentration of capital. The corporate form of business enterprise was used to set up the first railroads, steamships companies, etc.).

The above are the main forms of business enterprises. Businessmen seek the most suitable form for each type of business activity. However enterprises operate (produce, sell, provide the services of transport and other services) to serve anyone, all other economic organisations, that demand its products or services and are willing to pay the price. Each business enterprise engages in productive activities to achieve an objective return for its working team and a personal return for the entrepreneur. If the entrepreneur's return exceeds the normal compensation of his labour (wage) and his own capital (interest) it is called profit. The existence of entrepreneurial profit is the reason for the emergence of cooperatives which take the place of business enterprises. Cooperatives are discussed below.

Different forms of business enterprise are a response to economic need. Governments promulgate various legal forms of business enterprise (law of commerce) and entrepreneurs have a choice which one to select.

IV. ORGANISATION OF CONTACTS AMONG ECONOMIC ORGANISATIONS

A. MONETARY ORGANISATION

1. Metal Money

Contacts among economic organisations take place in markets. The organisational impact is either on individual markets (for goods, capital, labour) or on all markets. Money serves all markets and all contacts between economic organisations. That is why we start the discussion of the organisation of contacts between economic organisations with a discussion of monetary organisation.

We have seen that money came into being to satisfy a certain need, and that one commodity was selected to serve as money. Ultimately a precious metal was chosen and a certain amount of the metal became the technical monetary unit. To this day the names of monetary units recall weights (pound, sheckel). Because money serves all economic organisations on the territory of the state, the state itself assumes responsibility for organising monetary matters.

Monetary metal [sic: trh] was originally weighed in the market place, and later on in the home, it was divided into pieces, and the pieces only counted in the market place. Eventually–to promote general confidence–the government took over itself the function of weighing and dividing the metal into pieces of given purity and weight known as coins. The state strikes coins and reserves for itself the exclusive right to do so.

Coins are pieces of metal in money form (flat cylinder) certified by the government as to purity and weight. The government decides from what metal, e.g., gold, the coins shall be struck. It also decides, what the money unit shall be, what the coins shall weigh. However, the government also strikes coin on private account. Everyone used to have the right to bring natural gold to the mind and the government struck coins for him at a cost called [razebne seignorage].

Coins are not struck from pure gold or silver became these metals are too soft and wear out too quickly. Instead they are struck from an alloy but in such a way that the coin has as much pure metal as it is supposed to contain. If the coin should contain 1/3 of a gram of gold and it is struck from an alloy it must weigh somewhat more. It is impossible to achieve absolute exactness of weight and there exists therefore a technically allowable departure (remedium). When the weight of the coin drops, as the coin circulates below some (still permissible) weight, (circulation weight) the coin is taken out of circulation. The loss of metal that results from circulation is borne by the state. The loss of metal that results from damaging the coins is borne by their holders. Damaged coins are taken from their holders an replaced with a smaller amount.

If coins that weighed less circulated alongside coins that had their full weight, everyone would hoard the full-weight coins and spend the under-weight coins. The latter would then dominate circulation and everyone would be aware of the fact that he was selling for a cheaper money unit (less monetary metal). This would lead to higher prices. Bad money drives out good money (Gresham's Law).

Legislation of the state determines from what metal coins are to be struck, what is to be the amount content of the metal in the money unit, and what is to be the name of the unit (crown, mark, franc, dollar, lira, dinar, drakhma, lev, etc.). This establishes the monetary standard of the state. Depending on the metal selected, it may be either a gold standard or silver standard. The government then strikes the money units or multiples of the money unit if a single unit is too small.

How can small transactions be effectuated when only coins of a certain value are struck from the monetary metal? This also requires coins, and these are struck from less valuable metals–bronze, nickel, iron, etc. A coin worth one-tenth of a gold coin and struck from nickel should actually contain as much nickel as can be bought with the corresponding amount of gold in the gold coin. However, this relationship depends on the relative market price, and if the price of nickel rose, members of the public would melt down the nickel coins because they would contain more gold for the nickel than what they would get if they spent the coin whose monetary value is one-tenth of the gold coin. For this reason subsidiary coins contain less metal than their stated monetary value and they circulate because the government decrees that every one must accept them as payment in transactions at their stated monetary value. Despite this the public would not accept the subsidiary coins if the government placed extremely large quantities of such coins into circulation.

The government can therefore put into circulation only a limited quantity of subsidiary coins referred to as [kontingent], either an absolute amount for the whole country or in relative terms per capita. Coins used for minor transactions can be made of several different metals. They are minor coins.

Their value (purchasing power) is not determined by their metal content. It is derived value. Subsidiary coins are worth a fraction or a small multiple of the money unit. They can even be made of paper.

Because subsidiary coins do not contain as much metal as their face value, they cannot be coined for the accounts of private individuals. When the government strikes minor coins it makes a profit because the metal used in coining them is less than the face value of the coins when they are spent.

A monetary standard based on gold does not cease being gold-based just because it includes subsidiary coins made of other metals. The value foundation upon which depends the value of subsidiary coins continues to be the amount of gold contained in the money unit.

And what is the value of the money unit? That is not provided by legislation. It depends on the gold content of the money unit which is nothing but a piece of gold and has the value of the gold. After all, anyone may transform his gold (via the state mint) into as many money units as he wishes. Anyone can have his gold in natural form made into coins in the state mint and anyone can melt down gold coins. If gold were to become a common metal gold coins would buy less. The exchange value of gold and the exchange value of gold coins are identical.

And what si the price of gold in this case? The price is expressed in gold money units and a kilogram of gold has always the same price as the number of money units that can be coined from that kilogram of gold.

In the past there were monetary standards that involved free coinage by private individuals from both gold and silver (bimetallic standard) but this is no longer practical today. Countries (with exceptions in the Orient) have concentrated on the gold standard in response to international commercial relations. A unit of gold transfers a larger value from country to country than an equal weight unit of silver. If two trading countries have a monetary standard based on the same metal, this makes payments easier. This will be discussed further below.

2. Paper Money...Bank Notes

The function of money is to enable making all payments not only in buying and selling but also in transactions involving services, debts, transfer of capital, etc. What quantity of currency should be in circulation? As much as there are current payments that are not cleared in some center such as a bank.

If everyone had a deposit account in one bank everyone could make payments by ordering the bank (cheque) to credit the desired amount to whomever he designated as payee. If the payee also had his account with that bank, the bank would do so by debiting the account of the payor and crediting it to the account of the payee. Thee would then be no need for cash money. If this were true for all citizens throughout the country, there would be no need of currency; all payments would be made by moving deposit money between accounts. We would then have money of account transfers giro money. However, only some portion of total payments are actually transacted in this way. (In our country this purpose is served by the Postal Savings Bank [Postovni sporitelna] other payments are made in cash.

However, the volume of cash payments varies in the course of the year. It is large at the start of the month when payments of wages, salaries, rents, etc., are made, it is larger in the Fall when crops are sold, than at other times. Money that arrives in the household of a salaried employee, say 3,000 crowns, on the first of the month, returns gradually into circulation throughout the month as the household makes purchases.

If the only cash money we had was metallic money there would be sometimes too little money (when the volume of payments was large) and sometimes to much money (when the volume of payments was small). When the volume of payments was large, public demand for money would be large and high interest rates would be offered to borrow money. However, interest rates affect prices and wages and high interest rates tend to depress economic activity. The problem is dealt with by banknotes.

Every country has set up for this purpose a Central Bank or National Bank directly owned by the state or as a corporation that the government controls. The purpose of the Central Bank is to provide an additional quantity of money in the form of paper currency or banknotes to supplement the metallic money in circulation. When banknotes are introduced, the public actually no longer wishes to hold gold, since paper money is more convenient. The Central Bank thus issues banknotes, which are certificates of its indebtedness. They are denominated in round amounts (e.g., 500,1000, 5000) and bear no interest.

How do banknotes come into circulation? First, when the Central Bank exchanges them for gold coins held by the public or when it buys bullion, unminted gold. These banknotes are covered by gold, but they replace gold in circulation, they do not augment the quantity of money in circulation, and if there were no other banknotes the quantity of money in circulation would one again be sometimes insufficient and sometimes excessive. The quantity of banknotes in circulation would not be elastic. For this reason there is another way in which banknotes are issued.

Where there is a shortage of currency for current payments, members of the public approach the Central Bank requesting loans of "paper money," the Bank's notes, offering as collateral either movable assets (goods, securities, etc.) this is known as lombard loans (as distinct from collateral in the form of non-movable assets, real estate, known as mortgage loans).

Alternately they borrow against certificates of indebtedness, promissory notes which promise repayment on a certain date without specifying the reason that gave rise to the indebtedness (purchase, sale, etc.). The signatures of the two additional persons appear on the promisory note. They are jointly responsible for the repayment, in case of the original debtor's failure to repay the loan. Loans secured by promissory notes are known as discount loans.

In this way banknotes come into circulation by way of credit. But the Central Bank makes only short term (3-month) loans. When the shortage of money passes, when payments even out and diminish, loans secured by promisory notes or by lombard loans are repaid and banknotes return to the Central Bank. In this way economic life itself draws from the Central Bank, in the form of credit, the needed addition to the supply of money for the duration of the need.

The Central Bank does not make free loans. If it did everyone would apply for such loans. Instead the Bank lends at interest and it can decide what the rate will b because it can print money. It controls the demand for paper currency by means of the interest rate. This interest is known, in the case of promissory notes, as discount (deduction) because it is deducted beforehand.

If the management of the Central Bank notes that there is a shortage of (short-term) money in the market (interest rates rising, security prices falling) and if it believes that this is the consequence of an insufficient supply of money, it does not wait for members of the public to come to it requesting credits. Instead the Bank goes to the market to buy securities and thus increases the money supply, moderates the rise of interest rates and the decline of security prices. In the converse it sells securities. (These purchases or sales of securities by the Central Bank are called open market operations).

We have said that banknotes are certificates of the Central Bank's indebtedness. What does the Bank promise? It promises to exchange, at anytime, gold for banknotes. When one holds paper money that can be exchanged at any time for gold, it is just as valuable as gold. For this reason the public is willing to accept banknotes as it is to accept gold money, and banknotes are money that performs the same functions as gold money. This willingness assumes, of course, that the Central Bank is in a position to exchange gold for its banknotes. We know that only some portion of banknotes is backed by gold that part which comes into existence via purchases of gold and gold coin. That part which comes into circulation via credit operations (lombard loans and discounting of promissory notes) is not backed by gold, indeed it cannot be backed, by gold if it is to perform the function of an elastic supplement to the money supply. (We say that these banknotes are backed commercially.)

Therefore if all holders of banknotes demanded at the same time that their banknotes be redeemed for gold, the Central Bank would be unable to keep is promise. This will not happen however. If the public has confidence it requests gold only when it needs it to make payments abroad. (This is discussed below.) Otherwise the public is content to hold paper money. Nonetheless, if the Bank were to issue via credit too many banknotes, this would give rise to concern about the Bank's ability to redeem the notes, banknotes would be presented for redemption in large amounts, confidence would be lost. For this reason there are various legal limits on the Central Bank's ability to issue banknotes.

There may be a limit of the total quantity of all banknotes in circulation, or a limit of the quantity of banknotes not covered by gold (such limits tend to be too high and ineffective under normal conditions and too low and too stifling under abnormal conditions). Alternatively there may be set a required ratio of total banknotes to banknotes covered by gold (the gold coverage ratio, e.g., 25%). Possibly also there may be set a limit on the total volume of banknotes in circulation and when such limit is exceeded a bank tax is imposed on the excess issue of notes. This forces the Bank to raise interest rates to the level of the tax (otherwise it would lose money by issuing the banknotes). The government gets a share of the Bank's profit and plays a role in the Bank's management (appointing some members of the Board of Directors (Bank Board), appointing a supervisory commissioner, the Chairman of the Board, etc.).

Gold stored in the Bank's vaults represents the Bank's gold reserve. We have noted its importance for convertibility. Its importance for international payments is even greater.

3. Emergency banknotes and Treasury notes

Formerly, in times of war, governments that found themselves short of funds would print their own money, declaring
that they would accept it in payment of taxes and compelling the
public to accept it. Such money is known as treasury notes.
During the First World War governments did not print their own
money but compelled Central Banks to lend them banknotes
printed by the Central Banks. There were emergency banknotes.
They were not backed by gold, nor were they issued in response
to short term credit needs of the private sector to finance
current payments an therefore were not backed commercially
either. They came into circulation via the Treasury not because
there was a shortage of money in circulation but because the
state economy was short of funds. Such banknotes were issued
without hope that they would be redeemed soon. In either way
the government printed and thus created emergency command
over resources.

An economic organisation acquires warranted command
over resources by contributing something to other economic
organisations, by making a contribution to the national product
the conceptual basket of goods that represent the means that
sustain the nation's life. (It is "conceptual" because at any
particular moment the "basket" as such does not actually exist.)
For the value of his contribution everyone can then choose what
he needs in accordance with relative utility.

However, when the government creates unwarranted command over resources, when it creates unwarranted income
(without having itself contributed to the national product or
without having obtained such command from its citizens
through taxation or borrowing) it joins the ranks of buyers
alongside those who have acquired such command in a warranted eay. In so doing the government raises artificially the
level of nominal economic magnitude, it raises the price level
and reduces the value, the purchasing power, of money.

As domestic prices rise it soon becomes apparent, that it is preferable to redeem banknotes for gold and use gold to make purchases abroad. Th Central Bank loses gold, the gold reserve is reduced, the Bank is faced with the threat of being unable to continue to redeem its notes. To this the government responds by absolving the Bank from its obligation to convert banknotes into gold and by compelling the public to accept non-redeemable notes as if they were redeemable or as f they were metallic money. It imposes a forced conversion rate of banknotes. To be sure, if can compel the public to accept non-redeemable notes only when they are used to repay debt obligations (by refusing to grant judicial relief to creditors). But in the case of other transactions it must use administrative measures in attempting to prevent pries from rising.

The government thus bring s about inflation by creating unwarranted command over resources by printing inflationary issues of banknotes. When all prices rise, so does the price of gold. Its price is no longer stable. As opposed to the fixed price given by the gold content of the monetary unit, the price of gold rises in term of non-redeemable banknotes.

Th difference between the fixed price of gold given by the official gold content of the monetary unit and the price of gold in terms of non-redeemable banknotes is called agio. Gold no longer circulates. Only non-redeemable banknotes do. Their value reflects the relationship between nominal economic magnitudes such as nominal national income and real national product. The monetary standard is now a paper standard or "nominal" standard.

When the value of money thus declines, what becomes of the value of subsidiary coins? Their value is a function of the value of the monetary unit. This is now a paper unit whose value keeps falling. The purchasing power of subsidiary coins declines along with the purchasing power of the paper currency until it has fallen to the point where the value of the metal that they contain is lager than what they are worth as coins (this was not the case originally). At that point they began to be used as metal. They are melted down and eventually disappear from circulation (agiotage). They have to be replaced by subsidiary coins made from still less valuable metal (e.g., during the First World War, by coins made from iron), or paper, or some other material (leather, porcelain).

To correct this situation it is first necessary to stop the unwarranted issue of banknotes, i.e., to restore order in the public sector. Secondly it is necessary to eliminate the difference between the value of the gold monetary unit, which has an agio, and the paper unit whose value is lower. This can be done by reducing the gold content of the monetary unit to bring its value down somewhat closer to the value of the paper unit (devaluation). Alternatively it can be done by reversing the decline of the value of paper money until the agio of gold money disappears and the price level declines proportionately. This represents a deflationary process.

This is conceptually possible though a process that is the reverse of inflation. Because an unwarranted command over resources was created, it is now necessary to destroy it. The way in which this is done is for the government to take away command over resources from members of the public by taxing some portion of their income or by borrowing part of their income that had been acquired in a warranted way and destroying the banknotes thus acquired. In so doing the government reduces nominal economic magnitudes, it reduces the price level, and it raises the value of the paper monetary unit.

In practice the method of deflation is confronted by major difficulties. When prices are rising business profits are also rising and this stimulates business activity. When prices are falling profits tend to disappear. Unless businessmen succeed in lowering wages and salaries which their employees will resist they will incur losses because the amount of borrowed capital and business indebtedness have not declined. Business activity declines. Because of this it is not feasible to correct a major decline in the purchasing power of money, such as occurred after the First World War, via the process of deflation.

B. THE ORGANISATION OF GOODS MARKETS

Markets represent the coming together in time and place of buyers and sellers. Both the time and the place have to be agreed upon or mandated for the sake of uniformity and centralisation. Some markets are organised by agreement or custom of traders and producers (e.g., fairs in which only wholesale traders take part, such as the Spring and Fall Fairs in Prague). Others are organised by pubic bodies. Municipalities assume responsibility for market places and for other in those places, e.g., food markets and their cooling equipment. To encourage competition, municipalities have long exercised care that businesses engaged in the same trade should be located in the same neighborhood (streets of butchers, bakers, drapers, etc.). Some communities have periodic fairs (e.g., four times a year). The government regulates so-called commodity exchanges. These are markets that cover extensive areas where specific standard commodities, which are not physically present, are traded in specified minimum quantities (contracts). E.g., wheat trade on a commodity exchange wheat must be of a certain quality expressed in terms of the relative weight of the grain, etc. It follows also that much speculation takes place in such exchanges. Some exchanges are of world-wide importance, e.g., the London metals exchange. Markets are indispensable for the existence of competition and equilibrium prices.

The function of markets have been taken over–in part–by enterprises engaged in distribution (not completely because these enterprises are scattered and this makes it difficult to get a good picture of competitive conditions. This development is associated with the development of transport (railways, autobuses). The importance of periodic fairs in rural communities has declined because stores in towns have become easily accessible. In spite of this, new markets for specific goods are still coming into being, e.g., for glass products and ceramics.

And so, whether distributors supplement markets (they buy and sell in markets) or replace markets (members of the public make purchases in stores rather than in market places), they are an indispensable link in mediating and bringing together distant, and sometimes unknown producers, especially large-scale producers, and scattered buyers and consumers. There are no distant and unknown goods as far as the consumer is concerned. If it is true that exchange assists division of labour and that division of labour promotes labour productivity and prosperity, then commerce performs such functions also. Of course, commerce profits most from such mediation. The wealth of Venice, of the Low Countries, etc., stemmed mostly from overseas trade. Of course if there are two middlemen in the path between producer and consumer where one would be enough, then the producer or the consumer suffers. The middleman takes a larger share of value than is necessary.

Division of labour is also found in distribution, according to the type of goods (outlets specialising in distributing food products, hardware, leather goods, sundries, etc.). Alternatively division of labour develops along the lines of how much and to whom the establishments sell. Wholesalers sell larger quantities to smaller businesses, retailers sell smaller quantities to anybody. Of course, producers may have their own outlets where they sell their products (e.g., Bata).* Trading enterprises, particularly collective ones, may also assume different forms of business organisation, ranging from partnerships to joint stock companies.

The functions of distribution may also be performed by cooperatives. There are buyers' cooperatives (of consumers or producers, e.g., agricultural cooperatives that make joint purchases of seed or fertiliser, or cooperatives of craftsmen that make joint purchases of raw materials, etc. There are also sellers' cooperatives (e.g., dairy cooperatives of farmers or

---

* Translator's Note: BATA is the world's largest producer of footwear. The firm which is active in numerous countries

distribution cooperatives of shoemakers.) More will be said about this below.

Goods are sold in markets by the piece or according to weight and measure, and prices are quoted accordingly. Standardisation of weights and measures si desirable because it facilitates trade. In this respect the situation has evolved from private agreements and customs to mandatory standardisation decreed by governments and applicable to geographic areas that include entire countries and may even be applicable internationally. This facilitates commerce and reduces risks. For the same reason products are identified as to their origin (trade marks), their purity (hallmarks of precious metals), etc.

As we have noted, markets are organized either from below through agreements or customs, or from above by the government. Here the government plays a role through legislation. But legislation serves private interests, interest of individuals, to facilitate exchange and relationships between economic organisations.

C. ORGANISATION OF THE CAPITAL MARKET

1. Financial institutions

We have discussed financial markets where supply of and demand for capital are brought together. Such markets actually exist and they are known as security exchanges. However, security exchanges do not represent all of the financial capital market. As we shall see, only a portion of financial capital is brought together there.

----

started out in Czechoslovakia, Karel Englis' homeland, where it operated a large number of retail outlets. The headquarters of BATA are now in Canada and the firm is headed by Thomas Bata, Jr., son of the firm's founder.

The function of bringing together supply of and demand for financial capital is also performed by financial institutions (business enterprises). This is quite analogous with the way in which the function of goods markets is assumed by distribution outlets. It means of course that the market becomes decentralised. In a way therefore thee are as many markets as there are financial intermediaries to which flows the supply of capital and from which credit is sought. It could therefore happen that one financial institution experiences excess supply while another experiences excess demand. This would put pressure on the first to lower interest rates, while the latter would be encouraged to raise them. However, supply would then shift to the institution offering higher interest rates and demand would shift to the institution offering lower ones. The upshot is that financial intermediaries one again constitute a market even though supply and demand are not brought together in a single place. Because the greater part of capital flows (from capitalists to borrowers)) through financial intermediaries, we shall discuss them first when we discuss the organisation of the financial capital market.

The function of intermediary between supply of and demand for capital is performed by financial institutions, credit institutions, etc., (banks in the most general sense). Their task is to gather (acquire) capital funds and distribute them to those who require credit. The acquisition of capital funds si represented by deposits. There are different types of deposits and they can be distinguished according to what the depositors are given by the financial institutions when they deposit their money. They may be given pass books for savings accounts, certificates of deposit, i.e., documents certifying that an amount of money (a round sum) has been deposited and promising interest, letters of credit stating that the depositor has a certain credit balance in his current account, etc. (Current accounts are called current because the accounts are currently increased by amounts deposited and decreased by the amounts withdrawn.)

On the other side financial institutions lend the funds deposited in them to those who seek credit. Once again loans are differentiated according to the collateral given by the borrower to the bank. When the collateral is immoveable we speak of mortgage loans. When the collateral is movable we speak of lombard credit. When there is no collateral we speak of personal loans against promissory notes or IOU's (guaranteed by additional guarantors), etc. A distinction si also made between short-term and long-term credit, between investment and operating credit, etc. In addition to the credit functions, banks also perform the function of arranging payments, as well as buying and selling securities. This will be discussed below.

Division of labour also exists among financial institutions. Some are involved in encouraging thrift and in a safe placement of savings, e.g., by investing in immoveables up to a limit called "orphans' collateral"* (one-half of the value of buildings, two-thirds of the value of land). The are known as savings and loan associations (e.g., the Prague City Savings and Loan Association).

Others provide advantageous credit conditions to certain borrowers, e.g., to farmers, or municipalities, and they seek capitalists willing to lend them funds. This includes mortgage banks (Mortgage Bank of Bohemia) and banks for communal credit, e.g., the Provincial Bank of Bohemia in Prague.** (See discussion below.)

Credit for industry and trade (larger trade enterprises) is provided by commercial banks which obtain funds via saving deposits, certificates of deposit, and current-account deposits (an example is the Bank for Tradesmen or the Industrial Bank of Bohemia in Prague.***

---

* It is called "orphans' collateral" because a court of law may approve loans of funds belonging to orphans up to such collatoral limit.

** The two banks have now merged.

***Translator's Note: These were cooperative financial institutions of different types (credit unions). In Czechoslovakia

Commercial banks deal with larger business enterprises. Small businesses are served by mutual saving banks. They make similar loans and obtain funds in a similar way as do commercial banks, but on a smaller scale (e.g., the Mutual Savings Bank of Mala Strana). A rural type of credit union which make personal loans to the smallest borrowers on their personal security are known as Kampelik Credit Unions [kampelicky] or Raiffeisen Credit Unions [raiffeisenky]).**

Consumer credit secured by moveable collateral is provided by pawnshops.

In addition to business type financial institutions there are also credit cooperatives [zalozny] and institutions operated by the central government (Post Office Savings Bank) and other public bodies (The Provincial Bank, District Agricultural Banks, Communal Banks). Various forms of business organisation are involved in the field of finance: Individually owned enterprises (bankers), collectively owned enterprises ranging from partnership to joint stock companies.

---

before the Second World War they included in particular District Mutual Savings Banks [okresni zalozny hospodarske]. Tradesmen's Mutual Savings Banks [zivnostenske zalozny], General Mutual Savings Banks [vseobecne zalozny], and Kampelik Credit Unions [kampelicky]. Source: *Ekonomicka encyklopedia [Economic Encyclopedia].* vol. II, 649, Prague, 1972.

** Translator's Note: The Kampelik credit unions in Czechoslovakia before the Second World War were small credit unions that originated in the Czech provinces after 1890. Their name is associated with Dr. Cyril Kampelik who advocated the founding of these cooperatives on the model of their founder in Germany, F. W. Raiffeisen. Source: *Ekonomicka encyklopedia [Economic Encyclopedia],* vol. I, 360-361, Prague, 1972.

TERMINOLOGY*

kontingent -- Smi jich tedy dati dtat do obehu jen obmezene mnozstvi, kontingent urceny absolutene prop cely stat nebo relativne ha hlavu.

mince drobne -- minor coin

lombard -- Lombard loan

smenka -- promissory note

hypoteka -- mortgage

eskont -- discount

diskont -- discount

mimoradne bankovky -- emergency banknotes

statovky -- treasury notes

agio -- premium ?

agiotage

uzaverky -- contract (in the stock market or commodity market)–a specified round number of shares (e.g., 100 shares = 1 contract in the options market)

punc -- hallmark

vklady -- deposit

vkladni (usporna) knizka --passbook–but KE means savings account

poukazka -- papir znejici na zaokrouhlenou castku penezni a slibujici urok–*certificate of deposit*

sporitelny -- savings and loan associations

hypotecni banka -- mortgage bank

zalozny -- mutual savings banks

* This terminology chart was not included in the original text and is included for the reader's benefit.

2. Marketable securities

Those who lend capital funds prefer to have them repaid whenever they choose. Borrowers, on the other hand, prefer not to be obliged to do so (banks too prefer not to have deposits withdrawn). What is therefore needed is some way that makes it possible for lenders to mobilise capital without forcing borrowers to repay the loans whenever the creditors choose. The solution is found in marketable securities. When banks issue to depositors interest bearing certificates of deposit, the certificates have market value. Any bearer of such paper may request that the bank should pay to him the balance or that it pay interest The paper si a marketable security, a vehicle of transfer value.

Marketable securities therefore increase transferability and mobility of capital, and the willingness to lend. Several kinds of transferable marketable securities have evolved. Some are bearer securities (the owner's name does not appear on the paper). Others may show the owner's name may be shown in which case the paper is transferred to a new owner by endorsement and the paper is said to be a l'ordre. We can distinguish, in more detail, the following kinds of securities:

(a) Obligations (Bonds)
1. Partial bonds and priority obligations

When a large business enterprise (or government) wishes to borrow a certain sum, it divides it into smaller fractions in round amounts and issues against them debt instruments (bonds) promising to redeem them under certain conditions (e.g., on the basis of a draw the amounts shown in the instrument. In addition it promises to pay annual interest at a stated rate which is also shown in the instrument.

To facilitate the payment of interest, the instrument usually includes a coupon page to which is attached, at the bottom, a so-called talon. The coupons which entitle the bearer to interest for some part of the year can be cashed in at any financial institution, which is then compensated by the issuer of the bond. When all the coupons have been cashed in, the talon entitles the bond holder to receive another coupon page. Title to this type of debt instrument is usually issued in the name of the owner. They are called partial debt instruments in view of the fact, as noted, that the total amount borrowed is subdivided into smaller round amounts.

When debt instruments include a right to prior to redemption compared to instruments held by other creditors, we speak of priority obligations.

2. Collateral securities

Collateral certificates evolved from the need to reconcile the interests of capitalists who wish to have access to their capital at any time and borrowers who require long-term, non-callable credit that is paid back in installments, secured by a mortgage. When such borrowers come to a financial institution they receive the approved loan in the form of a collateral certificate whose nominal value* is equal to the amount of the approved loan. The borrower sells the collateral certificate to the capitalist at the market price. The financial institution therefore deals with capitalists who hold collateral certificates in their capacity as creditors, and with the borrowers. The capitalist cannot request that the financial institution redeem the sm stated in the collateral certificate on demand, but if he requires the funds, he can sell the certificate or borrow the needed funds against them (as a lombard loan). The borrower makes payments of interest and principal annuity. Interest on the collateral certificates is paid from the interest payments made to financial institutions by the debtors. In this respect the certificates resemble completely the debt instruments described under (1). Redemptions of collateral certificates are made out of payments of principal that flow into financial institutions, on

---

*   The amount stated in the instrument.

the basis of draws, in such a way as to keep balance between credits (mortgage debts) and debits (the nominal amount of circulating collateral certificates).

Collateral certificates also solve another problem that arises in connection with mortgage loans, particularly farm loans. The value of a farm is a function of the farm's net return and of the prevailing rate of interest, the rate at which a potential buyer of the farm–regardless of any other special reasons–capitalises this return. Assuming an unchanged return, the value of the farm may change as the rate of interest experiences lasting change. When the rate falls the prices rise and vice versa. A farm with an outstanding burden of debt of, say, two-thirds of some appraised value, and whose price then declines because of a change in the rate of interest, can suddenly become excessively indebted without any fault of the farmer. This gave rise to the view that farms cannot bear well a burden of debt that originates from borrowing for capital investment but only a burden that corresponds to the farm's rent with a fixed annual payment that the farm owner can still afford to make as long as the farm's return is unchanged. Whereas in the case of debt arising from borrowing for capital investment the debtor is also to some extent dependent on changes in the prevailing rate of interest.

Like the value of farms, the value of securities, e.g., of collateral certificates, also depends on changes in the rate of interest. The value of collateral certificates–abstracting again from other circumstances that affect speculation on the stock exchange–is once again a function of the return to capital which the security stipulates (i.e., annual return in terms of the current rate of interest). E.g., if a security yields an annual return of 4 crowns, and the current rate of interest is five percent, a savings and loan institution will pay interest of 4 crowns on a deposit of 80 crowns. An investor will therefore be willing to pay about 80 crowns from such security, though its principal (nominal) value is 100 crowns. Of course, this would be somewhat influenced by speculation. E.g., as noted above, when a collateral certificate sells below par (below its nominal value), it makes a difference that the investor has some chance, when the securities are redeemed by draw to receive the nominal, i.e., higher sum. However, it can be said that, given some return on either a security or a farm the values of both move in parallel.

When a borrower can repay his debt either in collateral certificates or in cash, it means in practice that his debt declines when the value of the collateral certificate declines, but that it can never exceed its original nominal value, even when the value of the paper rises above par (above its stated nominal value). As described, the borrower is thus freed from the harmful effects of changes in the prevailing rate of interest.

3. Perpetuities [rents]

Rents resemble in all respects the debt instruments described under (1), except that they do not promise repayment of principal but only the payment of annual interest, called rent. The payments may be partly restricted (to some period of time) or they may not be restricted.

4. Cashier certificates

These are not true certificates, but debt instruments issued by banks or by public treasuries. They are short-term interest bearing instruments stated in round sums. True certificates are discussed immediately below. If a certificate does not have a coupon attached (talon) and interest is deducted up front it is called a bon.

(b) Certificates
1. Cheques. Cheques are orders to pay on sight executed in prescribed form. They may be payable a l'ordre (endorseable) or to a payee. It is also possible for a cheque to be written not on funds that had been deposited with the bank but funds for which the bank is issuing credit. Cheques function as a means of making payments and as a device to economise on the use of cash in making payments.

2. Bills of exchange [notes]. Notes were already mentioned when the issuance of banknotes was discussed. They are instruments wherein one party (the issuer) instructs another to pay a certain sum to a third party whose name also appears in the note. Of course the issuer may issue an instruction that the payment is to be made to his own account and he also has the right, as creditor, to transfer the note to others by endorsing it. When the payor accepts the obligation stated in the note he becomes an acceptor and the note becomes an acceptance. For the note to be valid it is necessary for all formalities required by law to be fulfilled. Notes are abstract obligations because they do not indicate the reason for their issuance, i.e., whether they originated because an insufficient payment was made, because credit was granted, or for other reasons. If a note is transferred in sequence to several parties, then all who have endorsed it, including the original issuer, are liable for its payment to the last holder as shown by endorsement, in case that the debtor fails to fulfill his obligations. A note is therefore the more secure the more persons have held it. In other words, it becomes more secure as it circulates.

A note promises only the payment of a fixed sum of money. It promises no interest. For example, an individual who uses a note to borrow a certain sum of money repayable in half a year is issued a note that states this sum, but the cash amount that he receives as loan is reduced by a discount, i.e., interest on the sum that he in effect receives as loan. Loans evidenced by notes appear therefore on the books of financial institutions under the name of discount notes. An individual who holds a note that matures only after some time and who wishes to obtain funds right away will sell the note–of course after deduction of the discount. When the note is sold the second time it is referred to as rediscount.

Securities also include shares of stock which we have discussed.

3. The stock exchange. Just as there are commodity markets for trading in commodities so there are financial markets, security markets, where financial capital seeks placement, by

acquisition of various kinds of securities. These markets are operated by associations established for this purpose; they are self-governed by chambers of security exchanges, and they are supervised by the government.

Prices of securities are called course. Securities may be traded either in the spot market or for future delivery and settlement. Here the sellers speculate that prices will fall (a la baisse), while buyers speculate that they will rise (a la hausse). And so, speculation divides the market into two camps, where the camp that speculates on a decline is known as [kontremina]. There are many different varieties of futures transactions. If the object of trading is only speculation the parties are not interested in delivery of the securities but merely in the differential between the price at the time of the transaction and the price at the time of the future delivery. A speculator who has made an incorrect guess pays the differential without the securities being delivered (so-called differential trades). Unless trading in security markets is regulated by law it is governed by custom.

Trading in security markets includes buying and selling of shares of stock, fractions of debt certificates, perpetuities (rents), short-term paper (notes, bonds), as well as credit instruments secured by movable collateral (lombard loans), pre-selling of coupons (discounting of coupons, etc.). The security market provides a sensitive picture of the condition of the capital market. Given the great mobility of capital, the security market centralises the financial market for the whole country (a country needs several commodity exchanges but, as a rule, only one security exchange).

4. Organisation of the capital market. The capital market is organized bot˙ from below (by associations, agreements, custom,e tc.) and by government action, from above. Government is involved, first of all, in establishing forms of business enterprise that are also used in finance, and in setting up types of securities (e.g., bills of exchange, cheques, mortgage documents, etc.) used in financial markets. The government or state public bodies set up financial institutions (such as the state-

owned Post Office Savings Bank the Provincial Bank, district mutual savings banks. The government keeps records of mortgage liens on real estate in land title cadasters, it supervises the stock exchange, etc. We have already discussed the organisation of the National Bank.

The role of government is important in matters of credit, in that the government provides legal protection, so that debtors should live up exactly to their obligations. The government thus provides legal security to the capital market. All this the government does because it recognises the great importance of savings and credit.

5. The importance of savings and credit. Credit moves financial capital from capitalists to those (borrowers) who can make better use of it. This increases the effectiveness (productivity) of the nation's economic activity, provided that capital funds that were accumulated are used to set up and expand or to operate enterprises that turn out useful products. In this way takes place expansion of physical capital goods (machinery, motors) that facilitate the nation's productive activity; transport (roads, railroads) is improved; life is improved in other ways (hospitals, works of art, etc.). Had our ancestors consumed all that they produced, had they saved nothing, there would be no progress that is based on the fact that we can continue to build on the foundation of what they had built and what they had left to us. Saving and credit is the way of economic progress.

D. ORGANISATION OF THE LABOUR MARKET

The function of intermediary in hiring labour can be carried on as a business, as a separate professional activity. Large business enterprises hire workers directly through their employment offices. Hiring of labour is also carried on by employers' or workers' associations; because the latter are trades associations, their hiring activities involve separate trades. Public bodies (ranging from municipalities to the central government) assume the function of intermediaries in the labour market as a means to combat unemployment, this being a burden upon them because it requires that they make support payments to the unemployed. Hiring of labour may also be compulsory (mandatory reporting of vacancies, mandatory hiring of labour that had been assigned.

G. THE NATIONAL ECONOMY AND THE WORLD ECONOMY

A. Introduction

All economic organisations (both producing and consuming ones) that participate in the market are involved in the formation of prices (broadly defined: prices of goods, interest rates, wage rates). Prices are therefore the outcome of their interaction. Internally the activity of each organisation is influenced and determined by prices. Prices determine what the organisations consume and buy, what they produce and sell, what they save and lend, how much labour they hire and use. Economic organisations make their decisions on the basis of prices. Each therefore depends on all others, just as all others depend upon it. They are welded into a higher and broader complex, a whole make up of lower and smaller units, parts, separate economic organisations. This whole emerges from the market which binds the units together and from the market's outcomes. That is the most important point. In addition the whole has an external framework within which takes place the interaction of the separate organisations (a common monetary unit and other institutional arrangements). The latter represents an accessorial aspect of secondary, accidental importance. We refer to this higher entity as the exchange community.

The entire exchange community of a particular country is determined by a common legislative order and a common organisational framework created by government (monetary system, weights and measures, law and order, etc.). In addition, as we shall see, the government operates its own public economic sector built upon and dovetailed into the exchange community. The entity constituted by the exchange community of a country, as determined by its legislation and including the public sector, is referred to as the national economy. The national economy thus represents the sum total of the nation's exercise of care to preserve and improve life.. (We shall eventually return to the concept of the national economy after we have discussed the public sector and the state's solidarist activities.)

And so each nation (state) has its national economy. "National" refers to the territory of the country. However, national economies are not surrounded by impervious walls (though this is true to some extent, as we shall see when we discuss solidarism). There are contacts between economies, foreign economic relations. There are international movements of people, financial capital, and goods.

When government perceives its role to be one of merely facilitating relations between economic organisations (protecting persons and property and safeguarding contracts) and securing for everyone maximum freedom in the exercise of care for his welfare (an individualist state), it will not stand in the way of international relations either. It will allow movement of persons, capital, and goods–provided that foreign countries also pursue such policies (formal reciprocity).*

National markets for goods, capital, and labour are influenced by these international (inter-country) movements, and–as we shall see–it is mostly differences in prices (broadly defined) in the national markets which bring about the movement of people, capital, and goods across national boundaries. The movement tends to remove these differences (goods are ex-

---

* When the government of a country restricts international movement of people, capital and goods, or when other countries restrict such movements, then each will allow such movement as is allowed by the others (the principle of material reciprocity). Such behaviour is characteristic of countries that exercise care for the life, health, and culture of the nation, guided by the ideal of solidarism.

ported to foreign countries where they are more expensive, and this brings down prices abroad. This creates independence and inter-connection of economic organisations at home and abroad, so that changes originating abroad carry over to the home country and vice versa.

And so emerges an international community of exchange, a world economy, which is not subject, however, to a common government authority, nor does it possess uniform institutions that such authority generates (currency) unless countries reach agreement on these matters (international law of bills of exchange, etc.).

B. INTERNATIONAL MOVEMENT OF PEOPLE

People may travel abroad for very short periods and irregularly (trips for pleasure, business, medical reasons), for entire seasons and longer periods (seasonal workers, students), or for permanent   stay (emigration). Emigrants may retain legal association (citizenship) with their homeland or else become permanently associated with the foreign country (by taking foreign citizenship). Travel abroad represents an "invisible import" (travellers spend money of food and lodging in the foreign country).

Disregarding personal motives, emigration is caused by a country's poverty, whether such poverty affects classes of the population or only some classes. E.g., when land tenure is characterised by large estates, it pays to farm only by extensive methods, labour si economised, arable land is transformed into pasture, and people cannot make a living. Such was the case, e.g., in Ireland). On the other hand a country may offer great opportunities to make a living and is therefore very attractive for emigrants–as was the case with America. Indeed immigrants may be invited to cultivate land that is sparsely populated or because they possess certain skills (e.g., glass workers).

Large countries seek additional living space for growing populations unable to find sufficient opportunities to make a living at home–overseas colonies in uncivilised parts of the world–to be settled and civilized, the colonists remaining members of their own nation.

Some emigrants become naturalised, they take on foreign citizenship, others do not lose touch with their homeland, the send home their savings (remittances), buy land in the mother country or else save money to return home in their old age. E.g., Slovakia used to be a country of emigrants. The flow of Slovak emigrants went mostly to America where there is a large and well situated Slovak ethnic group.

How governments act to influence the movement of persons across national boundaries is discussed below.

C. INTERNATIONAL EXCHANGE OF GOODS

Goods are bought and imported from abroad when their exchange value is higher at home, when they are cheaper abroad than at home. In turn they are exported when the converse is true. Th exchange value of a good is expressed by the quantity of all other goods that can be obtained for a unit of the good in question. Exchange value therefore expresses the exchange relationship of one good with all other goods (the relationship of exchange) It follows that the motive for international exchange is the difference in exchange relations among goods. There is no reason for exchange if and when the exchange relations are the same in different countries.

In money terms a good will be imported from abroad when it is cheaper in the exporting country than the importing country. If a good that is expensive at home is imported at lower cost from abroad, the less expensive supply increases and the domestic price declines. Its relative price changes and adapts to the foreign relative price. When a good whose domestic price is low is exported its domestic price rises. International exchange si caused by differences in relative prices of goods in different countries and it leads to their becoming equal.

Therefore those goods are exported of which a country has a surplus (they are too cheap at home) and those goods are imported of which a country has a shortage (they are too expensive at home). A country thus exchanges a surplus of a good, that is less needed, for additional amounts of another good that is needed more. Th country therefore benefits from international trade. Indeed both countries benefit, both increase their welfare compared to what they would enjoy without foreign trade. International trade increases the welfare of all countries that participate in it. When foreign trade is interrupted the world's welfare declines.

It is usual to stress only exports because the public thinks of the returns of exporting enterprises and of their employment, whereas imports are regarded with disfavour as if imports made domestic productive activity more difficult. Such perception is one-sided. If it were correct, we would have to wish for nothing but exports to the exclusion of imports. But why should we export to foreign countries if we should get nothing in return? (If we owe money to foreigners, then we must export to service the debt; but when the debt is repaid or when there is no foreign debt to start with, then exporting without importing does not make sense.) We export so that we may obtain–by producing and exporting–some other goods that we import from abroad, goods that we either cannot produce at all (e.g., cotton or rice) or goods that we can produce only at much higher cost (e.g., rubber or petrol). In this way we "produce" rice in our glass factories and cotton in our machinery plants. We used to export sugar and import wheat, because we "produced"–with the same expenditure of labour and capital–more sugar beets than wheat per hectare than if we had produced wheat directly. Exports are not an end but a means of attaining the largest possible welfare effect via own production and foreign trade. Of course, by exporting we may also grant credits to foreign countries.

International trade is based on different conditions of production that have led to international exchange (e.g., Italy has an advantage in growing oranges while we have an advantage in growing barley). However, when there is foreign trade and when it becomes generalised, production in each country tends to develop accordingly, to become specialised, and international division of labour comes into being. The result is analogous to that which occurs in a domestic economy where separate economic organisations adjust to prices (opportunities to trade), where division of labour develops, and where productivity and welfare are thereby markedly increased.

International trade leads also to international competition and efforts of nations to compete through low cost and high quality of production. This leads to international economic progress but of course also to economic conflict which we shall discuss later.

In addition to merchandise exports and imports, foreign trade includes invisible exports of services to foreign tourists and other services rendered to foreigners (e.g., transport, postal services, etc.).

When we compare the value of a country's exports and imports, we get the balance of trade which is said to be active if exports exceed imports and passive in the converse case. An active trade balance implies a trade surplus; a passive trade balance implies a trade deficit.

D. INTERNATIONAL MOVEMENT OF FINANCIAL CAPITAL

Within a national economy capital moves between economic organisation by transfer of metal money, paper money or giro money (transfer of credits in a bank). How capital moves between countries is explained below, but the reasons for international capital movements are the same as those for domestic capital movements. It moves in search of returns expressed as percent yields. The motivation for foreign trade are differences in exchange relations and the motivation for international capital movements are differences in interest rates (assuming that risk is the same). If financial capital can get only a three percent return at home and six percent return abroad it will prefer placement abroad.

Why is the interest rate low in one country and high in another? Countries with high interest rates have a small stock of physical capital: railroads, electricity networks, machinery, engines, and other capital goods. Physical capital is in great

demand and promises high returns to those economic organisations that acquire it. That is why they can offer a high interest
return on money capital that they transform into physical
capital. The high returns are offered domestically, but if domestic savings are insufficient even with high interest rates, they try
to attract foreign capital. The converse is true for countries that
are capital rich.

Creditors have a claim (via financial intermediaries) against
borrowers who may have used the borrowed funds to build e.g.,
an apartment house, to receive interest and principal (on their
accounts in financial institutions) out of the apartment house
returns. By the same token creditor countries receive interest
and principal payments from debtor countries that have used
borrowed funds to build railroads, electricity networks, etc.

Individual capitalists who have saved some part of their
income transfer some quantity of purchasing power, some
command over part of the national product, to borrowers to
whom they have lend their saved capital. By the same token a
creditor country that lends capital abroad provides to the
foreign country some purchasing power in its own domestic
market, some command over a part of its national product. Th
debtor country can choose how it wishes to spend this purchasing power (borrowed capital) in the market of the creditor
country.

Usefulness of foreign loans depends on what the borrowers
buy. Suppose that the government borrows a billion abroad to
build a railroad and that it sells these claims against foreign
countries to private individuals for domestic funds (perhaps
paper money) that it then uses to finance construction of the
railroad. Suppose also that the private individuals use these
claims against foreign countries to buy expensive wines and
other luxury goods abroad. In that case, how did the foreign
creditor help in constructing the railroad? It helped by inducing
wealthy individuals to give up some part of their domestic
purchasing power to be used by the government to be transformed into a railroad. In return the government gave them
purchasing power against foreigners. If these wealthy individu-

als had saved this money, if they had abstained from using the corresponding part of their income on luxury goods, then the government could have built the railroad, it by going into debt only to its citizens. Interest and principal payments would not have flowed out of the country. The foreign loan was useful only organisationally (something that the country could have arranged itself) because building a railroad did not require expensive wines and other luxury consumer goods. When a country does not need from abroad the physical requisites for investment (e.g., machinery, metals, etc.) it pays to foreign countries for its inability to save. It is a different matter when a country needs material assistance from abroad (machinery, metals) and acquires these from abroad with claims that it has borrowed. In that case the investment would not be possible without foreign assistance, and if the investment generates returns out of which interest and repayment of the principal of the loan are made then foreign borrowing is appropriate.

Long-term loans are not the only foreign credits. There are also short-term credits, e.g., in the case of imports (imports credits) called remboursy.

A country may be a debtor of one country and a creditor of another. There are active and passive capital payments (interest, repayments of principal). Together they make up the capital account. It includes non-trade payments (payments other than imports–including invisibles–and exports). Also included are payments due to insurance, dividends (when foreign capital comes not as credit but as equity capital), retirement benefits, etc. Movements of capital between countries are called transfers.

E. BALANCE OF PAYMENTS

Payments for exports and imports constitute the country's current account. The flow of capital payments from a country (debts) and to a country (claims) constitutes the country's capital or financial account. The total of both payments from and to a country constitutes the country's balance of payments.

Kind of balance	Payments		Remainder
	active	passive	
trade	for export	for import	Trade + −
Capital (financial)	claims	debts	Financial + −
Balance of payment (total)	Payments into the country	Payments out of the country	Payment + −

As we shall see, everything tends toward balance and equilibrium of the balance of payments. But equilibrium of the balance of payments can be attained not only when the current and capital accounts are both in balance at the same time, but also when deficit in one is balanced by surplus in the other. A debtor country must have a surplus on current account to be able to use the excess of exports over imports to pay its debt. Creditor countries have a deficit on current account. The excess of their imports over exports signifies that payments from abroad are being made to service foreign loans. It follows that a surplus on current account is not a necessary goal. Such surplus is necessary if the country is a debtor. But if a country has large capital investments abroad and in spite of this attempts to have a surplus on current account, how could foreign countries pay their debt?

F. INTERNATIONAL CLEARING OF PAYMENTS

1. The technique of making payments

Every import should be paid for in gold because our banknotes cannot be used to make payments abroad. They can only be used at home. An importer therefore takes his banknotes to the Central Bank, exchanges them for gold and ships the gold abroad. The foreign producer has the gold minted into his country's coins or else takes it to his Central Bank to exchange it for banknotes. If gold coins are shipped abroad, this makes the payment costly. The cost includes packing, transport, insurance, and coin loss which occurs when coins that were in circulation are being shipped. (When a case of coins is shipped the most minute wear is taken into account; foreigners do not count our coins, they weigh them.) Finally thee is also the mind cost [razebne] (because foreign importers desire to have domestic coins). Therefore, given the very large volume of import and export transactions, gold would be unnecessarily moving back and forth.

The technique of international payments has evolved in such a way that payments to and from foreign countries–to the extent that they offset each other–are not made by moving gold, but that the only difference [saldo] is paid in gold. This is done as follows: Let thee be an importer I and an exporter E in Prague, and an exporter E and importer I in Rome. Suppose that we export shoes to Rome and that textile fabrics are exported to us from Rome–both with the same value of 100,000 Kcs. Let us suppose further that the Prague importer I does not pay cash but draws up a bill of exchange of 100,000 Ksc and forwards it to the exporter in Rome. Such bill of exchange, where the debtor is located in a different country than the creditor is known as devisa. The drawee in Rome takes the bill to the financial exchange in Rome in search of someone who is to pay 100,000 Kcs to Prague. He finds that Rome shoe importer I who is quite willing to buy the bill and thus save the cost of paying with gold. He forwards the bill to the shoe exporter K who in turn presents it for payment to the Prague importer of textile fabric. This can be visualized as follows:

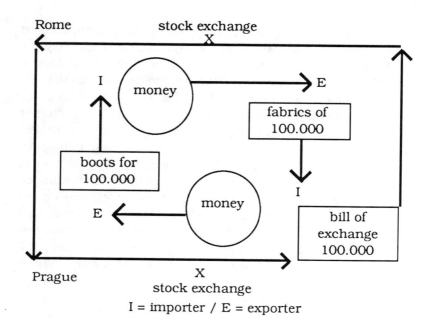

I = importer / E = exporter

Imagine now that there are many exporters and importers on both sides. Some sell devisas and others buy them, both in Rome and in Prague. They meet in the financial markets and create a market for devisas. Buyers of devisas are buyers of foreign money. The Rome importer bought and the Rome exporter sold the devisa drawn on Prague, drawn in our crowns. What then is bought and sold are crowns, and similarly in Prague are bought [and sold] Italian liras. In the devisa market are thus bought foreign currencies with domestic currencies; their price, the exchange rate, is formed (the price of devisas is the price of foreign currency).

2. Foreign currency securities

This is the way it is even when both currencies are based on gold. It is true that according to the law and the weight of the money unit, there corresponds to gold worth 100,000 Kcs some quantity of liras (with the same total content of gold) and that it forms the basic, parity exchange rate of the two currencies.

However, an individual who buys gold in Prague saves the costs of packing, transport, insurance, coin loss, and minting cost, which he would not save is he shipped gold from Rome to Prague to pay for the shoes from Prague. He may be therefore willing to pay for the devisa even more than the parity rate of exchange, but not more than the sum of these costs. If the devisa were more expensive he would not buy it and he would ship gold. It is the same way with the seller who will not sell the devisa if its price falls by more than these costs. If we add these costs to the parity exchange rate in both directions we get points where payment with devisas ceases and payment with gold begins. Gold begins to flow between countries. These points are therefore called gold points.

When one country has a gold based currency and another country a silver based currency there is no fixed exchange rate because the price relation of silver and gold changes in the metals market. It is first necessary to discover what this price relation is and the gold (an silver) points are then determined. When one country has a gold based currency and another country a paper currency, or if both countries have paper currencies, neither a fixed parity exchange rate nor metal points exist. Exchange rates may experience large, even very large, fluctuations in either direction.

3. Determination of the exchange rate of foreign currency

The exchange rate of devisas is a price. In addition to the three domestic markets (goods, capital, labour) there is a fourth market and a fourth price, the price of foreign currencies. Like every price it too has its constituents, supply and demand, among which it maintains balance. The constituents of devisa exchange rates are payments to and from abroad, i.e., the balance of payments. We may consider the balance of payments over some period of time, e.g., a month or a year, but as far as the devisa exchange rate is concerned, what is decisive is the relationship of payments on a given day. If a country's balance of payments is in deficit position, there is excess demand expressed by the difference [saldo] in the balance. Prices of foreign devisas are rising (and the rate of exchange of our devisas abroad is falling). When the balance of payments is in a surplus position the converse is true.

What is decisive is not only the relationship with one country but the relationship with all countries. Suppose that our balance of payments with Italy is in surplus position and the exchange rate of the crown in Rome is high, whereas the balance is in a deficit position vis-a-vis Greece and the exchange rate of the crown in Athens low. Importers in Rome who require our crowns to pay for imports from us, will then prefer to buy our devisas in Athens rather than at home. Their calculations will show that it is more advantageous . This is called arbitrage. The result is that the rate of exchange of our currency will not be high in one country and low in another (reflecting the [saldo] of the balance of payments) but that it reflects the entire balance of payments position with respect to all other countries.

How much will the devisa exchange rates fall or rise as a result of surplus or deficit in the balance of payments? When a country is on the gold standard and its devisa falls (foreign devisas rise) below the gold point gold will be required to be shipped abroad to cover the balance of payments deficit. Gold will be demanded from the Central Bank in exchange for bank notes. Thus there will be a decline of notes in circulation, and at the same time a decline of the gold reserves in the bank of issue. This will result in pressure in the money market and the rate of interest will begin to rise. The central bank too will raise the discount rate to prevent worsening of the ratio of banknotes to its declining gold reserve through a new outflow of bank notes (credit). Rising interest rates affect prices and the whole system of economic magnitudes in the country (deflation). This will lead on one hand to a favourable climate [spad] for inflow of capital from abroad (interest rates at home are higher than abroad) and for merchandise exports (declining prices make us more competitive).

In addition to that, as the devisa exchange rate of foreign countries rises in relation to the falling rate of a country, foreign countries become more expensive, because we perceive foreign prices only through the "crystal" of the exchange rate. When a lira equals 1.50 Kcs instead of 1.20 Kcs then lira exports become more advantageous and lira imports less advantageous than before. This leads to an improvement of the country's balance of payments and offsets the reason for the decline of the exchange rate.

But the reason for this was the fact that the Central Bank possesses a reserve of gold which it uses to temporarily cover the deficit in the balance of payments, and that this occurs as the quantity of bank notes in circulation declines and there is pressure on the domestic capital market and on domestic prices. The rationale for the gold standard and for gold reserves is thus the fact that they are able to maintain the exchange rate within the limits given by the gold points despite the fact that the balance of payments is temporarily in a deficit position. For this mechanism to function there must be gold reserves adequate with respect to the magnitude of payments to and from abroad. Gold is thus an international good that all countries accept with limit to "supplement" exports and to offset imbalances in the balance of payments.

When a country is on a paper standard and its bank notes are not convertible, it can nevertheless maintain a stable exchange rate, provided that it has sufficient gold reserves (and it must not pursue domestic inflationary policies, because rising prices would make exports more difficult). Of course, it must be selling gold to balance foreign payments. It need not have actual gold reserves, it can partly substitute for gold reserves of foreign devisas which it buys when their prices are falling (when the country has a balance of payments surplus), and which it sells when their prices are rising (when the country has a balance of payments deficit). In this way the Central Bank achieves stabilization of the exchange rate of its own currency.

If the Central Bank did not have sufficient gold or devisa reserves it could not moderate the fluctuations in the rate of exchange of foreign devisas and the domestic currency. However the rise and decline of the prices of foreign devisas tends itself to restore equilibrium in the balance of payments, because the rise of the price of foreign devisas makes foreign goods expensive which tends to reduce imports and to increase exports.

4. Clearing in international payments

It is conceivable that payments between countries–as long as they balanced each other out–would be settled in exactly the same way as happens in the case of payments between individuals. There could be a Bank for International Settlements (there is in fact one in Basle, but its functions are quite limited). The matter could be accomplished by crediting and debiting the account of each country, i.e., by means of clearing. Temporary deficit imbalances would be dealt with by credit issued by this bank and from an initial deposit of gold by each Central Bank. We are still far from such a situation.

However, such mutual settlements exist now among pairs of some countries whose central banks keep accounts of mutual debts and claims, and when these offset each other, settle them from such accounts. Such a relationship exists, for example, between country A (Yugoslavia) and country B (our country). An individual in country A who is supposed to make a payment to country B (for imports or to service a debt), makes the payment to the Central Bank of A which communicates with the Central Bank of B. The latter waits until individuals in B have made payments to it settle sums the owe to A. The central bank of B uses funds paid from A for settlement and the central bank of A proceeds in the same way. This settles mutual claims, provided they balance each other out, by clearing. However, when A (Yugoslavia) has a deficit in its balance of payments with B (our country), then B will continue to have a credit balance vis-a-vis in the mutual account, i.e., the claims of citizens of B on citizens of A who are waiting to receive payment, the longer the larger is the deficit balance. The claims are satisfied in the order in which payments for B are received in A. Waiting in B to be paid for exports to A means a loss of interest for the exporters and thus in effect lower export prices. The larger the imbalance and the greater the delay of settlement means that at some point exports cease to grow.

This is bilateral (two-sided) clearing. It results in the balancing of payments between pairs of countries, not in balancing of payments of a particular country vis-a-vis all other countries, even though its balance of payments may be in a surplus position vis-a-vis one and in a deficit position vis-a-vis another country. And this reduces also the volume of foreign trade. This type of clearing came into being during the world depression as a result of indebtedness of countries that led to deficit positions in the balance of payments and threatened monetary standards [ohrozovala menu].

5. The fourth point of equilibrium

We have seen that a country's domestic order and equilibrium among economic units are based on three points of equilibrium (prices in a broad sense)–in the markets for goods, capital, and labour. There is also the fourth equilibrium–the rate of exchange in the devisa market and equilibrium of the balance of payments with other countries. Just as the three domestic markets are interrelated so the fourth, foreign market, is related with all three domestic markets. This can be seen by imagining that equilibrium in the balance of payments is absent.

Suppose that there is a large surplus* in the balance of payments. at a certain exchange rate. There will be a flow of gold

---

* We say large surplus or deficit because small inbalances will not be felt.

into the country and this will be converted into money (metal or paper). The money will either begin to be used for purchases of goods–and this will lead to higher prices (exported goods have left the country but purchasing power stayed in the country)–or else the funds will enter the capital market, causing lower interest rates which will have the same effect. The system of domestic economic magnitudes will start to rise–because of inflation brought about by the surplus in the balance of payments. It will continue until the increase in the price level reduces exports and thus restores equilibrium in the balance of payments.

When there is a large balance of payments deficit the volume of money in circulation and gold reserves will start to decline–as long as the country follows a policy of fixed exchange rates and has sufficient gold reserves to cover the deficit. As already noted, there will then be pressure on the price level and other economic magnitudes to fall, the process of deflation will set in. This will reverse the flow of goods and payments and restore equilibrium.

These processes–inflation and deflation–are necessary if the country follows a fixed exchange rate policy, so that the rate cannot rise or fall, bringing about an increase or decrease of its constituents (supply and demand, exports and imports, etc.). It is as if the price of some goods were fixed so that it could neither rise nor fall and have an impact on its production and consumption, bringing them continuously into balance. Sometime it would be necessary to reduce production, another time consumption, to maintain both equilibrium and a fixed price.

Large domestic inflation and deflation–especially deflation–lead to serious disturbances and difficulties. The country can avoid them by substituting for inflation or deflation an intentional change of the exchange rate. When a country cannot maintain equilibrium in the balance of payments through exports it may avoid the painful process of deflation by lowering its exchange rate, and –when its currency has a certain gold content–this can be reduced, thus encouraging exports without domestic deflation. This is devaluation.

The reduction of the exchange rate will not cause domestic inflation (a general rise of nominal economic magnitudes) provided it merely achieves equilibrium in the balance of payments. But if devaluation is so large that it completely turns around the balance of payments position and brings about a large balance of payments surplus, then it will lead to domestic inflation.

Conversely if a country wishes to avoid inflation caused by a surplus in the balance of payments it can increase its exchange rate and the gold content of its currency. That is revaluation [valorisace].

We know that inflation si an increase of the set of nominal economic magnitudes which is caused either by creation of artificial purchasing power domestically (by printing paper money) or by an inflow of purchasing power from abroad due to foreign credit or a large surplus in the balance of payments–particularly when this was brought about by a previous devaluation or a fall of the exchange rate. Deflation is the opposite process and may be caused by intentional domestic pressure (destruction of true purchasing power) or by pressure from abroad, when there is a deficit in the balance of payments leading to a decline of gold reserves and of the quantity of money in circulation, especially when the rate of exchange was raised prior to that.

H. THE COOPERATIVE SYSTEM

A. Cooperatives

Recall the schematic representation of the circular flow of economic life. Business enterprises appeared on the right hand side of that schema. In striving for objective returns to working teams and personal returns to businessmen business enterprises produced, transported, and traded goods, and provided various services for the left hand side–consumers.

The cooperative system changes nothing as far as consumers are concerned but it attempts to replace the system of business enterprise. The subject of criticism is business profit (the excess of the businessman's return over the compensation of his labour and interest on his capital). The criticism comes, on the one hand, from customers and suppliers (buyers of the product or service, suppliers of milk, etc.) and, on the other hand, from employees. The former claim that profit increases the price at which they buy and reduce the price at which they sell. The later claim that profit reduces their wages. Both groups associate in cooperatives–bodies that attempt to eliminate the businessman and his profit.

Workers associate in producers' cooperatives, which are in fact workers' collective enterprises. The workers do not produce for themselves but, as enterprises, they produce for all who wish to buy their product. Out of the objective return of their cooperative enterprise they pay interest on outside capital while the residual increases the workers' share. And so we have producers' cooperatives of bakers, producers of meat products, etc. Producers' cooperatives transfer businesses to the workers but they are in fact themselves businesses.

The second group of cooperators includes customers and suppliers of business enterprises. They associate to replace business enterprise with self help and with cooperative enterprises which serve only their membership and eliminate business profit. As noted, this includes, on one hand, customers and, on the other, suppliers of business enterprises. Customers include, on one hand, consumers, and, on the other, once again, business enterprises. As a rule consumers buy from merchants (if producers are distant). If they associate to form consumers' buying cooperatives, they eliminate the function of the merchant. It is in particular white and blue collar workers who associate in this manner in order to increase their real wages. However, business enterprises also associate to form cooperatives which buy wholesale and eliminate the merchant. For example, farmers form cooperatives to buy fertilizers, seeds, machinery, etc., and tradesmen to buy machinery, raw materials (purchases of hides), etc. This group also includes individuals who seek credit from financial institutions and who form credit cooperatives. Since their members are personally liable, such cooperatives increase the willingness of capitalists to place funds in them and these funds are in turn loaned to members on terms that do not include business profit. The group also includes electrification cooperatives, and others.

Suppliers of business enterprises who feel that business profit depresses the prices that they receive, may form cooperatives to replace trading enterprises which they would otherwise supply. They form marketing cooperatives (marketing cattle, selling the output of footwear producers, etc.). Alternatively they may form producing enterprises to process the goods delivered to them (milk). Suppliers thus form producers' cooperatives which process only their own goods (milk, etc.). As in the case of marketing cooperatives they sell only their own products.

Cooperatives are thus active in all fields of business. Those engaged in the same activity tend to form federations with individual cooperatives as members. The law has also created various forms of cooperative organisations (with limited liability, unlimited liability, etc.).* Cooperative organisation is sometimes misused to actually operate business enterprise (a consumers' cooperative that sells to non-members). It becomes a front for business operation (because of tax advantages). Cooperatives are very widespread but they have not replaced business enterprise. The later still dominates the field. The system of cooperative enterprise is therefore only a partial system and is otherwise built on the foundation of the capital economic system (cooperatives use borrowed capital, pay interest, etc.).

---

* According to what the liability of the members of the cooperative is. They may be liable only to the extent of their share (deposit), or a multiple of their share, e.g., twice their deposit share, or–beyond that–all their assets.

B. Public Cooperatives

It is not necessary for residents of a community to set up specialised cooperatives for the provision of water, gas, electricity, etc., because that function is performed for them by local government of the community where they reside as if they were members of a cooperative. There is no need for separate administration, office, etc., because local government takes care of this. It provides the services to all residents just as a cooperative would. All residents may use the facility–they may use water, gas, electricity, etc.–but for this they must pay the local government–like the members of any members of any other cooperative–a price that covers cost. Such prices are known as rates [fees, charges].

In providing these services local governments do not make a profit. If they did they would be communal business enterprises. The difference between a communal business enterprise and a communal cooperative is that the former makes profits and the latter does not. Any service provided by local government to residents for which a fee is collected is cooperative in nature if in providing it the local government does not make a profit (e.g., schools, hospitals, sewers, public baths, etc.). Local government may also incur losses when it provides these services, not because of poor management but because it purposely charges lower fees to all the residents, or only to the poor residents (lower charges for health care, for tuition, etc.) to make the services accessible to all. This is done because of the solidarist objective of life, health, and culture of the nation. The loss is also recouped in solidarist fashion–by taxation. This is discussed below.

Much of the activity of local government is of such cooperative nature. Indeed local governments came into being because of such efforts to satisfy certain common needs by communal self help, originally by providing for highway safety, etc. Higher levels of government (district, province, central) also engage in a great deal of cooperative activity. District roads were operated cooperatively when they were toll roads, we have provincial hospitals, there are state schools that charge tuition, etc. And so there are public cooperatives in addition to private cooperatives. However they both replace only a part of business enterprise activity. They still represent only a partial cooperative system.

C. A SYSTEM OF CONSISTENT NATIONAL COOPERATION

A system of pure national cooperation would eliminate and replace business enterprise. All production (transport, etc.) would be concentrated in the hands of the state. It would be carried on by numerous state enterprises (not business enterprises!). Each would produce goods that the public wanted, of such design and quality as the public desired. Of course the public would pay prices that cover costs.

All enterprise installations (the real capital of the business enterprise system) would be state owned. The state would not have to borrow funds and or to pay interest to anybody. The only cost that it would incur would be labor cost. The money unit would be a unit of labour, e.g., an hour of labour. The wage and income of each worker would be as many labour units as he had contributed. Prices of goods stored in state warehouses would correspond to the number of labour hours expended both directly and indirectly in their production. (Directly–labour used in producing a good with a machine; indirectly–labour used to replace the machine because it is partly used up in producing the good.) The value of the good would not determine the value of labour, as is the case in capitalism, but the quantity of labour would determine the value of the good. There would be as much purchasing power in circulation as the value of the goods in the warehouses. Each individual would have freedom of choice of consumption, as he has now, and he would buy goods according to his relative utility (utility as related to price). Money would continue to be an indirect abstract good, but its unit would not be a certain quantity of one of the goods, but a unit of labour.

Individuals would have the right to work in state enterprises. They would not be forced to work (except by their need to survive–since no income other than labour income would exist). However, they would not be free to choose their work but would have to accept work that was assigned to them. There is a good reason for this restriction of the freedom to work. The state could not produce goods that were not in demand. It would have to produce goods demanded by the public free to choose goods in state stores and it would have to adjust to changes in the public's choices. It follows that it would also have to assign workers to produce different goods accordingly. As a result each individual could not produce what he wanted to produce and choose the kind of work that he wanted. Individuals would have to submit to the state production plan.

The function of the state would be purely technical and mechanical: Exercise of care to produce in the best possible way, with the least expenditure of labour, that which the public desires. State enterprises would be guided by the initiative of individuals, their subjective needs and valuations. The state would then exercise care to maintain balance between production and consumption and it would accordingly guide and assign labour. (The function of the state in pure solidarism would be altogether different.)

Because of the technological nature of state cooperative production, the movement that strives to establish such order is called technocratic. It is based on a critique of the capitalist system from the viewpoint of equity for the individual. It considers as equitable that the income of every individual should derive exclusively from his labour contribution and that there should be no other source of income (property income, income derived from the ownership of capital). Everyone should have the right to work and the right to the full return of his labour (undiminished by interest and business enterprise profit).* Carried to its logical conclusion, this then corresponds to the system of national cooperation.

---

*   This is not the only critique–as we shall see when we disucss pure solidarism.

This entire conceptual system is built on the assumption that there is a unit of labour which is an equitable measure of the compensation of labour and of the price of goods. Unfortunately, such unit does not exist. Technically speaking, labour is an expenditure of energy, but it is not possible to use ergs to measure the difference between the labour of an artist, a brilliant designer, and a day labourer. To say that an hour is a sufficient measure means that the wages of all workers must be equal which implies reducing productivity to a minimum. Russia had to abandon this idea.

PART 3
SOLIDARISM–
GOVERNMENT POLICY

A. INTRODUCTION. A CHANGED VIEWPOINT

We have described the system of economic individualism where–in principle–each individual exercises care for his own welfare. We have placed ourselves in the position of all such individuals exercising self care to understand how they obtain and use resources–goods–according to subjective valuations, according to relative utilities an costs, and accordingly, how they make purchases, how they sell, etc., and how they generate relationships between economic units (prices in a broad sense), as well as an equilibrium economic order among economic units both domestically and internationally.

When we speak of the state, we had in mind an individualist state which sees to it that self-caring individuals keep within their proper sphere of control (ownership), do not disturb others, abide by contractual agreements, and do not come into collision with others (rules of traffic); and that each of them has therefore a maximum of freedom and flexibility in exercising care for his wellbeing. The individualistic state assists in this by creating also an appropriate organizational framework (weights, measures, money, markets, etc.). However, the individualistic state does not pursue these policies in order to guide the nation's care to sustain and improve its life, but rather–once again–only to facilitate the economic "rules of traffic," to create (figuratively speaking) the "tracks" for a purely private "traffic." The state continues to perceive the totality of individuals as exercising care for their own welfare.

However, the state can also view the nation (which thus exercises care for its welfare) altogether differently. It may regard the nation as an organic body structured by age of the

172

population (this would be represented by a pyramid with the layer of two-year olds on top of the layer of one-year olds, and so on, all the way to the top layers of the highest age groups; by sex (the left- and right-hand sides of the pyramid); by occupation an social status, by cultural level, etc.

The state may examine the condition of this national body and the trend of its development. If it wishes to determine whether the condition and the trend are either good or bad, if it wishes to describe and evaluate the national body in this way, it must have in mind an ideal of a healthy, strong, and cultured nation–an ideal of the nation's life, health and culture. The state compares the existing condition an evolutionary trend with this ideal and finds them accordingly either good or bad; it evaluates them.* This kind of valuation, which regards the whole nation (society) from the viewpoint of a national (social) ideal, and which sees national (social) benefit as increase of the nation's life, health and culture, and national loss as diminution of these, is social valuation. The term "nation' is used here in the sense of the population of the state, society.

From here it is only a step to strive in practice for a change of the care for the nation's welfare, for sustaining and improving life, as it is exercised in the individualistic system, in accordance with subjective valuation of individuals, but whose

---

*   This may be illustrated as follows: Contrasted with the actual pyramid that describes the nation's age structure the ideal is a prism that is being replaced at the bottom by births and that ends at the top because members of the old age group pass away. The base becomes wider only when the number of births increases, not because the new borns do not all live to reach the top age but die before the reaching the age of one, two, or fourteen in short and in particular, before they contribute themselves to the nation's welfare by providing for the old and the young, by repaying the nation for the care which they themselves received. In the same way one may evaluate the nation's health from the viewpoint of health and the nation's culture from the viewpoint of culture.

outcome–as measured by the ideal of life, health and culture–is not satisfactory. In particular this will be the case when it turns out:

1. That the nation's condition and evolutionary trend are unfavorable when individuals exercise care for their own welfare; when entire groups of the nation are disappearing or weakening; when the social structure is very uneven (revolutionary*), (impoverished masses opposed to individuals of great wealth); when even, and therefore continued, progress is absent and there is only disintegration. What applies to life and health applies also to cultural achievement, etc.

2. That such condition and development are caused by the existing division of wealth which determines incomes and market power, by the freedom of each individual to do as he pleases–to produce, to consume, to export goods and capital, to import and buy abroad, etc., by the struggle of everyone against everyone else, in short, by all the elements of the individualistic order which have led to great technological progress due to competition and to great expansion of production but have not always resulted in the greatest social benefit of the people engaged in the competitive struggle.

This critique is entirely different from that which we encountered in our exposition of the system of national cooperation. There the distribution of the burdens and fruits of labour was viewed by the individual from within and found to be unjust for the individual. In the present critique, the state views from without (from a bird's perspective), not the division of the burdens and fruits of labour, but rather the nation and its quality, and finds that the individualistic order of care to sustain and improve life does not guarantee the optimum condition an evolution of the nation from the viewpoint of the nation's life, health and culture. It is somewhat like a father

---

* "Revolutionary" because the oppression of the people by a small class of the very wealthy (the top 10,000) causes an explosion, a revolution.

observing his children at play. He will let them play as long as it is good for their bodies and minds and he will arbitrate in their disputes. A child may want to change the game because not all children may have an even chance to speak or act. But the father will stop the game when he sees that they are getting overtired an neglect their studies. He wants to bring them up as healthy and educated citizens.

Presently the state ceases merely to care for the "traffic" among individuals, it is no longer only an individualistic state, but rather–proceeding from its ideal of the nation's life, health and culture–it views the nation as an entity, evaluates its condition and development, and considers how it might change the organization of care to sustain and improve its life. Such a state is solidaristic.

The state may be purely solidaristic. In tha case ir organizes acquisition and utilization of the resources necessary to sustain and improve life in accordance with the ideal fo life, health and culture, while suppressing the order based on individual and personal satisfaction of individuals and suppressing as well their competitive struggles and their control over goods. Alternatively, a solidaristic order may be built as a superstructure and complement of an underlying individualistic order. This is government policy that effectuates partial solidarism. Both will be explained.

B. CONSEQUENT SOLIDARISM
(COMMUNISM)

The essential features of solidarism were already described in the general part of this study (p. 00). A purely solidaristic state makes all individuals and the nation as a whole the object of its care which is directed towards the ideal of the nation's life, health and culture.

It follows that no individual can have free choice either in acquiring resources, in his work, nor in utilizing resources, in consuming. It is necessary that he be compelled to work and to consume in a particular manner (like a child or a sick person).

It follows further that no individual can have control over goods, both those that serve to produce other goods and those that serve final consumption. He can neither donate nor sell the goods allocated for his consumption because they were allocated solely for his own objective use. This is no different from children who are the object of their parents' care. Control over goods must be in the hands of the state as agent who exercises and manages care. The logical outcome is communism–total state control over goods. (In national cooperation each individual is master of consumer goods because he has freedom of choice in consuming.)

All care for the nation's life, health and culture is concentrated in one single economy, indeed the only economy, whose systemic purpose is known to us. It follows from this purpose that increments of the nation's life, health, and culture represent utilities, whereas decreases of culture, health and life represent losses and costs. This economy is confronted with a dual task: The first is material the second personal.

1. The material task concerns allocations of the nation's resources to production (and hence consumption) of various goods–where and how to limit the nation's production of food to have sufficient resources left for housing, clothing, culture, etc. In the individualistic system the task confronts every consumer. He solves it according to the principle of equalisation of relative marginal utilities (one cannot continue to produce and consume one good if further output brings less relative utility than the production of another good). Accordingly, all material needs in an economy and their satisfaction (this applies to the whole economy in solidarism, and to the consuming sector in the individualistic economy) are linked in a nexus of material solidarity [vecnou solidaritu]. Each separate need is satisfied while all other needs are taken into account. The result is some composition of the aggregate national product. In the individualistic system it is determined by individual and subjective valuation, because only personal satisfaction and willingness to buy goods determine how far one proceeds n satisfying different wants and therefore the appropriate structure of

aggregate production. On the one hand, in a purely solidaristic economy the composition is the outcome of an objective valuation (attribution of utility) that follows from the ideal of the nation's life, health and culture. The structure of production and consumption, i.e., the composition of the national product, will be therefore quite different in a purely solidarist system than in an individualistic system. We shall see, therefore, that one of the main tasks of government policy (partial solidarism) is to bring about a partial restructuring of the competition of the national product as it emerges from subjective valuation, in the direction of objective social benefit–the life, health and culture of the nation. (A portion of individual income is taxed–which depresses consumption as determined by personal satisfaction–to provide more schools, hospitals, etc.)

2. The second task is personal. It concerns the question of how to allocate the burden of labour required to produce goods to different individuals, and how to allocate these goods to be consumed by different individuals who form, in the aggregate, the object of state care–unless goods directly serve the whole society (e.g., defence goods). This task (which is not faced by the individualistic economy) involves once again two problems:

a) When resources are acquired, when labour is allocated, one must consider the diminution of life, health and culture that the burden of labour causes to workers, because–as we know–such diminution represents a cost to the solidarist state economy. This point is that in the aggregate such diminution (cost) should be as small as possible. This will be so when each labour task is assigned to the individual to whom it causes the least harm. When one considers to which of two individuals one should assign a particular task, one decides to assign it to the one to whom it causes less harm. This individual has greater capacity for such work. Allocating labour according to capacity therefore implies minimizing the costs of the solidarist economy and maximizing output with given costs. (When there are several beasts of burden with different burden-carrying capacities, one cannot place the same burden on each because some would then be overloaded while for others the load would be too small; when allocating the loads according to burden-carrying capacity one utilizes this capacity to the maximum. Th strong will labour much, the weak little.

b) When the application/use of resources is considered, preserving life and health brings more utility than does culture. To assist the very weak, the ones who are most removed fro the ideal, is more important than raising the very high cultural level of the very strong. Allocation of goods si therefore not guided by individual contribution, by merit (as in the system of national cooperation) but rather by objective passive need (see p. 000). The very strong who contribute most to producing the national product may possibly receive very little if their needs are very small, and the very weak who contribute very little to the creation of the national product may receive a very large share of state care. Th strong and the weak are thus linked for mutual assistance and even developments of the whole. This represents the nexus of personal solidarity which means neither an equal burden of labour nor an equal share of its fruit, but rather even development of all with respect to health and culture. The nexus of personal solidarity characterizes state solidarism.

All citizens of the solidarist state are thus guaranteed a livelihood (the right to a livelihood) through the assistance of others, but at the same item they also have an obligation to work according to their capacity–otherwise the right to a livelihood could not be realized. In the solidarist economy there would be rationing tickets for some goods and services, but these would no longer be money because they would not make possible free choice of goods.

Pure solidarism introduced forcibly in a society of selfish individuals means that the strong are unwilling to put forth greater effort while the weak tend to increase their claims. The principle "Let each contribute as much as he can (according to capacity) an receive as much as he needs (according to objective passive need)' degenerates easily into "Give as little an take as much as possible." This means lower aggregate productivity and a lower living standards. Pure solidarism–which is of course not realized in practice in such ideal way–is also opposed by the natural desire of all to be free as far as labour and consumption are concerned. Nations are therefore satisfied with partial solidarism in government policy and they reject pure solidarism (communism). There is a trend toward such partial solidarism that aims at the life, health and culture of the nation and attempts to make such tendency prevail not only as the state is concerned but also with respect to the motivation and behaviour of all citizens whose initiative and freedom are preserved. This is so because of the growth of solidarist ideas in the public mind (awareness of belonging to the nation, social responsibility, respect for one's neighbours).

C. PARTIAL SOLIDARISM
GOVERNMENT POLICY

1. INTRODUCTION AND OVERVIEW

The government views population as an entity, paying attention to numbers (state), its reproduction (natural change–deaths and births), movement across borders (emigration and immigration), its structure according to natural criteria (age, sex, health, illness) and social criteria (occupation, social class) etc. All this is the concern of the science of demography. The finds become the basis of valuation and of practical efforts to improve the population so that it develops in the direction of the ideal of health and culture.

However, to accomplish this, the state does not totally abolish the individualistic economic system and replace it with pure solidarism. Instead it preserves the basic framework of individualism, but it constrains–using its legal order–the freedom of individuals who would otherwise pursue only their personal satisfaction. It does so both positively and negatively: It forbids individuals to do certain things that they would otherwise do, and orders them to do certain things that they would not do. It thus interferes with the individualistic system, with equilibrium prices and their constituents, it restricts the freedom to enter into contractual agreements, it erects barriers between home and foreign countries (tariff duties), etc. The sum of all these legal norms constitutes public law–as opposed to private individualist law which we encountered in our exposition of the individualistic order.

If decrees and prohibitions are insufficient, the state goes further and establishes its own supplementary solidaristic economic sector built upon the individualistic exchange society as its substructure. Resources for this sector are obtained from subordinate private economic units, both producing and consuming ones, on the basis of their capacity to pay. The government uses such resources according to social usefulness. The law and the economy are two chief methods (two arms) of government policy (state solidaristic activity). They complement one another an they are integrated. (As a father disciplines and provides for his children, so government either instructs parents to have their children educated or provides itself for their education in state schools.) It is especially important to become acquainted with the state economy.

The legal system and the public sector of the economy constitute the two chief methods of government policy which has three main systemic objectives. These are of course derived from the ultimate objective–the ideal of life, health and culture of the nation. The government:

1. Strives to maximize the national product as the basis of all care for preserving and improving life. The set of all measures directed to this end constitutes government production or economy policy in a narrower sense.

2. It also strives to bring about a distribution of the national product and of the burden of labour among individuals which is better suited to the nation's progress toward the ideal of health and culture than that which emerges from individualistic struggle. This concerns the realization of the principle of personal solidarity in the individualistic (capitalist) order. This is social policy.

3. Finally, it strives to restructure the composition of the national product, as determined in the individualistic economic system by subjective valuation of individuals, so bring it closer

to the ideal of the nation's life, health and culture. It realizes the principle of material solidarity within the capitalist system. The set of corresponding measures constitutes industrial sector policy [politiku odbornou] which consists of–according to the sector with which it is concerned–health policy, cultural policy, and defence policy.

The individualistic system permits uncontrolled relations with foreign countries (personal relations, capital movement, merchandise trade). Countries develop in competition with other countries. Solidaristic interference shapes the life of each nation individually. This leads to restricting international competition and relations with foreign countries. Economic nationalism emerges.

Accordingly, Part Three deals with the following:

1. Population.
2. The public sector.
3. Content of government policy, etc.
   a) Economic policy in a narrower sense.
   b) Social policy.
   c) Industrial sector policy.
4. Economic nationalism.

II. POPULATION

By and large, the development of the state has tended to the formation of states based on nationality, nation states. However, there are also states that are nationally mixed. Th solidarist state perceives this population and exercises care for this population in its entirety. Such population is denoted as "nation," in the political sense of the word (belonging to a given state), rather than the ethnographic sense of the word.

Each nation is different. There are big and small nations with respect to population size, but all nations differ with respect to race, intellect, traits of national character, levels of education attained, age structure, social structure, etc. Valuation and care for the nation in its entirety is guided accordingly, as are the methods applies in the exercise of that care, which must correspond to all this. Each nation also possesses its own ideal toward which it progresses.

The Czech nation is not among the smallest. It is advanced, healthy, it has attained a high level of general education, it has a highly perfected language as instrument of thought testifying to a great sense for order and organization. It is also exceedingly had working and frugal which guarantees, given its intelligence, that it can stand up to foreign competition and to preserve a high level of culture and welfare. It also possesses a high sense of mutual solidarity, willingness to make sacrifices for the whole, but also a high sense for justice. This is shown by its history.

Every nation is endowed with a territory that constitutes its living space and its base, with its natural resources and living conditions. The significance of this space diminishes when there is free movement of people, capital and goods. For example, our textile industry imports raw material from thousands of kilometers away while it exports its labour in the form of textiles to the farthest corners of the earth). However, it becomes very important when these international relations are interrupted (war, trade barriers). It may then happen that the nation, which now becomes dependent on its base, experiences a decline in its standard of living. The country becomes overpopulated and the nation tries to expand its living space, it exercises pressure on other nations, and this leads to wars.

The question of overpopulation is of major interest to demography. When we say that a certain country (and this statement can only be made with respect to a certain geographic area) is overpopulated or underpopulated, we express a value judgment that the size of the population–from the viewpoint of the ideal of life, health and culture–is either too large or too small relative to possible living standards. Overpopulation is a situation when the living standard of the population of a geographic area is lower than it would be if the population were smaller. Conversely underpopulation is a situation when the living standard is lower than if the population were larger. (A region that is too sparsely populated lacks the advantages of a concentrated division of labour and of contracts among economic units; its population lives rather primitively.) Sometimes a given population could also enjoy higher living standards if it would better organize its productive activity by means of the legal and economic order. A region where ownership of land is too concentrated (latifundia) can provide livelihood for fewer people than a region with middle- and small-size farms. (This is why Ireland was overpopulated and experienced large-scale emigration; this is why land reform in our country opened up opportunities for a livelihood to an additional population. As Pliny wrote: Latifundia perdidere Italiam.)

If we find therefore that a certain country is overpopulated, this may be because it presses against limits of production which it is in its power to shift because they are caused by its economic and legal system, in which case we speak of relative overpopulation. Alternatively, the population may press against limits of production that cannot be shifted because they stem fro the niggardliness of nature, in which case we speak of absolute overpopulation.

The world's population is growing rapidly. During the 19th century it doubted but it succeeded in overcoming the niggardliness of nature by better organization of production and technological progress so that present day living standards are much higher than those enjoyed by half that many people at the start of the 19th century. This fact represents a failure of the teaching of Malthus (dating from the end of the 18th century) that poverty in his day was caused by overpopulation and that mankind always faces overpopulation because it tends to grow more rapidly (in a geometric progression) than it is capable to increase the means of subsistence (in arithmetic progression). As we noted, a growing world population succeeded during the 19th century to secure from nature means of subsistence at a rate not only equal to but higher than the rate at which it grew.

It appears also that this alleged reproduction tendency of mankind is not immutable. When nations attain higher levels of culture and affluence birth rates decline and average life spans rise. This too is taught by history and by comparison of more advanced with less advanced nations.

But demography is not only concerned with the size of the population but also its structure and quality–matters that claim more and more attention as solidarism grows.

III. The Public Sector

A. THE STRUCTURE OF THE PUBLIC SECTOR

1. The economic structure of the public sector is not uniform

As we noted the government carries out policies affecting the nation through legislation (decrees and prohibitions), and by means of its own public economic sector. We shall now discuss this sector.

The public sector does not represent a uniform economic organisation. An individual's household and his business each represent an economic organisation but it is not a uniform organisation whose revenues and expenses could be added up and juxtaposed. On the contrary, they represent two distinct organisations, one–the business–generates business returns (the result of revenues and expenses) for the businessman. This becomes his household income to be juxtaposed with his household expenses. The two are interrelated because the income base of the household is derived from the return of the business whose purpose is to make money for the household. However, each economic organisation has its own purposive order, its own way of acquiring and utilizing resources (income and expenditures) and its own material solidarity (interrelationship of various needs).

For this reason it is necessary to distinguish various branches of the non-uniform public sector.

2. Government enterprises

The government owns (is an agent that controls) numerous enterprises engaged in different types of activities. In the first place it owns a number of enterprises which it administers and manages just as any other collective entrepreneur such as a corporation. For those willing to pay the government operates enterprises that produce goods (e.g., farm products on state farms, iron in state iron mills, weapons, books, newspapers, etc.): enterprises that provide the services of transport and communication (mills, railways, busses, airplanes, telephones, radio, etc.); enterprises in the field of credit and finance (State Bank of Issue, Post Office Savings Bank, state pawnshop); as well as enterprises that provide services (hospitals, state spas, etc.), and others.

State enterprises make money, they earn returns on the capital that the government has invested in them. However the government does not operate them for the sake of the return. Making money is not the government's objective, and state enterprises never earn sufficient profits. The government is not a good businessman. It is not sufficiently flexible, it must depend on civil servants, it is subject to political (party, etc.) pressures. Why then does it continue to run enterprises? Either because their scale is too large for the private sector (railways), or because it is necessary that their activities, such as production of goods, transport, services, etc., should not only be monopolised (to maximise returns), but so that they may best serve the nation. Railways are arteries of "circulation of economic blood"; they are instruments of regional progress and should be built with regional needs considered, not just in regions where they would be profitable; mail must be delivered even to the smallest locality, hospital services should be available to all, etc. From the viewpoint of promoting the ideal of life, health and culture, as service in the interest of the public, they are public business enterprises. They are business enterprises because they still earn returns, but their returns are subordinate to the public interest. If they serve no public interest they should not be operated by government. There is no reason why government should operate them.

State business enterprises fit in the individualist-capitalist system; they represent state capitalism. They serve individuals and economic organisations, according to their desires and interests—of course at competitive or monopolistic prices. (There is monopoly when there is only one producer with no competitors, e.g., the tobacco monopoly.) Etatism is the term used to describe efforts to expand the public business enterprise sector.

3. Public cooperatives

The returns of public business enterprises may come under so much pressure of the public interest as to be eliminated altogether. Prices then cover only the costs of goods used in production, of labour, and out outside (borrowed) capital. These expenses are met from the objective return (see p. 00). This means that public business enterprises become public cooperatives (p. 000). Once again they serve members of the public, producing what they want to buy, provided of course, that they are willing to pay. However the price they pay does not include profit; it only covers costs. Prices charged by cooperatives are called fees (tuition fees, hospital user fees, court cost fees, etc.).

Public interest may lead to a situation where the selling price charged for the good or service is reduced still further, so as to make the good or service accessible to a wide circle of individuals, including the less affluent, because the good or service tends to promote the nation's life, health and culture (lower hospital user fees make hospital services available to the less affluent).

And so it may happen that prices (charges) that have been reduced in the public interest do not even cover the full costs of the good or service. This means of course that such public enterprise is no longer operated for profit, that it is purely cooperative. As long as the charge covers the full costs the enterprise is still a cooperative. When costs exceed the amount charged, the excess is due to the fact that the government wishes to charge less than cost in the interest of the nation's life, health and culture. This excess cost has a solidarist aspect and the resulting arrangement (e.g., schools that charge tuition that does not cover the entire cost) represents a mixed organisation, that is partly cooperative (up to the amount of the charge) and partly solidarist (up to the amount of the cost).

4. The solidarist economic organisation

What we have just discussed–a mixed cooperative enterprise–can be pushed further, to the point where the government does not ask that citizens pay anything (not even a partial payment) for the good or service that it provides. The good or service is available to all without charge. However the prices charged by business enterprise and the charges made by cooperative enterprises perform the function of regulating consumption, the demand for the good (or service) in question.

Let us suppose that the government is the sole (monopoly) producer of footwear for its citizens. In that case it could produce footwear in state factories operated like business enterprises (capitalistically) and it would produce such quantities and qualities of footwear as members of the public would demand, in view of their subjective satisfaction and the prices charged which would include cost plus business profit. Prices would regulate demand (according to relative utility). Demand would be depressed by higher prices an encouraged by lower prices.

The government could also carry on production in cooperative enterprises. Price would then become charges that would not include business profit. From the viewpoint of the consumer, however, the charge is just as much a price as the price charged by business enterprise. The government would again produce quantities and qualities of footwear corresponding to the subjective wants of individuals, provided that they were willing to pay the posted charge (cooperative price). Once again the charges would regulate consumption as did prices, and to a particular charge (based on full cost) would again correspond a particular demand and level of consumption.

However, if the government wished to supply the public with shoes in the solidarist way, it would not ask for payment or impose a charge for the shoes. Prices or charges would then no loner regulate demand and consumption, and since shoes would be available without charge, everyone would want to get too many in too many varieties. Now the government's objective is to provide the public with free shoes (in practice its objective would be to provide free education, free hospital care, free therapy in spas) because the postulate of the nation's health demands that everyone should have shoes and that paying fro shoes should not discourage the poor from getting them. However, the postulate of the nation's health by which the government si guided does not require that everyone should have as many shoes of all varieties as he wants. It only requires that individuals should get goods required to maintain their health, i.e., in accordance with objective passive nee (p. 00)–one pair of shoes for the winter, one pair for the summer, perhaps a pair of work shoes, and no more. The regulatory function of prices in capitalism an of the cooperative charges in the cooperative system has to be replaced in the solidarist system of government regulation aimed at achieving the purpose of the solidarist economic organisation: the ideal of life, health and culture of the nation and the objective needs that follow from it.

From what was said, it is already clear that the taking over by the government of some productive activity (in this case to supply the nation with shoes) says nothing about the systemic principle according to which the government will exercise this activity. It may do so in the capitalist way (in state-owned business enterprises), in the cooperative way, or in the solidarist way.

There must be constraints of solidarist consumption because the government must face the question of how to cover the cost of the good (or service) which it provides for free. It may have available for this purpose certain revenues that are coincidental, such as the short-term deposits, from the proceeds of fines, tariffs (duties collected on merchandise imports), gifts, inheritances, etc. Such revenues are coincidental or accessorial because they are not set up for the specific purpose of covering solidarist needs, with respect to either their level or the way they are obtained. Also, such revenues may not exist. The government may not operate any business, it may have no revenues from fines if the public obeys laws, gifts and inheritance may be insignificant and irregular, collections of import duties are a function of the volume of imports which depend on private initiative, etc. In any case, such coincidental revenues would cover only a portion of solidarist needs.

The question remains how to cover the residual part of these needs, or–if there are no coincidental revenues–how to cover them in total. The state solidarist sector acquires the needed resources from its individualist substructure, from private economic organisations, both producers and consumers. It does so by siphoning off, in various ways, a part of their returns, incomes, or wealth. It goes without saying that this can only be done by compulsion because the contributing economic organisations receive nothing in return. For them it is a pure sacrifice. Such contributions are taxes. When private economic organisations buy goods or services from the government an pay prices (tobacco) or charges (hospital care) then such prices or charges are not a sacrifice, just as prices paid are not a sacrifice in private transactions. But a contribution without corresponding counter value–a tax–is a sacrifice, a loss to the private economic organisation. The question then arises: What principles should be followed when such sacrifices are imposed (principles of taxation)?

The solidarist government orders it public sector according to the postulates of life, health and culture of the nation as its purpose. In its use of resources it aims to maximize objective utility, which in this case means increments of life, health and culture. In acquiring resources it aims at minimizing losses–costs–which are decreases of culture, life and health. It follows that taxes are imposed sequentially in order to cause the least losses in this sense. This is the only correct principle of taxation which shall be discussed in detail below. It is a principle that follows from the systemic purpose of the state solidarist economic organisation. The government makes use of money as a resource, it acquires monetary resources at a cost (sacrifices of life, health and culture). The relative utility of the money unit is falling and the relative cost of the money unit rises, until the lines of diminishing utility and increasing cost intersect and the boundary of rationality is reached at the point of intersection (see p. 00). To levy additional taxes would be irrational because relative cost (decrease of life, health and culture) exceeds relative utility (increment of life, health and culture).

5. Overall survey

In a broad sense, the public sector of the economy consists of:

a) a set of independent business enterprises each of which is an independent economic organisation, with its revenues (from prices), its expenses and its enterprise returns;

b) a set of cooperative enterprises each with its revenues (from fees or charges) and its expenses (without business profit);

c) one solidarist economy with revenues (from taxes) used for expenditures up to the boundary of rationality.

It would be incorrect to add together the expenditures of all these economic organisations because they do not use resources in the same uniform way an they do not represent a single uniform system (material solidarity of individual uses is absent between the three different groups). It would be equally incorrect to add together their revenues because they do not obtain resources in the same uniform way, in accordance with the same systemic (purposive) principle.

There is first the solidarist sector whose resources are derived from taxation (unless it has coincidental revenues). Then there are state business enterprises which cover their expenditures from the prices they charge and whose enterprise returns represent coincidental revenues of the solidarist sector. Finally there are public cooperative enterprises whose charges are the revenues from which they cover their costs, and if the charges are insufficient, then the part of cost that is not covered represents a part of solidarist expenditures. We can represent this by the schema on the following page (p. 192).

B. THE SOLIDARIST SECTOR OF THE PUBLIC ECONOMY

I. Obtaining resources. Taxes

A) The bearing capacity in paying taxes

Unless the resources required by the public solidarist sector are derived from coincidental, accessorial revenues, they must be obtained from compulsory transfers–taxes–paid by subordinate private economic organisations, producers (business enterprises) and consumers (households). They are levied so that the loss to the nation's life, health and culture is minimized. Of two economic organisations facing a given tax, the one that suffers the smallest loss by paying the tax has a greater ability to pay. When we say that taxes are levied in accordance with ability to pay, we say in effect that they are imposed in a way such that the detriment which they cause is as small as possible.

Through taxation the government obtains control of a part of the national product that it takes away from private use (thereby narrowing the basis of the nation's life). Of course, it then uses the resources to generate more utility, more protection of life and health, than the loss caused by collecting the taxes. By collecting taxes the government causes, in principle, two kinds of losses: direct and indirect.

It causes direct losses to individuals by reducing their incomes an their consumption, and therefore also their opportunities to develop a life style that they desire. A given tax will cause smaller loss to households (of the same size) with higher income than those with lower income. In the case of high

SURVEY OF THE PUBLIC SECTOR OF THE ECONOMY

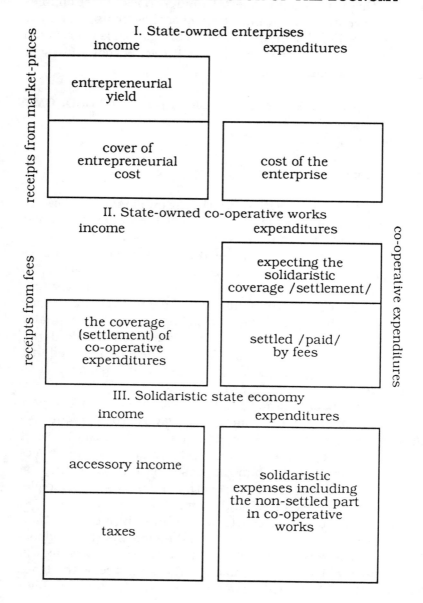

income households it will merely reduce their higher level of culture; in the case of low income households it may affect health and perhaps life itself. It follows that with respect to such direct loss, individuals with higher incomes have a higher relative ability to pay than those with lower incomes. If we were to impose only one unit of tax we would tax the individual with the highest income. Imposing additional units of tax would thus eliminate extremely high incomes and make income distribution more equal from the top down, affecting lower and lower income groups and causing increasing losses. We are thus concerned with and we compare directly the losses of different individuals and the ability to pay of different individuals whose consumption and foundation of their livelihood are reduced. That is why we refer to this ability to pay as personal ability to pay. We are concerned here with losses that the tax causes to individuals' life, health and culture by diminishing their income and consumption. The losses with which we are concerned are direct losses. If the system of taxation were based solely on this personal ability to pay it would lead to more equal distribution of income from the top down.

Direct losses result from taxation of earned personal income (and business returns). Indirect losses involve the formation of future incomes (and business returns) and therefore also future losses. For example, if a tax were to reduce inequality of income by taking away from all individuals any income about 50,000 crowns, such individuals would lose their motivation to earn more than that amount, to be productive and put forth effort–as compared to their behaviour before the tax was imposed. This would undermine business activity and the formation of the national product–the foundation of the nation's existence. Even the tax base would be eroded since no income about 50,000 crowns could exist and the government would have to reach deeper to tax lower income brackets. This would have similar results–until the entire business enterprise (capitalist) system stem would disintegrate.

Personal bearing-capacity is an element of consequent solidarism. If consistently applied it would necessarily destroy the individualist-capitalist system and it would have to be replaced by pure solidarism, i.e., communism. That is why, when introducing any tax, one must: consider its effects on the activity and productivity of business enterprise and the formation of the national product. The set of such considerations–of the impact of the tax upon business activity and productivity, on the capitalist foundation of the state solidarist sector–constitutes a set of principles concerned with material productivity effects. These principles affect and modify the principles concerned with personal ability to pay, as an aspect of pure solidarism, so that the tax becomes the outcome of both.

Taxation of incomes (the income tax) cannot simply reduce the inequality of income distribution. It must also take into account material productivity effects and appropriately change the structure of the tax so that recipients of higher incomes should be left with more after-tax income than recipients of lower incomes even after the tax is collected. A tax on business returns cannot siphon them off in such a way that the businessman receives no reward for his labour and no interest on his capital because business activity would then cease. When considering any tax, one must pay attention to both personal ability to pay and to material productivity effects.

The tax is then imposed on its base (income, return, property) as some percentage, some tax rate. The rate may be the same for all bases (e.g., all incomes), in which case we speak of a proportionate tax. Or else the tax may be different. When the tax rises as a percentage as the base rises, it is progressive. When it falls as a percentage as the base rises, it is regressive. Progressivity and its converse are not principles of taxation but methods of taxation. When choosing one or the other one should pay attention to the correct principles of taxation–personal ability to pay and the impact on productivity. For example if the business turnover of all enterprises is taxed three percent (turnover tax) the tax is a proportional tax. If low incomes (there may be a tax-exempt minimum–e.g., 6,000 crowns) are taxed two percent, higher incomes three percent, and still higher incomes four percent, the tax is progressive. If a tax–e.g., a tax on business returns is in principle four percent (regardless how high the return), but the lowest business returns receive tax concessions in the form of a lower percent tax, the tax is progressive.

b) The tax system

If it were possible to ascertain precisely the income of all individuals (including those who do not draw upon all the income from their business because they immediately reinvest some of the returns) the entire system of taxation could be reduced to a single income tax. Because this is not the case, the government introduces many different taxes (including some that are introduced in order that the public does not realise how much tax it pays and therefore does not oppose it). But in the end taxes are paid from three sources: household income, the objective returns of business (in the aggregate it amounts essentially to the same thing), and property.

In more detail one can distinguish:

1. taxes imposed on incomes

a) direct taxation of incomes by means of the income tax. Here the income of the household is ascertained, as is the size of the family which depends on the income. The tax is then assessed according to personal ability to pay (progressively) but with consideration of material productivity effects (recipients of higher incomes are left with more after-tax income than those in lower income tax brackets).

b) indirect taxation of incomes by consumption taxes (taxation of consumption expenditures). Direct taxation of incomes reduces money incomes, indirect taxation reduces the real content of the incomes. The government levies taxes on goods and services that businesses produce for households; it collects the taxes from producers or from distributors. The taxes are assessed per unit (per litre, per kilo) or as a percent of the sales price. The businessman is compelled to raise the sales price of the good or service by the amount of the tax. At the higher prices consumers buy less of the goods or services an they are therefore indirectly taxed. Consumption taxes are levied in all areas of consumption expenditures, in particular:

a) food, beverages, combustibles. This includes, e.g., taxes on sugar, meat, wine, beer, mineral water, tobacco products, etc.

b) housing, light, heat. This includes taxes on apartments based on the size of the dwelling, not on the returns of residential buildings–such tax would be classified as a tax on business income), taxes on coal, electricity, light bulbs, gas, etc..

c) clothing, footwear, underwear. There are relatively few specific taxes in this area because it is difficult to impose taxes on these consumption expenditures. Here might be included taxes on raw textile materials, on jewellery, etc.

d) other expenditures. This category includes various kinds of entertainment (theatres, motion picture theatres, dances, playing cards, billiard tables, riding horses, tennis courts), taxes on transportation tickets, etc.

2. taxes imposed on the objective returns of business

The objective return of business enterprise is the difference between the price of the product and the value of goods used in its production. It is the source of the compensation of labour (wages and salaries) and outside capital (interest, rental, lease payments). The residual is the return to the businessman. The objective return is not taxed as a whole. It is its individual components that are taxed: the return to labour, the return to capital, the return to the businessman. To this correspond three kinds of taxes:

a) taxes on wages and salaries. As a rule these are levied only on higher labour incomes (tax on higher salaries).

b) taxes on the return to capital. There are three forms of capital: land, buildings, and financial capital. To this correspond:

c) taxes on land. In our country it is not the actual returns of land that are ascertained. Instead estimated returns (corresponding to lease payments or ground rents) are recorded in cadastes and taxes are then assessed as these cadaster returns (i.e., not with perfect accuracy).

d) the tax on residential buildings that is supposed to tax the return of residential buildings. If the building is rented out the tax is levied on the rent. In rural areas where few buildings are rented, the tax is levied on a roughly estimated base according to the size of living quarters (number of rooms). It is called a classification tax.

e) the taxon on rentier income falls upon the interest income from financial capital, either the capital of the owner (n case of private loans) or the capital of financial institutions (deducted when interest is paid).

f) tax on business returns (tax on business earnings): Direct taxes on business returns, taxes on business earnings, involve quantitative appraisal of the returns and levying of the corresponding tax. A distinction is made between individual and collective enterprises. In the case of the former, where labour and personal effort of the individual businessman plays a significant role, the tax is called a general tax on earnings, and is rather low, especially in the case of small business where returns are mostly returns to the labour of the businessman. In the case of collective business, which involves the use of large capital to conduct the business, the tax is known as the special tax on earnings. Its rates are higher in view of the predominance of the capital component in the return of the business. (The tax is not suitable for cooperative enterprises. It assumes a certain interest on the invested capital and it impose some percentage of this assumed interest as tax. It is then of no consequence whether the tax is assessed according to the size of the capital or according to the fictitious return.)

g) Indirect taxation of business returns by taxing transactions. The government does not need to wait until the formation of the entire business return is completed before it ascertains what it is and taxes it. Business activity can be divided into separate transactions–purchases and sales–and when they occur taxes may be collected on the sale price, etc. (sometimes the tax is collected in the form of a fiscal stamp attached to a document; fiscal stamps are also used to pay fees, e.g., stamps attached to verdicts or to report cards). In this way are taxed purchase as and sales of real estate, as are receipts, security transactions, etc.

A tax that is a percentage of sales–a turnover tax–may have different incidence. When it is shifted to the consumer in the form of higher price it becomes a general tax on consumption. It is a different matter when it affects the returns of businesses that do not succeed–because they operate in a competitive environment–to raise prices of their products by the amount of the tax. It then becomes a tax on business returns, but one that is assessed on sales.

3. Property Tax

a) Direct taxation of property assumes once again that the property is appraised and the tax levied on this appraised value. A tax on property may be a one-time (large) tax imposed for such purposes as currency reform or national defence, etc.) or a (moderate) tax collected periodically to supplement the income tax. Its purpose is to capture more income derived from property (which may be the source of a family's livelihood father the breadwinner has passed away).

b) Indirect taxation of property. This involves taxation of certain transactions that do not involve productive activity (unlike indirect taxation of business returns), e.g., gift taxes, dowry taxes, and inheritance taxes.

II. The use of resources. Government expenditures.

Government makes business expenditures and cooperative expenditures when it provides goods and services to individuals (individual private economic organisations) to whom it sells at a price or to whom it charges a fee. The solidarist sector of the economy buys goods and services that do not serve separate individuals (and cannot be sold in the market) but serve the public as a whole (central administration, international diplomatic relations, defence). Or else the government buys goods and services that do serve separate individuals, economic organisations and groups of organisations, but it provides them without charge, either because individual benefit cannot be measured without major difficulty (the benefit derived from public roads), or because the benefit falls within the scope of the ideal of the nation's life, health and culture, and the betterment of the individual along these lines. The sum total of all these tasks is state administration, but this includes also public cooperative activities that are not completely financed out of fees and charges (e.g., schools, hospitals). The main areas of state administration (embodied in various ministries) represent different main needs of the solidarist economic sector.

Because the solidarist sector must pay attention to limited resources (we shall see below why they are limited) it follows that one need confronts another just as it does in the private consumption sector. A particular need cannot be satisfied without consideration of other needs. One cannot proceed further in satisfying one need if the objective utility derived from another one is higher. (One cannot have excellent schools and inferior hospitals.) This leads to a kind of harmony (according to the law of equalisation of relative marginal utilities). Government purchases in the goods market and the labour market, together with private demand, make up the aggregate demand in the corresponding markets, where prices (broadly defined) have of course, once again, a feedback effect on government demand.

III. The boundary of rationality. The subsistence minimum.

It is said that the public sector differs from the private sector in that its revenues are guided by its expenditures (if expenditures are given, revenues must be found), whereas in the private sector it is the other way around. Is is true that expenditures of the public (solidarist) sector can be set without considering possible revenues? Of course not. And what does it mean that expenditures are set without consideration of revenues? Nothing more than that the utility of increased spending is being compared with the disutility (cost) of increased taxes. The public (solidarist) sector has its own boundary of rationality, just as any other economic sector (cf. p. 00). The boundary lies at the point where the line of declining utility (here it is objective utility, given by increments of life, health and culture) intersects the line of increasing relative cost (here it is objective cost, given by diminution of life, health and culture). To acquire additional resources would be for the most part harmful. And this is how limitation of resources is given in the public sector.

To raise additional taxes would mean to tax lower incomes which serve more important needs and it would therefore cause greater harm (to life and health). This is justified as long as the utility from spending such tax revenues is greater and predominant. But when this is not the case, then taxing lower incomes is not justified. Incomes on the critical boundary of rationality should be free of tax. They represent a subsistence minimum that should not be taxed. The subsistence minimum is not determined without considering the utility that the expenditures yield. It is different in different countries and it may be different, at times, within the same country. When the defence of the nation's freedom is involved, the minimum may be drastically reduced in view of the importance of the defence expenditures. It is true, after all, that the government demands even more sacrifice of its citizens' life of its citizens for the national defence.

C. CREDIT AND BALANCE IN THE PUBLCI SECTOR

1. State enterprises and public cooperative enterprises.

State enterprises, like other business enterprises, make two kinds of expenditures for goods and services. The first kind si returned to the enterprise (is reproduced out of the value of output), in the course of a single accounting period. (For example, wage expenditures are returned from the sales of the output of iron, an the sales cover all wage expenditures made while the output is produced.) The second type of expenditure is returned, or reproduced, over a number of periods, because the goods acquired with such expenditures (investment goods) yield their productive services over several periods. These expenditures are once again returned from sales of output, but the output of a single period covers only a portion of the investment expenditures corresponding to depreciation. The former are operating expenses the latter constitute capital or investment expenditures.

The value of goods or services produced in the course of a year must therefore cover total operating cost of that year. It must also cover that portion of past and current investment expenditures corresponding to depreciation during the current period. In addition to this it must, of course, cover profit. When the value of output does not cover operating and investment expenditures, the enterprise operates at a loss.

Businessmen may operate with their own capital or with borrowed funds and they may use credit for both operating and investment expenditures. However, they must repay operating credit during the same accounting period, whereas investment credit may be repaid over a number of periods during which the corresponding capital goods yield their service. When a businessman is unable to repay operating credit in the course of the accounting period, it is so because his sales were not as expected and that the business operated at a loss. Losses diminish the assets (capital) of the enterprise and creditors' claims are threatened. The continued existence of the enterprise is in jeopardy.

All this applies also to purely cooperative enterprises whose charges cover their expenditures in full (except that the charges need not cover profits since there are not profits).

2. The public solidarist sector

Expenditures on goods and services currently used and capital goods that wear out over time and yield their services over several accounting periods are also found in this sector. The former are called ordinary expenses, the latter extraordinary expenditures. However, the purpose of these expenditures is not to make money, as in the case of business enterprises–via production and sale of goods. Their purpose si rather to serve individuals or society as a whole through activities directed toward improving the nation's health and culture. These expenditures are not reproduced in the same way as they are in the business sector because goods and services produced in the solidarist sector are not sold in the market.

The situation is somewhat like that of households that buy goods and services for current consumption as well as durable household goods that will serve over a number of years. Of course expenditures on new durable goods, representing investment that will serve for a number of periods, are not extraordinary when the acquisition of such goods merely replaces that part of the stock of previously acquired investment goods that was used up during the current period. If, for example, the government owns 1000 buildings with a life of 100 years, then total depreciation equal the value of 10 buildings and the expenditure on the construction of 10 new buildings signifies merely the preservation of technical balance and stability of the stock of buildings. Only expenditures on buildings that go beyond this are extraordinary. True investment is expansion of the public sector's wealth, and the condition of the public sector's wealth is not made any worse when it is financed by borrowing.

However, borrowing is sometimes used to finance current expenditures rather than investment expenditures (e.g., unemployment benefits or war effort). Once again these expenditures are financed by reducing current consumption of the population. However the burden that the public assumes is voluntary.

It represents savings placed at the government's disposal. When the public lends the funds, it expects to be repaid in the future, but the fact that it was able to assume the burden at the time when it did, shows that, in principle, the expenditures could have also been financed by taxation. We say that the nation has spread the expenditures (burden) over a number of years. The nation has to assume the burden of reduced consumption or increased labour at the time when they occurred, but the government was able to cover the expenditure by borrowing and repaying the loan over a number of years. The only way that the nation could spread the burden of the expenditure over a number of years would be by borrowing (and buying the needed goods) from foreigners. However, when expenditures are financed by domestic borrowing, the public assumes all of the current burden of the expenditures. Also, when the government covers a portion of its expenditures by inflationary methods (cf. p. 00) then–because prices are rising–it reduces individual consumption just as it does when it levies taxes.

Another question is whether there may be too much resistance to increased taxes, which would force the government to borrow and repay the loans over time, even though the expenditures are not capital expenditure. When current expenses are unusual and large, and when they are financed by borrowing (because of resistance to increased taxation) they are also called extraordinary expenditure.

Otherwise one should follow the rule that ordinary expenses (on goods and services used during the current period, including depreciation) ought to be financed from ordinary revenues–taxes. Can such spending be financed by borrowing? Yes, but only by short-term credit which helps to bridge over the time difference between spending and revenues in a given month.

The total of ordinary spending over a whole year may be fully covered by ordinary revenues, but in the course of a particular month there may be a discrepancy between revenues and expenditures–sometimes a treasury deficit, at other times a treasury surplus. However, should the total of ordinary spending over a whole year exceed the total of ordinary revenues thee would be a budget deficit which would be financed by borrowing rather than by tax revenues as it should be.

The government turns for sources of credit to be money market where its demand constitutes a major part of demand for loanable funds. This makes borrowing by the private sector more expensive and difficult, and in turn impacts on the country's productivity. The government must therefore weigh the utility an the cost of this method of financing.

Short-term government borrowing uses various forms of financial instruments such as certificates[1]* or bonds** (with no interest coupons attached, the interest being paid beforehand), bills, or even credit current account credit. Long-term borrowing utilises bonds, perpetuities (which pay interest but no principal), premium loans (which pay everyone a premium, when there is a draw, in addition to repaying the borrowed capital), lottery loans (which do not pay special awards–prizes to everyone ut only those who won a draw, etc.

Long-term government loans that incurred at a time when credit was light and interest rates high are paid back over a

---

* Translator's Note: The term Treasury Certificates [Treasury Bills] is used to describe short-term government obligations issued to cover the treasury deficit of the state budget, the so-called transitional debt. *Ekonomicka encyklopedia [Economic Encyclopedia]*, vol. 2, 155, Prague, 1972

** Translator's Note: bon–term...used for certain forms of transitional government debt (state treasury bons), a form of state treasury certificates or treasury bills. *Ekonomicka encyklopedie [Economic Encyclopedia]*, vol. I, 65, Prague, 1972.

bons–a name given to documents, such as French Treasury Bonds, upon which is printed the word "bon" in conjunction with the amount of the bond e.g., "Bon pour cent francs" good for one hundred francs. *Thomson's Dictionary of Banking*, 12th edition, 109.

number of years. It may happen that in the meantime there is a general decline of interest rates. The government will take advantage of this and ask that its creditors accept lower interest. Those who do not agree are paid back their principal right away. Such reduction of interest payments is known as a conversion and is voluntary. There is also forced conversion, when the government does not offer to pay back the money it has borrowed to those who do not agree to accept lower interest.

D. THE BUDGET OF THE PUBLIC SECTOR

Each year the government works out a plan of expenditures and revenues of the public sector known as the government budget. This is embodied in special legislation, the Finance Act.

Of course, the plan must reflect economic conditions. The plan of the enterprise and cooperative sector is different from the plan of the solidarist sector. Because the elements and the structure of the two sectors are different, one type of plan is suitable for public enterprises and public cooperatives and another for the solidarist sector. In the case of public enterprises revenue from market sales of goods and services compared with the cost of goods used in production (including depreciation of capital goods) results in the enterprise objective return. The entrepreneur–the government–must deduct from this the shares of labour (wages and salaries) and outside capital (interest) to arrive at its return and its profit. This is also true of public cooperatives, except that profit is not involved since there is no profit here. The economic plan of public enterprises and public cooperatives includes also a plan of investments (true investment expenditures, expansion of capital stock) and how they are financed (from the returns of public enterprises, from accumulated reserves, from borrowed funds).

The solidarist segment of the public sector consists primarily of the expenditure plan. It includes ordinary expenditures (current expenditures including depreciation and spending on new plant and equipment corresponding to the wear an tear of the existing capital stock). It also includes extraordinary expenditures. The latter include true investment expenditures representing expansion of the capital stock (not merely bringing worn out capital stock up to its required level) as well as expenditures that are extraordinary (though they are for current use) only because they do not occur regularly (e.g., spending on war), because they exceed the ordinary level of spending, and because they are financed by borrowing due to opposition to higher taxes.

It follows that one cannot add, simply and mechanically, all the revenues and expenditures of the separate segments of the public sector. In practice it is difficult to separate mixed (partly solidarist) public cooperatives from the solidarist segment of the public sector precisely because of the mixed nature of public cooperatives. (E.g., the government budget of this country [Czechoslovakia] includes a separate plan for public enterprises, whereas mixed public cooperatives are combined with the solidarist segment in a unified public administration budget in which both are included.)

However, budgets of the separate segments of the public sector differ also in another respect, namely with respect to how binding the plan is. The budget of public enterprises (and public cooperatives) cannot be binding–except for true investment expenditures. It is not possible to decree that only so much and no more tobacco will be purchased. After all, it is a matter of market sales of tobacco products and this can only be estimated in the budget. If more tobacco products are used, more tobacco will be bought and buying tobacco will not cease just because the budget did not foresee the larger sales.

It is different in the solidarist segment of the public sector. Its expenditures are not a function of sales but material and personal capacities. These are estimated on the basis of prior conditions of income, returns, and wealth (revenues too are estimated accordingly). However, when we start out from this, it becomes necessary to restrict solidarist spending so that it would not depart from the boundaries of rationality. It is therefore constrained in a mandatory fashion, and that is why the budget takes the form of legislation passed as a Finance Act.

However, a total spending of the solidarist segment of the public sector total expenditures is not the only thing that matters. Classification of expenditures according to different purposes (health, culture, defence, etc.) is important too. The importance of these purposes determines the utility as well as the marginal utility of expenditures which–confronted with the disutility of taxes–(increments and decrements of the nation's culture, health and life) leads to the boundary of rationality. That is why the budget must be classified into categories according to these purposes and why this structure must be adhered to when it is put into effect. Otherwise there would be no violation of the budget as a whole if funds were shifted from one budgetary purpose to another, while no change occurred in total expenditures. The economic structure of the public sector would be disturbed nevertheless. Such shifts are known as virement. They may be prohibited altogether when it is a matter of basic importance for the program (it is not permitted to take funds that ar to be spend for education and use them for social assistance). Alternatively when shifts of lesser importance, within the basic program, are involved they may be restricted by requiring that certain conditions be met (e.g., approval of the Minister of Finance, the Supreme Office of Accounting Control, etc.) E.g., expenditures budgeted for one school may be shifted to another one.

The government operates according to the budget under the supervision of the Supreme Office of Accounting Control, and the results of these operations are submitted in the form of an accounting statement. ·

E. AUTONOMOUS BODIES

Our discussion has thus far dealt with government as if the private exchange sector was faced only with the policies of the central government, its decrees and prohibitions (the legal system) and its public economic sector. The state is a political body of all citizens residing on its territory. The central government represents its supreme authority. However there are other, more narrowly defined, political bodies subordinates to central government, ranging from municipalities (such as Brno) to higher bodies–districts (e.g., the district of Kyjov) comprising the territories of several municipalities, and still larger bodies, provinces (e.g., Moravia), comprising a number of districts. Higher political bodies have larger territories.

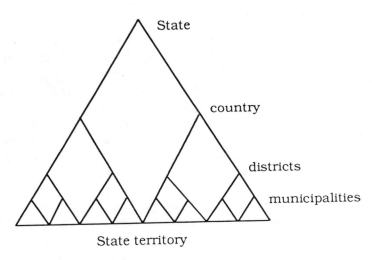

State territory

A municipality consists of a territory and its residents. The same is true of districts and higher bodies. Citizens are compelled to be members of particular political bodies. They are its subjects (the body compels them to pay taxes). Because such bodies consist of the residents of a certain territory they are known as territorial political bodies.

There are other corporate bodies (chambers) which do not comprise all but only some citizens of a given territory, those who belong to certain occupations, e.g., farmers, small businessmen, lawyers, notaries, engineers, physicians. They share common private interests and such corporate bodies are therefore known as private interest corporations. Membership in these corporations is also compulsory and members are obliged to pay dues to finance their activities.

Both political territorial bodies and private interest corporations are called self-administered. Some are natural, e.g., municipalities, others artificial. (Depending on circumstances, there may be more or fewer, larger or smaller political bodies between the municipality as the lowest natural unit and the central government as the highest sovereign unit.

Self-administered political bodies also pursue policies vis-a-vis their members (or territorial area). By authority of the central government they promulgate legal norms (e.g., municipalities promulgate traffic, safety, and market rules and regulations). They do so, of course, within the framework of the central government legal system. They also operate their own economies. The economies of self-administered political bodies have the same structure as the economy of the central government. First, they operate public enterprises (e.g., municipalities operate electricity generating plants, gas plants, electric streetcars, etc. , which earn profits for them; municipalities and provinces operate forestry enterprises, they own buildings, etc.). Second, they also operate public cooperatives (water works, schools, hospitals). And finally, they engage in solidarist activities of their own (making up the deficits of mixed cooperatives, poor relief, public roads, etc.). Depending on the nature of various political bodies one or the other element may predominate.

Enterprises and cooperatives of self-administered political bodies may compete with enterprises and cooperatives operated by the central government just as they compete with other business enterprises and cooperatives (unless this is not possible for natural reasons; e.g., in the case of roads). However, solidarist activity of self-administered political bodies must be coordinated in a planned fashion with the solidarist activity of the central government. A municipality cannot simply impose a tax without considering the taxes levied by the central government, and the government cannot tax its citizens without considering the taxes they pay to self-administered political bodies. Sources of tax revenue and taxes must be divided between self-administered political bodies and central govern-

ment in a reasonable fashion. The existence of self-administered political bodies means that solidarist activity which
would be otherwise unified is decentralised. This leads sometimes to rationalisation (municipalities build schools according
to local circumstances and at lower cost than if the central
government built them. And finally, healthy competition between self-administered political bodies stimulates their willingness to bear sacrifices.

Self-adminsitered political bodies may independently impose some taxes–those that are not collected by central government (e.g., some consumption taxes that can be more easily
collected on a local level, such as taxes on games of chance, or
taxes related to the local character of the political body, such as
taxes on apartments). Alternatively, self-administered political
bodies may join in levying taxes imposed by the central government by imposing e.g., a 100% or 200% surtax on the central
government profits tax.

Why do we refer to these political bodies as self-administered? The citizens and members of political bodies administer
them themselves and bear themselves the responsibility for
their administration. From the viewpoint of the municipalities
the authority of central government si external, whereas authority within the municipality derives from its citizens. When
the central government is an elected one, then t too is an self-
administered body of all citizens on its territory. It is the apex
of autonomous administration.

IV. THE CONTENT OF GOVERNMENT POLICY

A. INTRODUCTION

So far we have discussed the method that the government uses in pursuing its policies, the use of legislative norms (orders and prohibitions) and the public sector (acquiring and using financial resources). We now ask what is the content of government policy, i.e., what does the government wish to accomplish by using these methods. We can illustrate the relation of method and content by taking an example fro another field. Let us suppose that we want to acquaint the population with hygienic practices. That is the content of our effort. We can proceed to do so by spoken or written word, pictures, instructions or prohibitions, financial assistance, etc. That is the approach or method used in our effort. What then does the government want to accomplish with its legislative norms and its public sector?

Actually this was already explained. The basis of the nation's existence si the national product. In capitalism it is produced in accordance with subjective preferences of individuals (according to what they buy, their valuations). The government starts out from this basis but uses its policies to modify the national product so that it might conform to the ideal of the nation's life, health and culture. It modifies it in three directions:

a)   it strives, in general, to maximise the national product. The complex of measures directed to this end constitutes production policy or economic policy narrowly defined.

b)   in the interest of balanced development of the whole, it strives for a more equal allocation of labour and of the national product among individuals. it implements the principle of personal solidarity in the capitalist system. That is social policy.

c)   it strives to restructure the composition of national product, so that it might conform more closely to the ideal than if it were determined by individual preferences. It implements the principle of material solidarity in the capitalist system. That is industrial policy. Let us represent it schematically:

I. ECONOMIC POLICY NARROWLY DEFINED

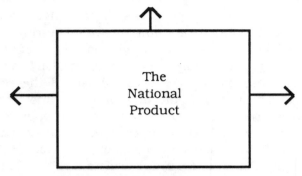

Endeavour for its maximizing

II. SOCIAL POLICY

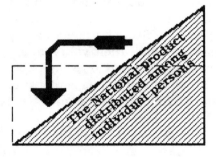

Endeavour for its equitable distribution

III. SPECIAL POLICY

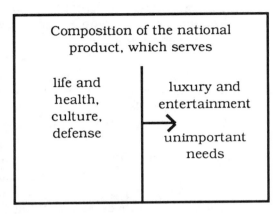

Composition of the national
product, which serves

| life and health, culture, defense | luxury and entertainment → unimportant needs |

Endeavour to expand important goods and
narrowing less important ones, see from the
point of view of the State's purpose.

In each category we must distinguish external, foreign policy which impacts on international integration of the economy under one of these headings (production, personal solidarity, etc.) and domestic policy which impacts domestically on the national body and the national product.

B. ECONOMIC POLICY IN THE NARROWER SENSE

1. International integration

An individualist state knows no restrictions on the movement of persons, capital, and goods across national boundaries. The solidarist state may find various restrictions and intervention desirable, primarily in the interest of the nation's productivity.

This concern above all the movement of persons–emigration and immigration. The solidarist state restricts both emigration and immigration whenever it perceives that they weaken the nation. It restricts emigration of members of certain occupations that are considered vital for domestic production, defence, etc. At other times it fosters emigration of individuals for whom it cannot find a livelihood, persons who are undesirable, etc. It may seek to attract immigrants if the country is too sparsely populated or when it wishes that certain trades, skills or the labour force should grow. (It seeks to attract them by offering them various inducements such as tax incentives or–in earlier times–grants of religious privileges, etc.) It restricts immigration when it wishes to prevent entry of unwelcome elements, overpopulation, etc.

The solidarist government si also concerned with the movement of capital. A country's productivity requires that thee should be a sufficient supply of capital to carry on business activity and undertake capital investments. What is therefore involved are restrictions or outright prohibitions of the outflow of capital that may be due to higher returns abroad or fear of disturbances at home (inflation, war). The government may require approval of loans to foreigners, it may restrict foreign payments (transfers) by requiring permits, it may restrict trading in foreign exchange, it may resort to clearing arrangements for foreign payments to prevent disequilibria in the balance of payments (only those payments are permitted that are compensated) so that a balance of payments deficit would not result in capital outflow, etc. Th government may also try to attract foreign capital to undertake business ventures and capital investments (to build railroads, waterways, gas plants, etc.) by guaranteeing returns, tax holidays, etc.

Finally, the government is also concerned with the movement of goods–imports and exports. Exports may be encouraged (by export subsidies, lower exchange rates, tax rebates, etc.) in order to increase domestic employment and maintain equilibrium in the balance of payments (indirect protection against capital outflow), perhaps also to encourage capital inflows via balance of payments surpluses. On the other hand exports may be discouraged (by embargoes, export taxes and duties) if goods are urgently required to feed the people, for defence, to avoid strengthening adversaries, etc. However, intervention si more common in the case of imports.

With imports it is a question of general or of special restrictions, of a total import embargo, or merely discouraging them by taxing imports (import duties) or by permitting imports only on the basis of special government permits (issued by an agency designated for that purpose–so-called permission procedures).

General import restrictions may be imposed because the country's exports are not sufficient to maintain equilibrium in the balance of payments, or because the government strives for autarky, self-sufficiency. (It may be preparing for a time when the flow of imports will cease, causing serious disturbances, unless the country is prepared to produce substitute raw materials.) Accordingly the government will impose different restrictions on the imports of different goods. If there are difficulties due to balance of payments disequilibrium, restrictions will be imposed on imports of luxuries, so that only imports of urgently needed goods continue. If the government pursues a policy of autarky, restrictions will be imposed on the imports of goods that the economy is subsequently compelled to produce as import substitutes. Imports in the aggregate can be restricted simply by depreciation of the exchange rate, which makes all imports more expensive, or by using clearing arrangements for foreign transactions. This slows down payments for imports so that the foreign exporters suffers loss of interest and that lowers their revenues.

Special restrictions concern particular products and the rationale for them are the circumstances under which such goods are produced in a particular country. Therefore the severity of restrictions will be different for different goods. Restrictions usually take the form of tariff duties, i.e., taxes on the imported product. Tariffs may be assessed per unit, per unit of measure or weight (e.g., per centner)–in which case they are known as specific duties. Alternatively they may be assessed according to the value of the good and are known as ad valorem duties (ad valorem duties depend on the information provided by the parties about the price of the good and this information is not reliable.) Different goods may therefore have different duties.

If a good si subject to a domestic consumption tax (e.g., a tax on sugar) then imports must also be subject to the same tax. Consumers would otherwise buy imported sugar that was not taxed. Such tax si levied in the form of a duty and its purpose is merely to collect from imports the tax to which domestic consumption is subject. Such duties are known as financial duties and their level is determined by the level of the domestic consumption tax. Other duties are known as economic duties. Their rationale is found in the circumstances under which the good is produced.

Importers must pay the duties in addition to the price of the import. Foreign goods become more expensive because of the tariff. If the good was imported because it was produced abroad at a lower cost than at home then imports may disappear altogether, because the incentive for imports was the price difference which has now disappeared. Such tariffs are prohibitive an their effect is the same as if imports were prohibited. Even when the tariff does not he such drastic effect, the fact that foreign products become more expensive means that they will be used less both by consumers and producers. Domestic producers will be able to produce more and at higher cost than if the country was supplied by cheap foreign goods. Domestic production becomes more profitable. This means that some domestic production manages to survive at all (otherwise it would be destroyed by foreign competition) or else that it operates on some level of intensity (e.g., agriculture, which could not succeed, given low prices of farm products, to cultivate the soil with sufficient intensity–its productivity would decline). It may also mean that domestic production can develop and overcome the difficulties connected with every new productive activity (the "infant industry" argument).

Of course, when a country seeks protection via tariffs against imports, then other countries will also seek production by imposing counter tariffs against exports of the first country. Excessive tariff protection would lead to tariff war and to ruining international exchange of goods, international division of labour, and the benefits that they bring. For this reason, individual countries erect tariff barriers (autonomous tariffs) but lower those barriers by mutual agreements, commercial treaties, with individual foreign countries. When one country signs a commercial treaty with a second country it obtains a so-called most favoured nation clause which provides that any favourable treatment that the second country might grant in the future to a third country will apply to the first country as well.

When several countries unite to form a tariff community (common tariffs apply to imports from outside the community) this is known as a customs union. This means that an internal exchange community is established which tends to unification of currencies, tax systems, etc.

When countries strive for autarky or when they are concerned about their balance of payments, they may directly restrict the volume of imports that may be admitted (quotas) or they may regulate the volume of imports according to the volume of exports (compensation).

2. Domestic economic policy

a) Two viewpoints.

Domestic economic policy is sometimes directly concerned with the economy as a whole (e.g., as we saw, with protection of the domestic capital market) but it often deals with particular industries, such as agriculture, manufacturing, trade, transport, etc., and it is accordingly classified as agricultural policy, manufacturing industry policy, domestic trade policy, transport policy, etc. However, these separate economic activities are often served by the same means, e.g., education, etc. It is therefore possible to provide an exposition of domestic economic policy by describing the instruments that it uses. This is the approach that we follow. As we discuss particular policy instruments we pay attention to different economic activities. We shall only touch on the main groups of instruments without going into detail because the instruments are very numerous and varied.

b) Persons of economic activity.

Man's labour and is works depend on what kind of person he is, and what is true of the individual si also true of the nation. When one wishes to improve the nation's production, to increase and improve the national product, one must begin with people. Everything that improves man's health and fitness, that raises the level of his education an technical training, his attitude to work and enterprise will, in the end, surely lead to improvement of his work.

Parents, employers, professional associations, and autonomous public bodies strive–in educational institutions of all types and levels–to promote physical, spiritual and moral advance of the population, its general education, professional training, and economic literacy. The proper function of central government is to oversee such efforts which stem from the initiative of private individuals, self-help organisations, or autonomous political bodies, to dovetail them and to complement them. It is not its function to nationalize everything and thus annul the forces that place themselves voluntarily in the service of the public interest.

Economic success requires economic education:

1.   Above all, young people should be guided toward truth, honesty, fairness, and tolerance–even vis-a-vis adversaries and strangers. This applies to businessmen (producers, merchants, etc.), blue-collar and white-collar workers, teachers, politicians, and scientists. This is a cultural axiom–but one that is of special importance for the economy–that there should be mutual trust, better relations among individuals and among classes, among both us and foreigners with whom we have economic contacts. Fraud in business, usury in credit, demagogy in politics, dishonesty in argument in the press with one's

opponents–all of these corrupt. Their converse gives rise to a great sense of truth, honesty and decency, in everything and everywhere.

2.   Next it is a matter of solid preparation for any kind of work, both general education and professional training (including professional training for manual labour) so that everyone should have an understanding of his work and be capable of improving it, sine this is the only way of attaining greater work efficiency, which makes in turn possible adequate compensation. Though there are shortages of qualified workers, there is unemployment of unqualified labourers who can only find employment as a certain proportion of the qualified workers. It is neither possible nor desirable that people should be concerned with matters that they do not understand, to make decisions about such matters, perhaps even to instruct others about them. The greater the intensity of competition the better must be the preparation for competing. Fortunately in our country we have a high level of general education of the population. Only a well educated population is capable of major achievements. Knowledge of foreign languages, too, is of major importance.

3.   We need a positive attitude to work, a sense of duty and responsibility. We must love our job, our occupation, our work, without consideration of compensation (we do not say that there should not be adequate rewards). We believe however that young people should not be brought up to ask first what they can get and to make claims on society, without considering the contribution that they make, but that they should become fond of some work, try to improve it, find out whether they are adequately prepared for it and whether they merit the reward for their labour. Work must be ennobled by a perception that each contributes something to the common work of the whole nation that he works for the whole upon which he is himself vitally dependent, and that the is a member of the national working community.

No great undertaking was ever accomplished without such positive approach to work. A young man's ideal should be to make something, create something, improve something–not just to make money. This is true of all work, physical and mental, and it relates, of course, to faith in work, faith that work can accomplish much, indeed all, including adequate reward. Making money cannot be the only ethical principle of truly successful work for anyone, be he a manual or mental worker. Love of work, indeed passion for work, will call forth outstanding world-class specialists in all fields. e shall need many of them.

We require also a positive attitude to entrepreneurship and enterprise. This is our greatest deficiency and there are perhaps historical reasons for it. For centuries we have been a nation of peasants, labourers, and later on white-collar workers, but we did not control commercial and industrial enterprise. Hence our somewhat unkind attitude toward business. And yet, without these leading centres of economic activity not even the best possible qualities of workers will be enough. This was made abundantly clear during the Great Depression when the profitability of a large part of business enterprises was destroyed, their activity declined and employment fell. It is precisely because our resource endowment is not favourable and we are therefore compelled to make our living only with labour that is well organised by business and well equipped technically, that our country must pursue–willingly or not–a policy that puts no brakes on business but encourages business and thus also economic activity. This concerns also our tax system which must not destroy the motivation for business investment and business operation. After all, business activity is the source of the entire national income (including tax revenues of public bodies). We need entrepreneurs in the field of foreign trade and many others. We must not make them dislike this responsible activity which deserves to be respected and recognized. We must train our young people not only to be technically proficient in their work but to acquire also a feel for enterprises and management.

    5. We require finally a great deal, a very great deal of capital to keep our production at a world level of technical equipment

and achievement (as well as to be in the position to provide necessary export credits). The capital can only be created by savings from the results of productive activity–from income. Unlike the Western countries we have no individuals with milliards. What we have is a healthy social structure, a strong middle class, but we are dependent on the savings of the middle class and less affluent groups for capital accumulation. Fortunately our people are not only intelligent and hard working but also extremely thrifty and this explains the secret of our economic success. However it imposes upon us an obligation not to destroy our people's propensity to save but, on the contrary, to provide our young people with additional incentives to encourage this propensity.

Given that it is necessary to bring up our young people in this economic spirit, then such spirt must permeate, above all, our educators–from elementary schools to universities. Educators of the young have in their hands the future economic and cultural destiny of our nation. They are responsible for the education, attitude and spirit with which our young people will approach their life's calling and the management of economic affairs that they will take over from the present generation.

General education on a lower level is provided by a dense network of elementary and junior-level intermediate schools and on a secondary level by academic and technical senior-level intermediate schools. Institutions of higher learning (universities, technology institutes, mining technology schools, fine arts institutes, etc.) are conceived as institutions for specialised study Specialised schools are devoted to economic and technical studies on all levels.

In addition to the system of educational institutions there are expositions, museums, books, journals, courses and lectures (radio) financed from both private and public sources. Special voluntary organisations are devoted to the scientific management of work. Personal activity and diligence are stimulated by grants of patents (to secure for the inventor the economic fruits of his idea), trade marks used to designate products to show that they are not falsifications or imitations, copy right, etc.

c) Units of economic work

In our time when farmers have full private ownership of agricultural land and there is no corvee or other obligations imposed upon agriculturalists, it is important to have farms of optimal size from the point of view of productivity. Experience teaches that in this respect the most advantageous are neither excessively large farms (latifundia) nor farms that are too small (dwarf farms).

Very large farms require a large number of hired labourers. These are not employed under one roof, as in a factory, so that it is difficult to supervise them. Their low productivity means that labour is expensive. For this reason large farms tend to dispense with hired labour. As a result they may use less intensive methods of production requiring less labour (e.g., shifting from a type of husbandry where cattle roam in pastures). Alternatively they may tend to replace labour with machines, shifting from labour-intensive to capital-intensive methods of production. The trade-off is of course lower employment of labour.

On the other hand on very small farms (dwarf farms) the soil cannot be properly cultivated, in particular crop rotation cannot be very well practised. Such dwarf size holdings always produce the same product (e.g., some grain and some potatoes) which exhausts the soil and reduces its productivity.

In our conditions the optimum farm is of middle size, particularly if it can manage with a labour force consisting of family members, or if members of the family constitute the backbone of its labour force. Under these circumstances the farm will have a satisfactory level of productivity because its profit is the family labour income.

Farms that are not well managed are likely to become indebted and broken up. This is what happens with large estates belonging to individuals (the former landed nobility) who are not personally engaged in farming. It also happens when farms are divided among several children by farmers who had operated them themselves. Formerly, governments endeavoured to preserve large estates in order to sustain the position of the nobility (so called fideicommissum–estates that could be neither divided nor excessively indebted). In our time there is discussion of protecting middle-size peasant farms.

In our country we have thus far undertaken a reform of land tenure–forced redistribution of the land of large estates for a moderate compensation. It was an intervention in private ownership but it actually strengthened the institution of private ownership by increasing the number of proprietors of land. It benefitted the nation's social structure (it strengthened the middle class) and contributed as well to improved productivity because the middle class is characterized by high labour productivity (intensive animal production).

In addition to owner operated farms, there is also frequently encountered the leasing of agricultural land, especially large estates. If the lessee is endowed with sufficient capital, if he is an efficient businessman, and if his lease si guaranteed for a number of years, he is often able to operate the farm better than the land owner. At times of emergency lessees are given special protection.

Collective enterprise is of little significance in agriculture which is the home ground of individual enterprise. There have been occasional attempts to organize cooperative production, but they have not been successful.

On the other hand, in manufacturing and other industries (trade and transport) the possibility of strengthening the capital position by collective forms of business enterprise plays a major role. By setting up and facilitating such forms of enterprise the government thus promotes business activity. To the extent that mergers promote higher productivity b concentrating production in large enterprises and by merging several enterprises into one, the government can be of assistance, in particular by not levying taxes on mergers like the taxes that it levies on business liquidations.

Government may also promote productivity by engaging in business activity itself, e.g., when private individuals do not possess sufficient capital resources or when they are unwilling to engage in a particular enterprise because of excessive risk (as was the case, e.g., when railroads were first built). Sometimes government must itself engage in activities (such as operating steamship lines) that are carried on elsewhere by the private sector.

Central government (or other government bodies) may finally join with private business in mixed enterprises in which the government–though it may control 51% of the capital–leaves management to the more energetic private participants. The latter must however serve the public interest because the government holds a majority of capital shares (e.g., in the field of electricity generation and transmission in our country).

d) The technical equipment of enterprises

Given present day levels of technology the productivity of human labour depends on technical equipment with machinery and engines. Those who introduce improvements and lower costs of production succeed in the competitive struggle. An old pice of machinery becomes useless not only when it is physically depreciated but also when it is overtaken by technological progress. This applies as well to other technology (chemical processes, methods of processing raw materials and auxiliary materials). Technical improvement in agriculture includes land improvements (drainage, irrigation).

How well enterprises are equipped depends on research and knowledge of technology, on conditions in the capital market, an finally on prospective returns. The businessman must know what kind of technology his enterprise requires, he must have access for this purpose to his own or someone else's capital, and he must perceive that the new equipment is profitable. (The equipment must bring about such savings and improvements that it will exceed interest on the invested capital and the depreciation of the investment.)

This is the heart of government programs directed toward improvements of productivity via technology used in business enterprises. Programs directed toward technological advance exist at educational institutions of all levels, state research institutes, museums of technology, etc. Governments show concern with the conditions of investment credit as well as operating credit by organising capital markets (to be discussed below). To finance land improvements there was set up special amelioration credit which uses land improvement collateral certificates. These are like other certificates of indebtedness except that they have priority even vis-a-vis existing creditors who are however not harmed because land improvement makes the land more valuable. Governments also show concern for the profitability of new investments by not taxing or taxing at lower rates a part of net profit used to finance such investments.

Government also promotes overall technical advance when it encourages or undertakes itself investment projects that serve all business, but cannot be undertaken by individuals (highways, railways, electricity installations, improvement of waterways, hydro projects, etc.).

e) Financial capital for business enterprises

We have already discussed the general need for capital accumulation (under point 5.). To conduct business businessmen must have access to operating and investment capital. To finance their capital requirements businessmen may use their own financial resources, they may admit others (expansion by means of shares of capital stock) or they may borrow for operating and investment purposes. Government assists in this by organising financial markets, which we have already discussed. However, it may also intervene in financial matters more profoundly in the interest of promoting the country's productivity. After all, interest represents a burden on producers, a part of production costs, a component of price. Anything that reduces the interest burden facilitates productive activity. New investment is more profitable when interest is lower than when it is higher. It is primarily a question of lowering the charges of financial institutions that form the difference between the (lower) interest paid to depositors and (higher) interest charged to borrowers. Facilitating rationalisation of the financial industry (mergers, cf. p. 000) is therefore helpful to other producing industries as well. Sometimes it is necessary to strengthen monitoring and regulation of financial institutions which might otherwise incur losses (because of poor judgement or speculative investments), that are eventually borne by depositors or creditors.

Government may influence financial markets indirectly through its own credit operations which compete with the private sector, it may make it easier to get credit in domestic financial markets by obtaining foreign loans, it may affect trade and payments balances (e.g., by prohibiting capital outflows) and this is again connected with domestic financial markets). When interest payments are taxed this does not, of course, make the conditions in the loanable funds market easier.

Finally, the government may interfere in financial markets by regulation, i.e., by imposing legal controls of interest rates–obviously lower interest rates–to assist borrowers, to promote investment and business activity. Of course, government cannot impose lower interest rates at will (it cannot outlaw interest) because this would undermine willingness of the public to make their savings available in the financial markets.

In some cases government goes beyond this. It offers loan guarantees to businesses that find themselves in difficulties (but are otherwise healthy and important from the viewpoint of the economy as a whole). In this way the government reduces risk premium as part of interest and makes borrowing less expensive (a case in point are exporters whose costs are reduced in this way which makes it easier for them to compete abroad), etc.

The government may finally stimulate economic activity by using unemployed capital to finance its own investment projects. It may obtain capital from abroad, for itself or for the private sector, or it may create additional credit artificially (outside financial markets) by printing additional money (which is of course inflationary).

f) Promoting employment

We have already seen (cf. p. 000) how government assists business by organising the labour market. Governments may intervene in the labour market by controls of the movement of persons across national boundaries (cf. p. 000), by itself competing for labour in the public sector, by reducing its investment activity when times are prosperous (high levels of employment in the private sector) and expanding it when workers are being laid off in the private sector.

When government intervenes in the labour market by direct controls (wage controls) it does no for the benefit of workers–as we shall see in our exposition of social policy. When government pressures business to employ workers (even though business may derive no economic advantage from it), it subjugates the interest of production to social concerns.

g) Markets and prices

Businesses produce for the market and for exchange. Therefore anything that facilitates prompt and smooth operation of exchange also promotes production and sales by business enterprises. Knowing how to produce is important but so is knowing how to sell, how to realise the monetary results of production. We have seen how markets and exchange are organised on the basis of technical institutions of exchange (money, currencies, weights) markets, forms of business enterprise, types of commercial agreements, etc.

Encouragement of enterprises engaged in trade (through specialised education, etc.) also promotes, indirectly, the country's productivity. Trade brings products closer to consumers who might otherwise not be even aware of them. However, trade ceases to make a contribution to the formation of the national product when there are more middlemen on the path between producers and consumers than is necessary, because this causes an excessive differential between the prices received by producers and those paid by consumers.

The higher prices paid to merchants b consumers regulate and depress consumption, while the lower prices paid by middlemen to producers regulate and depress production. It is therefore in the interest of productivity that trade should be as efficient as possible and that it should exclude those who manage only by competing unfairly, engaging in dishonest activities that hurt consumers (false weights and measures, adulteration of food, etc.). Government therefore punishes unfair competition, restricts or prohibits certain kinds of trade (sale of poisons, of alcohol), and regulates others by special legislation (installment purchases entered into frivolously because purchasers need not pay right away and are not concerned about the future). Only persons of good character and who possess adequate training may be permitted to engage in certain trades (e.g., pharmaceutical dispensaries, public houses).

The volume of production of a particular product depends on its price which determines the cost that can be incurred in producing the good as well as the producer's return–his motive to increase production. Lower prices tend to reduce, higher prices to increase both. Does it then follow that government should strive for a general increase of prices to stimulate overall productivity? Not at all. A higher price of even a single product lowest both its sales and its consumption and therefore, ultimately, its production. Higher prices of all goods eventually mean higher nominal levels of economic indicators and a lower value of money. Such artificial increase of all prices, brought about e.g., by lowering the exchange rate or by creating artificial purchasing power (printing money) stimulates production while prices are rising (during inflation). But once the process stops there is a reaction and a decline. The process represents an economic injection obtained at the cost of a decline in the value of deposits and savings.

It follows that the government should pursue a policy of higher prices only as an exception, that such policy should involve only some goods, and that there should be special reasons for it. For example, the government may be concerned with the possibility that imports maybe stopped. It may therefore seek self-sufficiency in food production by preventively excluding cheap foreign competition (e.g., by tariffs) thus artificially raising domestic prices to stimulate higher levels of production. In this way it may assist entire branches of production (e.g., agriculture) but this occurs, of course, at the expense of other branches of production. For example, it may establish a grain monopoly which acquires all the grain produced by farmers at prices set by the government. The grain monopoly thus performs the function of an agricultural producers' syndicate which cannot be established by agreement among them because their numbers are too large.

When some branch of production succeeds in raising (cartel) prices by organising a syndicate and production is restricted (by quotas) even though the industry is quite profitable (cf. p. 00), then the higher prices resulting from the syndicate organisation actually lead to lower level of production. If the government then exerts pressure to lower prices (and therefore the profits of the syndicate members) it also promotes overall productivity.

h) Transport

Transport moves freight–on the instruction of producers, distributors, or consumers–from one location to another. Transport costs constitute a part of the price paid by consumers, and higher prices tend to depress consumption. Transport moves goods from where they are produced and where there is excess supply to where they are consumed and where there is excess demand, from locations where prices are low to locations where they are high. Transport thus facilitates exchange and price equalisation and therefore promotes production and productivity. The faster and cheaper is transport, the greater is its contribution to this end. Government economic policy should be directed to this end. There are different policies corresponding to different modes of transport.

The most important means of freight transport includes railways, lorries on highways, and steamships on rivers and oceans. If railways would be part of the private sector, entrepreneurs would choose to build profitable lines, serving industrial centres of commerce (to the most important cities), and the rest of the country would have no railways. It would lag behind because its natural wealth from quarries or forests would not reach distant markets. Railways make the natural wealth of a region, as well as the products of its labour, more valuable and they are therefore a vehicle for its development. That is why they should be operated by government as commercial or cooperative enterprises, and to be located so as to lead to balanced development of the whole country. Excess profits generated on profitable lines should be used by the government to cover the losses of unprofitable lines. That is why railways are public enterprises, even when they are operated as commercial enterprises.

Railways are faced with money costs of labour, loading, unloading, coal for locomotives, lubricants for waggons and engines, depreciation of track–rails, sleepers–of structures, engines, waggons. The costs are a function of the freight mass, the space occupied by freight, and the distance over which freight is carried. Some freight has small mass but occupies much space. Its transport involves much dead weight–the mass of the waggon needed to transport it. Other freight occupies little space but has large mass; in this case it is its own mass which is important.

One must also consider the ratio of the value of freight to its mass and space (cf. goods suited for circulation, p. 00). Transporting goods of the same mas and space from A to B costs the same, but the cost may represent different proportions of value. If the transport charge is 10 while the value of one good is 100 and of the other 1000, the transport cost si 10% in the first case but only 1% in the second case. Transport charges make goods more expensive and, from the point of view of businessmen or consumers, they are a cost of production. Goods are moved from locations where they are less expensive to where they are more expensive. However, transport charges must not absorb the entire differential, otherwise there would be no point in moving the goods. Transport charges therefore determine the distance over which it pays to move goods. The charges determine the radius for the benefit of the economy as a whole, especially for goods less suited to circulation (goods with a relatively small ratio of value per unit of space and mass–e.g., coal, ore, lumber), charges are not set as high as they are for goods more suitable to circulate (goods with a high ratio of value to mass and space–e.g., silk, watches, jewellery). It is precisely this value ratio that is taken into consideration.

A set of transport charges based on mass and space is a specific set, whereas a set based on value is an ad valorem set. Attempts to derive optimum economic benefit from transport lead to a mixed set of transport charges. To be sure, such set should be designed to cover the costs of the railway (whether it is operated commercially or as a cooperative).

Railways have recently begun to face competition from motor vehicles which are taking over part of their transport tasks. Motor vehicles are not confined to the railroad track, they can travel on all highways. Railways must construct their roads whereas the roads used by motor vehicles are constructed by public bodies. Fairness in competition demands that operators of motor vehicles should contribute to road maintenance (motor vehicle taxes). Competition between railways and motor vehicles will lead to greater transport efficiency of both and to a rational division of labour between them. Development of automobile transport represents still another great step on the path of progress and is therefore welcome and encouraged by government (note its importance for national defence!). Government itself is introducing mass transport by busses which complement railway transport.

As for steamship transport it is primarily river transport that is relevant for our country (on the Elbe, Vltava, Danube, and Oder rivers). River transport is operated by both private business and the government. It requires no rails or highways and is less expensive. It enables therefore transportation over large distances of freight with a low ratio of value to mass and space (stone, ores, brick, lumber). River transport depends on the natural course of rivers but it is possible to build canals and makes rivers navigable (by constructing locks),e tc. Nations with access to the sea have an enormous advantage (aside from the wealth of the ocean depths) in having access to ocean navigation and to inexpensive connection with the rest of the world.

A most recent development has been air transport. It is relatively expensive and serves primarily the transport of persons and mails. Here too are being introduced rational connections (including international ones) and governments everywhere encourage air transport either by granting subsidies to private companies or by providing air transport themselves through government airlines.

i)   Spreading business losses by insurance

Any business can suffer losses that mayh have very serious consequences. Losses may affect persons (illness, accident, death), material objects (fire, flood, hail,cattle diseases), or business operations (strikes, bad debts, fluctuations of the exchange rate). They may cause damages to the economic organization which they affect. For example, when the head of a household passes away, the family suffers loss of its income, an the business suffers loss of its executive officer; when a family member passes away or falls ill the family faces unexpected expenses; fire may destroy business property an interrupt its operation; bad debts may destroy the assets of the business, cause insolvency of the enterprise and bring to an end its operation. We are concerned here with losses that affect business and may bring their operation to an end.

As far as individual businesses are concerned, such events are random, unexpected, and uncertain. Many businesses may not be affected at all, while others may be struck over and over again. Individual businessmen are therefore unable to take protective measures against such events, even if they would set aside reserves against such contingencies. Misfortune does not wait till they are ready. However, when we compare the number of such events with the number of businesses that could be affected and that are thus faced with certain risks (e.g., the risk of fire), or when we compare the amounts of monetary losses that take place (e.g., losses caused by fire) with the value of the properties that face such risk, we observe a kind of relative regularity (buildings destroyed by fire as a percent of the total number of buildings). Death or accident are thus events that affect the individual one a lifetime or once in many years, but the number of deaths is a relatively constant percent for the total population. The relative constancy of the phenomena indicates that its cause is constant. Westergard placed a black and a white ball in a container, then drew balls from the container and noted the colour of the ball he had drawn. In a given draw he naturally obtained either a black ball or a while ball, but as the number of draws grew larger and larger the number of white balls grew closer and closer to the number of black balls drawn. This result is not unusual. On the contrary, a different outcome would be peculiar. After all, the conditions for drawing either a black ball or white ball are the same. But this cannot manifest itself in a single draw which has to be either black or white. It manifests itself however when there are many draws, and this suppresses the conditions that apply in the case of a single draw, and the conditions applicable to all draws becomes relevant. This phenomenon is known as the law of large numbers.

Knowledge of this characteristic of business losses had led to the scheme of bringing together businesses facing a given risk to jointly cover losses that have actually occurred, as if they had afflicted all businesses, in return for the assurance that losses which strike individual businesses at random will be shouldered by all businesses. This is the idea of insurance. It can be carried out by large commercial enterprises (joint stock corporations) whose operations are based on calculations of risk and which collect payments from individual businesses (primarily) that are larger than what is required to cover the losses, in order to create reserves and to make profits. Alternatively it can be carried out by private cooperatives (mutual insurance companies) or public cooperatives (e.g., the Provincial Cattle Insurance Company).

These services, which provide stability for business, may be supported by government through supervision (regulation) of insurance companies, through subsidies and guarantees (as in the case of insuring losses in the export business) or through provision of insurance services by government operated cooperatives. The latter can be operated by the central government or by lower level autonomous political or private interest bodies.

j) Yield as the motivating force of business activity

The residual of the objective return (cf. p. 00) which accrues to businessmen after compensation of labour and of the capital of others is the entrepreneur's return. It is the compensation for his labour and interest return on his capital. However, businessmen wish to receive as their return a lager compensation for their labour than they would pay to someone else and a larger interest return on their capital than they would receive if they deposited their funds in a bank account. After all, they bear risks and perform managerial tasks in their businesses. This extra compensation si known as entrepreneurial profit. It is the motivating force for their activity and stimulus for efficient management. If a businessman values his independence very highly he may be content wit a return to his labour and capital that does not include profit because if he did not go into business for himself he would have to hire himself out as an employee. Businessmen may be content for a time with lower returns to their labour and capital if they see the future in a favourable light. However they find it difficult to face operational losses because such losses diminish their capital and worsen their future prospects–all the way to eventual liquidation of the business.

Under exceptional circumstances the government may supplement the profitability of business, e.g,, by guaranteeing some percentage return (this used to be done, for example, when railroads were built). However, government ought not to supplement business profits directly through subsidies because it would undermine business concern with efficiency. Government contributes to profitability indirectly when it assists business in acquiring technical equipment, lowering the cost of credit, etc. Because business returns are the source of business taxes, government must set up these taxes so that they would not undermine interest in entrepreneurship (concern with the material ability to pay).

k) Conclusion

We have examined how the government promotes productivity. The list is not complete, it is meant to show the main approaches, which are intended to operate through business enterprises engaged in productive activities. What applies to commercial business enterprises is also true of cooperatives, to the extent that they take the place of businesses. Just as all government activities that we have discussed, this too is divided between the central government and autonomous public bodies within the central government, both territorial bodies and private-interest corporations. Provinces and municipalities are concerned with agriculture, trades, markets, education, etc. There are also voluntary organisations (societies, associations) whose purpose is to encourage in various ways overall productivity (e.g., the Economic Institute of the Czech Academy). Alternatively they may support productivity in specific areas (e.g., the Society for the Encouragement of Industry, The Agricultural Union) or foster certain types of encouragement (e.g., education: schools, museums). The central government (and lower level public bodies) may then assist productivity by supporting this self-help.

C. SOCIAL POLICY

1. Introduction

Social policy is the implementation of partial solidarism in an individualist economy, directed toward more equitable distribution of the burdens and fruits of the nation's labour. it is not intended to displace and abolish the individualist economy but to build on its foundations, in order to modify the individualist social system, established by competition and consent, through government intervention (legislative norms and the public sector). Its purpose is to achieve greater equity in the distribution of the burden and fruit of the nation's labour.

Social policy can be classified as general social policy which seeks to achieve equity among the population as a whole, without consideration of specific classes and groups of the population, and specific social policy which is concerned precisely with particular classes and groups, with social classes and their special problems (small business, the working class, the poor).

In implementing social policy (like all other policies) the government uses two instruments: Legislative norms–directives and restraints that guide the behaviour of citizens–and the public solidarist sector of the economy. In discussing social policy, we are of course aware that it is implemented by central government and by autonomous public bodies. In addition there is also voluntary self-help which the government may support.

Social policy may also be implemented by government participation in international organisations and by its international relations. This may take negative form–restrictions of the movement of goods, capital, and persons to protect domestic labour, employment, etc. Or it may take affirmative form–negotiation of international treaties for the protection of labour (length of the work day, etc.) in order that working conditions in one country should not be better than in other countries, because the competitive environment would be less favourable in countries with higher standards of labour protection.

2. General social policy

a) The standard of living

When the national product is divided by the number of citizens of households, we obtain the average standard of living. It consists of the set of goods that the nation has produced an consumed and forms the basis of national as well as individual existence. We should distinguish its level, measured in terms of value (price), and its composition, of what goods and in what proportions it consists. The standard of living of each individual is a function of his income and of prices which he faces in the market. Recipients of higher incomes enjoy higher standards of living; lower incomes make possible lower standards of living.

Suppose that an individual has an income twice as high as another. This does not mean that he will consume twice as much food, etc., as an individual whose income is half of his. He may eat better quality foods but he will also enjoy more and better housing, attend the theatre and take trips–activities that the individual with half his income cannot afford. In short, the composition of consumption expenditures that make up the living standard will be different at different levels of income and therefore at higher or lower living standards. Indeed the composition will also be different because of the preferences of individuals who are free to choose. However individuals who are in continuous contact tend to develop similar patterns of consumption behaviour. There is a tendency for the emergence of different types of living standards depending on income levels, occupations and educational levels, rural and urban residence, etc. Individuals who become accustomed to certain living standards will try to maintain them and they will resist having them lowered.

From the solidarist viewpoint, which is concerned with the nation's life, health and culture, the government may disapprove of the composition of consumption expenditures as a whole, on the average, or in individual cases of consumers who spend their incomes on goods that are objectively worthless, indeed harmful (narcotics, alcohol, artless literature, vulgar entertainment, etc.). However, to correct the composition is the task of specific social policy to the discussed later.

For the most part social policy is concerned with income differences. Individuals have different living standards because their incomes are unequal. Some can afford luxuries, others cannot afford even goods needed to preserve life and health (minimum subsistence). The price of the luxuries enjoyed by some is diminution of the life and health of others. From the viewpoint of the ideal of life, health and culture a small gain is obtained at the cost of a major loss. That is why social policy aiming at more equal living standards and more balanced development of the whole is directed toward more equal distribution of income.

b) Distribution of income in the individualist economy. Income equalisation.

In an individualist economy all incomes are formed as objective returns of business (the difference between the value of output and the value of goods used up in the process of production). Incomes are derived from the value of output and therefore from labour and business activity. The source of income of all who participate in producing iron is the value of their product. Depending on the prices of iron and of other goods they use their incomes to choose what they need in the market.

The objective return of business is the source of income of individuals who participate in business activity–of entrepreneurs who contribute labour and capital and receive entrepreneur's return; of workers who contribute labour and receive wages, of capitalists who contribute capital that they invest in the business and receive interest. This can be represented as follows:

Value of agricultural produce and products

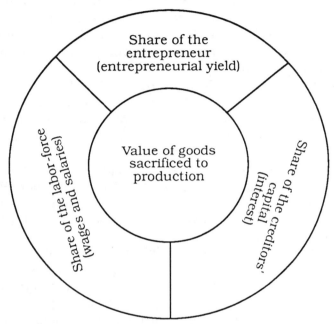

The outer ring represents the objective yield
of the enterprise

The shares of the objective returns of business flow to households as incomes. A household may receive income from several businesses and several sources. E.g., the head of a household may receive income from his business, his wife may receive interest on her dowry, and a daughter may earn income from writing. Incomes which have their direct source in business are direct or original incomes. Incomes derived from original incomes (e.g., alimony payments) are indirect or derived incomes.*

---

* When we discuss objective returns of business enterprises we include conceptually objective returns of cooperatives which do not include profit, but which include objective returns

Indirect incomes which have their source in direct incomes, are therefore ultimately derived from objective business returns as well. When we consider that entrepreneur's return represents compensation for his labour and capital, we can say that labour and capital (wealth) are the sources of income in the individualist economy.

Income differentials can be therefore traced to differences in labour compensation and differences in property ownership which makes non-labour income possible. Major income differentials are not so much due to differences in wages and salaries as they are to differences in wealth.

Policy whose objective is greater equality of income will therefore attempt, in the first place, to bring about a more equal distribution of wealth either directly, e.g., through reform of land tenure, or indirectly, e.g., through property and inheritance taxes.

Government may also intervene with income distribution directly. Some individuals may be compelled to transfer directly some part of their income to others (e.g., alimony payments). Alternatively the transfers maybe indirect, via the public purse and taxation–welfare payments, unemployment compensation, youth programs, etc. The solidarist principle of taxation (progressive taxes) reinforces indirect equalisation of income by government.

c)   Allocation of the burden of labour

In general the question of how the burden of labour is allocated is synonymous with the question of the length of the working day. Low levels of labour productivity were responsible at one time for the long work day. Workers had to work long hours to produce enough to live. When they became equipped with machinery and motors the burden of human labour was eased. Following introduction of machinery and motors the

to the working team–the difference between the value of output and the goods used up in the process of production.

length of the work day was not immediately reduced. On the contrary the time worked tended to become longer because of the desire that each day the machines should be operated long hours because of the interest cost. As labour was replaced by machines and motors this caused unemployment and downward pressures on wages. Low wages forced the workers to work longer hours to earn a living. Excessively long hours of work destroy the worker's life energy. What is the ideal duration of the work day?

The ideal means, first of all, that labourers should work as much and have as much rest each day to be able to come back to work sufficiently rested the following day. Otherwise their fatigue will become so great as to cause illness. But the ideal also includes sufficient leisure–in addition to the time they spend working for a living–for education and entertainment. They need to time to live a little for themselves. To what extent this is possible depends precisely on aids to human labour, the energy of natural resources that drives machinery and motors. It would be unwise to shorten the work day and increase the time devoted to entertainment and culture at the expense of productive activity. Technological progress makes possible reduction of the burden of labour without lowering the standard of living.

We need not be concerned about a shorter work day of those who decide themselves how much they wish to work (businessmen). We need to be concerned about those for whom the decision is made by businessmen (manual and white-collar workers). Workers have engaged in a drive for a shorter work day through trade unions. However, general and pervasive results can only be obtained through government action. This follows from the fact that the length of the work day plays a role in competition. Businesses that operate longer–e.g., stores that stay open longer–have a competitive advantage. There must be uniform regulation of this factor for all competing businesses. Given a shorter work day, the desire of businessmen that machines should be operated continuously can be accommodated by workers taking turn. For an enterprise to operate continuously, given an eight-hour work day, there can be three shifts per day.

The length of the work day can be set directly–as some maximum number of hours per day (or week or month–when the hours of work cannot be same each day, e.g., in the summer in agriculture). Alternatively it can be set indirectly by establishing periods of rest–the day may be split by rest periods, the work week by Sunday rest, or–if work must be done on Sunday–by substitute rest. The work year may include vacations lasting a number of days. In our country the general rule is the eight-hour work day. Even shorter hours apply in mining. The most advanced businesses have already gone beyond this.

As we have noted, duration of the work day also plays a role in foreign competition and countries therefore enter into international agreements, or conventions, about the length of the work day. This makes the position of business easier. The International Labour Organisation in Geneva which prepares these conventions has assisted in the formulation of the social policies of individual countries.

Government cannot reduce the time spent at work if it wishes to avoid lowering production and reducing living standards. Social policy may therefore be in conflict with productivity policy. However if social policy increases workers' health and education it also increases their work performance For this reason, when there are extraordinary circumstances demanding the exertion of all the forces of the nation, government may actually lengthen the work day.

3. Special social policy

a) Introduction. Classes in Society

Specific social policy is concerned with social classes. Social classes emerge in the individualist-capitalist economic system from the normal competitive struggle in the market. We have noted that producers and consumers, debtors and creditors, workers and employers stand opposed in the market. The opposing sides are engaged in struggle over prices, interest, wages. However, struggle, competition for buyers, goods, capital, work, positions, exists also within the opposing sides. The common thrust of the competitive struggle, the common and concurrent concerns of the participants, generate among them an awareness of common concern for their living conditions. This is a lasting concern and it molds them into social classes that are united by the common concern about making a living and opposed to other classes in a conflict of interest.

All this is most apparent in the case of workers who do not own the means of production. They seek wage employment from employers (business, households). They want high wages and low prices of the goods they consume. Because of strong common interest in their living conditions they constitute a strong social class.

Facing the workers is the business class which is engaged in competitive struggle on several fronts, in markets for goods, capital, and labour. Its interests are no longer so concurrent as those of workers. Tailors want everything low priced, and only garments to fetch high prices. Farmers want to buy manufactured products at low prices and sell their products at higher prices. However, within the class of business that emerge additional groupings from the competitive struggle of big business with small and middle-size business. Small and middle-size businessmen are aware of the competitive pressure of big business which operates with large capital. They are concerned that their independent existence is threatened and they form a social class of small and middle-size business opposed to big business.

Employees of the central government and other public bodies whose position depends on legislative norms, individuals whose income is derived from their financial investments (rentiers), etc., tend to become associated–depending on their income level–with one or another class. They may join that class in political life (elections), but they do not constitute a separate class emerging from normal economic struggle in the capitalist economy.

The population is thus divided into social classes according to productive activity and share of the national product. But there are also those who are not productively active because they are unable to work (or cannot find work) and who own no property off which they could live. There is no place for them at the individualist-capitalist dinner table. They do not participate in economic struggles, they are not part of the set of the economically active population. They are the poor.

This can be represented as follows:

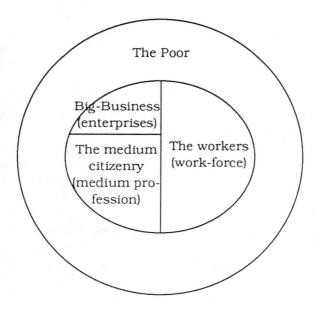

Special social policy thus involves three social problems:
1. the problem of small and middle-size business
2. the problem of workers
3. the problem of the poor.

b) The question of small business and small business policy

aa) What is the small business class?

The middle class is not coextensive with recipients of medium incomes. If it were it would include workers whose wages are sufficiently high to classify them as recipients of middle incomes. Policy toward small and medium business would not have to be concerned with preserving medium business, if individuals received mid-size incomes. That is not the case however. The small business class consists of persons who are independent and receive medium incomes, i.e., medium and small businessmen faced with pressures from big business.

In agriculture large estates do not threaten the existence of small and medium farms because they cannot replace their output. Even if large estates produced at lower cost than small and medium farms (which is not the case because small farms are worked, for the most part, by the farm family itself) they could not expand their output without incurring higher costs. This follows from the law of diminishing returns to land which states that to double the crop from a given area of land requires more than double the input of labour and capital.

Nor can big business displace small business in the distribution sector because continued ramification of the division of labour always demands more intermediaries between producers and consumers. Consumers want goods to be conveniently available and that leads to continued splitting of businesses active in trade. Here we encounter the competition of large department stores with unit prices.

On the other hand big business tends to displace small business in manufacturing industries because it operates on a large scale and at lower cost. It has available more machines and motors, it buys raw materials and other material inputs wholesale and therefore at lower cost, it has large visible assets and can therefore obtain credit more easily and at lower cost; it employs large numbers of workers and can therefore make better use of the advantage of the division of labour, etc. Small-scale industrial production is handicraft production, large-scale industrial production is factory production. Many crafts have already disappeared and were replaced by factories which produce at lower cost and sell at lower prices. They have taken over the production of craftsmen and they have continued to reduce production costs still further. Th term used to describe both handicrafts and small merchants is small business.

Concern for preserving the small business class follows from the fact that social policy has a double objective: to modify the operation of the individualist order and to preserve it. In the case of the class of small businessmen it aims both at a more equitable distribution of income (solidarist concern) and at preserving entrepreneurial independence (individualist concern). The individualist system can survive only if there is a large number of businessmen who prefer it. Who would have a stake in being a businessman if the entire nation consisted of wage labourers employed by a few factories? Small business is therefore mostly concerned with the survival of small and medium business. In following this objective it also promotes middle income because small and medium businessmen are recipients of middle incomes. Th crisis of small business is due to competition of big business. The approach to small business policy follows from this fact.

bb) Two principal approaches to small business policy

When to parties, one strong and the other weak, are engaged in struggle, we may assist the weak by erecting a barrier between them, reserving to the weak an area which the strong may not enter, or by making the weak stronger, equipping him for the struggle, etc. This holds also for small business policy.

The first approach means that a barrier to competition is erected between big business and small business. This is the case when big business is prohibited to produce some goods or when it is made difficult for big business to do so. That is why small tradesmen demand that big business should provide certificates of competence.* When such certificates are not required it is the small producers who suffer, not the big factory. They demand that repair shops operated by big business (e.g., factory operated shoe repair shops) should not be allowed. Small merchants demand that large department stores with fixed prices, such as ASO** should be prohibited, that distribution networks operated by large factories should not be allowed, etc. In this way even businesses less capable to compete could survive–of course, by producing at higher cost and selling at higher prices, i.e., at the expense of overall productivity.

The second approach consists of government policies that strengthen small and medium business in its competitive struggle with big business and thus keep small businesses alive and encourage growth of their numbers. There are various ways of doing that. The simplest but least viable would be for government to increase the revenues of small businesses by subsidies from the state treasury. This would amount to assistance, at government cost and at the expense of productivity, to those enterprises that are least efficient, and it would also undermine their own efforts to operate more efficiently. In taxing the income of small business the government may of course take into account the fact that its source is mostly labour (whereas the source of income of big business is mostly capital) and therefore impose lower taxes on small business.

We need to ask why small business exhibits competitive weakness and why big business is superior. Without doubt the explanation lies in the large scale capitalisation and intensive

---

* Translator's Note: The authors seems to allude to an incident in Czechoslovakia in the 1920's when operators fo small footwear businesses demanded that Thomas Bata, Sr., the head of BATA, the giant shoe manufacturer, should demonstrate his competence as journeyman shoemaker. He did.

** Translator's Note: A department store in Prague, Czechoslovakia, before the Second World War.

organisation of production of big business. Small business must compensate for the superiority of large capitalisation through association (organisation) and for the superiority of intensive organisation of productive activity by superior quality of its output. While big business has easier access to cheap credit due to the visibility of its assets, farmers and tradesmen can gain access to affordable credit by organising credit cooperatives. While large scale purchases can be made at lower prices, small businessmen can reduce purchase price by making joint purchases. Small businesses can even buy and operate machinery jointly. Electricity makes it possible for even a small producer to use electric motors.

Government may assist the self-help organising efforts of small businessmen to obtain credit by providing loan guarantees for some part of the loan, thus reducing the cost of credit, etc. It may also enforce mandatory membership in small business associations (known as gremia in the case of small merchants). These have taken the place of the former guilds. As yet they have not be introduced in agriculture. In the cities they are limited to particular trades whereas in rural areas they include a number of branches. They are combined into higher federations that protect their members' interests. The government may also enforce compulsory membership of small businessmen in more widely based estate organisations.

What is most important is the quality of output. Even if the machine-made product is sold at a lower price than the hand-crafted product, the latter is not more expensive if its quality is better in construction, solidity, design, and taste. When these characteristics are important, particularly when the product is of individual character, for example furniture–because individuals are different and because they desire to have special design, for instance in their footwear, made-to-measure clothing, etc. , handicrafts survive and prosper alongside factory production. This purpose is also served by certificates of competence which do not serve as barriers to factory production by increase the quality of output of small producers and protect it against incompetent rivals. The government requires such licensing certificates and thus regulates competition in the small business sector. Government organises courses for craftsmen, expositions, etc. in order to raise their level of education and quality of their products.

The complex of measures of this second approach which aims to strengthen the small producer in his competition with big business constitutes the so-called improvement campaign. While the first approach–the approach of artificial barriers–reduces productivity, the second approach is in harmony with promoting productivity because it assists small and medium producers in their competitive struggle and enhances their productivity.

cc) Special measures.

Special measures may be suitable for specific groups of small and medium producers. For example the distribution of land ownership in agriculture is important from the viewpoint of the interests of small and medium farm operators. Land reform which consists of buying outland owned by large estates, to be sold at low prices to small farm operators, strengthens small and medium farms and, if it increases the number of farms, it strengthens the class of farmers.

All that was said about government productivity policy (economic policy narrowly defined) naturally benefits small and medium business because it strengthens it in the competitive struggle.

Small businessmen want security through mandatory old age and disability insurance schemes. We shall deal with analogous insurance schemes for workers when we discuss the working class. Because small business is so varied, the introduction of such schemes meets with considerable difficulties. In the case of those small businesses whose income is derived mostly from the labour of the owner, old age security is more important than in the case of other small enterprises, e.g., in agriculture where land ownership provides security to the aged farmer (the institution of farmer's retirement pension [vyme-nek]).*

c) The working class and working class policy

aa) Introduction

Workers constitute that portion of the nation who make a living by earning wages working for others in businesses or households. Consequently, unlike businessmen, they are not independent. They do not own land, a business, or other property that would provide them with a living and they are forced to offer their labour to businesses or households for a wage or salary.

The problem of the working class involves three questions and three concerns for the government:

1. The first question is: How to create jobs for them, how to bring them into the process of production. If one fails to achieve this unemployment ensues.

2. The second question is: How to formulate the content of the work agreement for those who do have jobs. Such agreements actually determine the entire life of the working class.

3. The third question is: How to care for members of the working class who are no loner able to work or not yet able to work. This is largely the question of social insurance.

---

* Translator's Note: A contractual arrangement for the care by his successor of a retiring operator of a farm or other real estate. It was usually arranged among very close relatives (e.g., children and parents) and involved a claim to housing, payments in natura or in money, and perhaps also various services. It is an old institution on the territory of Czechoslovakia and had the character of custom in feudal times. In the 18th century it was codified in legislation and the relevant arrangements were recorded in land cadastres. *Ekonomicka encyklopedie [Economic Encyclopedia]*, vol. 2, 596-597, Prague, 1972.

These questions cover the problem of the working class.

bb) Recruiting workers in the process of production. Unemployment

This takes place in the labour market, through labour recruitment. The government assumes this function so that it may be conducted systematically, for the whole country and for all occupations, and impartially. This reduces unemployment caused by the fact that employers and employees are not aware of each other or do not get together.

There may be full economic activity with all workers employed, or there may be less than full activity with part of the labour force unemployed. This may occur at regular intervals (especially in winter time) because productive activity and employment do not proceed evenly through the year. Because some production is seasonal (e.g., agriculture, construction, sugar refining) economic activity follows seasonally ascending and descending waves. The result is seasonal unemployment which the workers take into account and for which they make provisions (they have resources on which to live in winter time: their savings from the summer, their own dwarf-size farms).

There is also unemployment that occurs at regular intervals and may affect some or all branches of the economy. The economy is in a cyclical decline which may have various causes. Introduction of machinery and motors have displaced many workers permanently (rationalisation). Speculative production leads to overstocking of inventories in warehouses and subsequently to declining production (overproduction). Deflation means lower prices, growth of real indebtedness and declining profitability. But the number of workers does not decrease just because fewer workers are employed. Unemployed workers are a problem for the central government (and other public bodies).

The government considers first the cause of the disturbance of employment and the obstacles to business activity. If it is within its power to remove these causes and obstacles it will do so. If the cause of unemployment is rationalisation the government will shorten the work day, so that the newly introduced machinery becomes a blessing for all. If the cause is an excessive burden of taxation it will lower taxes, etc. Only then does the government look for ways of artificially increasing employment, either by itself undertaking public works and making investment expenditures, or by making financial contributions (subsidies) to stimulate production in the private sector or the activity of autonomous public bodies (emergency public works, production care).

Unemployed workers who cannot be absorbed in this way must be cared for by means of unemployment benefits. The existence of unemployment benefits leads an unemployed worker who is not very anxious to work to the following reasoning: When I work I earn a daily wage of 20 crowns; when I do not work my unemployment benefit is 10 crowns. Therefore I really work for only 10 crowns and that is not worth it. We must therefore distinguish voluntary from involuntary unemployment. The distinction cannot be easily made by the government or other public bodies if they themselves directly provide the unemployment benefits. The distinction is better made by trade unions which collect contributions to unemployment benefit funds from the workers and then disburse benefits. Another reason for this approach is the desire of trade unions to prevent the unemployed from lowering wage rates of all by offering their labour at low wage rates. Workers will resist paying benefits to those of their comrades who do not wish to work. The government therefore also participates in supporting the unemployed by augmenting the benefits paid by trade unions, thus easing their burden. This indirect method of paying unemployment benefits is known as the Ghent system (after the Belgian city where it was first introduced).

Before special care for the unemployed was introduced, they were treated as paupers without means to earn a living. They were assigned "to the community" for poor relief. This will be discussed below. The government assists the unemployed because there is significant interdependence of individuals, economic organisations, and regions with the exchange economy as a whole. Government assistance means that the cost of assistance is allocated to the economy as a whole in accordance with ability to contribute.

cc) The content of the labour agreement

Labour agreements contain provisions about (1) who are the parties to the agreement, (2) what are their obligations, and (3) what are their rights. There is also the question of monitoring the agreement.

(1)   Who are the parties to the agreement. Government regulations prohibit that some persons to work for wages because work is harmful for them. This includes children under 14, young persons under 18 (to perform certain kinds of work, e.g., in factories), women (to work at night in factories) and pregnant women (to do any work). It is not enough, of course, merely to prohibit work, because these persons are under pressure to work due to personal or family circumstances. It is also necessary to exercise care that persons who are not allowed to work do not suffer from poverty. Very recently there has also been a tendency for married women (whose husbands earn enough to support their families) to be excluded from working in both the public and private sector. The rationale for this is that they should not take away jobs from male workers who support families.

(2)   What the workers agree to give in the labour agreement. They agree to perform work of a given kind and duration. But in doing so they also agree to give some of their freedom, some of their selves. They agree to be present in the place of work (the workshop) during the hours of work and to be exposed to its environment (the heat of the mill or the rubber factory, the dangerous machines). They use their mental and physical energy. They expose their bodies to health hazards, they may perhaps expose their souls to moral damage, etc.

It follows that damage to the worker's life, health and (moral) culture should be minimized. The government's principal concern is with the length of the work day–a topic with which we have dealt in the general discussion of allocation of the burden of labour. The government is also concerned with the worker's in the work place. It issues directives and prohibitions to employers about how workshops must be equipped (light, air, ventilation, wash rooms, work clothing, protective measures against accidents, toxic exhalations, poisons, etc.). It regulates workers' conduct (prohibition of smoking when there are explosive on the premises), etc. Different regulations exist for different industrial branches where there are different dangers to the worker's health (working with lead, blast furnaces). This concerns in particular work in factories where large numbers of workers are gathered, where significant danger to their health exists (machinery, chemical processes) but thee is also greater ability to pay for the required safety equipment.

(3)   What the workers get for their work. Workers may receive wages in kind (in natura allowances in agriculture, e.g., some quantity of grain, milk, etc.) or else money wages. These are the rule, except in agriculture (and even there the entire wage is not paid in kind). Wages may be simply a function of time spent at work (per day, per hour) or they may be a function of physical output (by the piece—piece wages, such as the meter, e.g., cubic meter of earth dug, stone quarried, etc.). Piece wages are an incentive for workers to strive for greater productivity, to make better use of working time.

What the worker gives molds his life in the environment of the work place. The wages that he receives mold his home life, the life of his family, his household, because they determine the standard of living that he can afford. Workers attempt, through their syndicates (trade unions) to raise wages above the level resulting from the operation of a freely competitive labour market. The government may assist by enforcing the wage bargains that the syndicates have negotiated for a particular type of work, and perhaps extending their applicability, in a material sense, to non-union shops (to enterprises whose workers are not trade union members). The government may also intervene with respect to the duration of wage bargains by extending their applicability beyond their expiration date if a danger exists that the workers may not be able to negotiate an extension themselves.

The daily struggle between unionized and employers' syndicates deepens the antithesis between the working class and the rest of society and lead to "class struggle." Efforts to suppress the class struggle tend to bring about forced unification of employers' and employees' syndicates in corporate organisations (e.g., the Italian fascio). Such associations must of course be headed by persons who are neutral and who are endowed with public authority so that they may deal with confrontations and resolve conflicts.

There are branches of production where it is difficult for trade unions to be organized. This is true when workers are too scattered, cannot get together, and cannot therefore make agreements–e.g., workers in cottage industries who are employed in their own dwellings by outside entrepreneurs–tailors, or (in earlier times) stocking makers, etc. They process materials, such as textiles, supplies by the entrepreneur or his agent (known as factor) who acts as intermediary between them and the entrepreneur. Here the government plays a direct role through legislation that takes the place of trade union agreements since such agreements are not possible. The legislation specifies minimum wages either directly, or indirectly through appointed district wage commissions that set up (and modify) mandatory minimum wages. Government wage regulation is discussed below.

(4) Supervision. The set of legal norms that restrict and regulate labour contracts constitutes so called legislation for workers' protection. It is important that the legislation should be observed. This is primarily in the interest of workers (and of employees in general, including white collar workers). Workers must be informed about the regulations that govern their working conditions, and the regulations are therefore recorded in written form as work rules that must be available for public inspection on the business premises.

According to the law, workers also elect work committees and workers' trustees who act as their spokesmen vis-a-vis management and monitor the observation of legal norms for workers' protection. In this respect they act a equal partners of management.

Finally, the government also appoints special control officials known as business inspectors to monitor the observation of laws for workers' protection in certain wider areas. Their function is to supervise the observation of regulations pertaining to working time, facilities for health protection, accident prevention, etc.

Government may assist the self-help organising efforts of small businessmen to obtain credit by providing loan guarantees for some part of the credits, thus reducing the cost of credit, etc. It may also enforce mandatory small business associations (known as gremia in the case of small merchants). These have taken the place of the former guilds. As yet they have not been introduced in agriculture. In the cities they are limited to particular trades whereas in rural areas they include a number of branches. They are combined into higher federations that work for their members' interests. The government may also enforce association of small businessmen on a wider basis as estate associations. Because small business is so varied, the introduction of such scheme meets with considerable difficulties. In the case of those small businesses whose income is derived mostly from the labour of the owner, old age security is more important than in the case of those small enterprises, e.g., in agriculture where land ownership provides security to the aged farmer (the institution of farmer's retirement pension [vymenek]).*

Only then does the government look for ways of artificially increasing employment, either by itself undertaking public works and making investment expenditures, or by making financial contributions (subsidies) to stimulate production in the private sector or the activity of autonomous public bodies (emergency public works, production care).

---

* See previous note, p. 250.

Very recently there has also been a tendency for married women (whose husbands earn enough to support their families) to be excluded from working in both the public and the private sector. The rationale for this is that they should not take away jobs from males workers who support families. In the above passage the author alludes to a (short-lived) movement during the so-called Second Republic period, after the Munich agreement when fascist tendencies came out in Czechoslovakia. One of the forms that this took was what would be called "male chauvinism" today.

dd) Persons unqualified to work

The third and last aspect of the workers' question concerns those members of the working class who are not yet able to work (children, minors) and those who no loner are able to work (the elderly, the handicapped, the sick). Workers' children, like the children of others, are cared for by the central government (or other public bodies) if there is no one else to care for them, i.e., if they are orphaned, abandoned, or if their parents are not competent to care for them (for financial or moral reasons). This is discussed below.

There remains the problem of workers, male and female, who have lost their ability to work. They cannot be assisted by being included in the ranks of the employed (points dd and bb). If they own no property, they must receive supplemental income. Might this not occur also outside the working class? It might indeed. A businessman may also become unable to work, or an individual may be unable to work from birth on, never having been a worker. These and analogous cases are the concern of public bodies that provide poor relief to such persons.

However, workers do not wish to be a burden to the community when they get old, sick or handicapped. They want security as a matter of right, not as a handout. They do not ask that society should care for members of the working class unable to work. What they want is to assume the risks of work, as a group, through workers' social insurance against accident, sickness, infirmity, old age, death of the bread winner–perhaps with contributions by employers.

Employers and employees pay premiums to insurance plans–health insurance, accident insurance, a central social insurance scheme against old age and infirmity. The premiums finance periodic payments to workers who are sick, who have had an accident, or who are handicapped, as well as widows and orphans. In turn, ever worker who contributes to the insurance scheme has the certainty that he too will be taken care of if the need should arise.

Whether such premiums are paid by workers or by employers they are always a labour cost, a cost of production, a component of price. Ultimately they are paid by consumers who must bear the labour risks that their consumption causes. Those who smoke cigarettes with bronze mouthpieces must bear the risk which production of such cigarettes carries for the worker's health. If the government contributes to social insurance benefits (e.g., old age pensions or benefits for the inform) it allocates the burden of such payments by collecting solidarist taxes.

Such insurance scheme must be compulsory. Otherwise there would not be complete coverage (persons who face small risks or those with insufficient foresight would avoid participating in the scheme).

Payments from old age and infirmity insurance schemes are made in one of two ways. Either by ascertaining what the losses have been and covering them from contributions made during the current year. The level of premiums is set according to the level of losses that have occurred. This is known as the schedule approach or repartition approach). Alternatively payments are made by setting up for each worker a capital fund sufficient (according to the calculus of probability) to provide for his care. Premiums are fixed, and calculated to crate and maintain the necessary fund, whether the losses incurred in a given year are larger or   smaller. The system is known as the capital fund system. The size of the required fund depends on the rate of interest, because payment of a given life annuity from interest and from capital requires a larger capital sum if the interest (the interest component of annuity payments) is lower than if it is higher.

Social insurance schemes thus generate large savings and large accumulations of financial capital. They assume the existence of interest and of the capitalist economic system. Like any other capital they seek investment opportunities. Whether invested in the private sector or public sector (roads, hydro projects, electrification), they help to raise the country's productivity just as any other investment. The national product is therefore increased and the payments made to elderly and infirm workers do not depress the living standards of the rest of the population, whose share of the higher national product is not less than heretofore, while the increment of the national product is received by workers who are beneficiaries of the insurance scheme. It is therefore very important that the capital funds of the social insurance plans should be invested productively.

d) Care for the poor

Individuals who own no wealth, are unable to work, and whose care is not provided in any other way, become the concern of public bodies whose solidarist responsibility is to assist the weakest. The government tries first to find someone who would be responsible to care for such persons (e.g., children for parents). Secondly, it considers which public body (local communities, districts, provinces, central government) should provide such care. The task falls primarily to the local community where the poor reside and where they have, as a rule, lived and worked when they were able to work. Care for the poor is primarily the business of local communities.

Large municipalities can provide good care for their elderly poor citizens. They provide them with homes for the elderly (where they receive room and board as well as health care). On the other hand, small communities cannot afford this, and the care that they provide tends to be inadequate and sometimes undignified. They find it particularly difficult to care for those who require medical and other health care, due to old age or infirmity (institutions for the elderly and the infirm) or due to some defect or illness (institutions for the sick, blind, deaf and dumb, epileptics, mentally ill, etc.). These institutions are operated by higher-level public bodies, including central government.

In some countries all poor elderly citizens are simply taken care of by the central government which pays them old age pensions.

Support of the poor is an element of pure solidarism and to some degree it represents realisation of the right to existence. It is not however a full realisation, because the level of care for the poor depends on the state's ability to provide such care. Consequently the poor are not given the right to sue for such support. It is not possible, in capitalism, to grant to individuals a general right to existence because many would prefer a small handout without working to receiving wages for work. Otherwise it would become necessary to establish a general obligation to work and change the whole system. Because of this under capitalism relief of the poor always involves some harshness and odium (being excluded from the right to exercise the franchise).

That is why poor relief is a separate issue from youth care because there is no need for harshness in this case (children cannot work as yet and they cannot therefore shirk gainful labour). Harshness would be harmful in this case because the development of children requires that they should not go hungry and that they should be properly brought up. Care for the young is exercised at all levels of government from local communities to central government. In addition private associations and private citizens are called upon to participate (youth care commissions on the level of local communities, districts, and provinces).

Poor relief involves rational principles and requires a feel and understanding of the poor. Large urban communities set up bodies of volunteer workers (called "fathers of the poor") who divide among themselves areas of the city. Each volunteer visits the poor in his area and extends to them aid financed from communal resources. Together the "fathers of the poor" constitute a corps that directs all matters pertaining to poor relief–of course within limits of resources that the community devotes to this purpose. Urban communities thus have special poor ordinances. The city of Prague has been a model for the world in this respect. Poor relief n Prague was organised by parishes and parish priests were "fathers of the poor." The model was emulated by the city of Elbefeld where it became separated from the Church. From thee it has spread as the so-called Elberfeld system.

As in all areas of social welfare, support of the poor too is being carried on increasingly through private efforts, through numerous associations that are very diverse with respect to the direction of their endeavours. Individuals too have made numerous gifts of property for the relief of the poor who are beneficiaries of the incomes from such gifts. Capital that is to be used for the poor (bank accounts, securities, buildings, land) is earmarked for this purpose (under government supervision) and constitutes an endowment. Endowments can also be set up for other purposes, e.g., to support scientific work. They are nobody's property. They represent non-personal wealth to be used for a particular purpose. But if an association, a business enterprise, a community, or the central government segregate part of their wealth which they continue to direct and manage, but which they earmark for a certain purpose, then this part constitutes a fund.

4. Social policy and productivity

Both productivity policy and social policy are motivated by the desire to guide the nation toward the ideal of life, health and culture. Productivity policy strives to increase the national product, the basis of the nation's existence and development. Social policy strives to achieve a more equitable distribution of the national product (and the burdens of labour) in the interest of a more balanced and therefore also a lasting development of the national whole.

It follows that productivity also serves the social interest. For something to be distributed it must first exist. The larger the pie the larger each piece into which it is divided. By the same token social policy also promotes productivity because it improves the health and culture of the weakest, and because anything that makes men into better human beings makes them also into better workers.

Of course each policy may also be in conflict with the other. If we tried to increase production by excessively extending the work day, or if we tried to increase it by excessive accumulation of capital (which reduces consumption too much and causes harm to the health and culture of the population) we would be trading off the nation's energies and talents for an increase of the national product. If we should interfere with the structure of business returns, attempting to make the distribution of income an the burdens of labour more equitable, so as to depress or bring to a halt the operation of business or to undermine willingness to work, we would be equalising poverty rather than wealth.

Both the national product and its rational distribution promote the ideal of life, health and culture. Both productivity policy and social policy therefore promote this objective. However each has its limitations: The limits of productivity policy are given by social concern; the limits of social policy are given by consideration of productivity.

D. STRUCTURAL POLICY

Structural policy is directed toward changing the composition of the national product that would otherwise result from the activities, preferences, demands, etc. of individuals who make decisions about what is produced, how much is produced or, as the case may be, how much is exported and imported, by making purchases in accordance with their subjective utilities. A solidarist government may find such individualistically determined composition inappropriate. It may note that the composition of national product determined in this fashion and the corresponding composition of national consumption places too much emphasis on luxury, amusements, harmful products and harmful consumption, and insufficient emphasis on health, education, etc.

The government therefore intervenes in the formation and composition of the national product and private consumption to guide them along the lines of the solidarist ideal of the nation's life, health and culture. It is always a question of allocating more of the nation's resources for purposes of health and culture than would be otherwise allocated by private initiative. In addition there is also the concern of defense against external enemies, so that it becomes a question of directing labour, production, and consumption to promote national health, national culture and national defense. We refer to this aspect of government policy (striving to change the composition of the national product) as industrial policy. It includes health policy, cultural policy, and defense policy.

The central government (and possibly other public bodies within the state) pursues such policy by using both instruments of its power, legislation and the public sector (the solidarist sector and the mandatory cooperative sector).

The government uses legislation to promulgate positive directives addressed to the citizens, e.g., that they must care for their children, that they mus be vaccinated, that they must obey the rules of hygiene, that they must send their children to school, that they must be ready to serve in the armed forces, etc. Alternately, it promulgates negatively stated prohibitions, e.g., that citizens must not consume harmful things such as opium or worthless literature, that they must avoid engaging in any activities that would jeopardize national defense, that they must not import harmful substances, etc.

Through its solidarist economic sector the government takes away from the public a portion of national product that corresponds to the public's preferences and uses it to provide that which the public would otherwise neglect but which is nevertheless important from the viewpoint of the ideal of the nation's life, health and culture. The government uses the portion of national product removed from the citizens' free disposal within the public sector to finance institutions of national health and culture as well as the armed forces and defense expenditures. (An example of mandatory cooperative activity is illustrated, e.g., by compulsory education where attendance si compulsory but where tuition is paid.)

Structural policy must be distinguished from social policy. It does not involve the distribution of income (and the burdens of labour) among individuals and assistance to the most disadvantaged. It involves either institutions serving directly the entire public (e.g., national defense) or those serving all individuals (including wealthy ones). However some institutions may be operated in such a way that the most disadvantaged can be benefitted without being charged. This follows as a matter of course when such institutions (schools, hospitals) are operated in a completely solidarist fashion (when they are available to everyone without charge and are financed from taxes). When they are operated on the cooperative principle (payment of tuition, payment of hospital user fees) then the socio-political aspect involves lower charges for the poor.

V. ECONOMIC NATIONALISM

In as much as government intervention raises domestic costs and prices it undermines the country's position in foreign competition. Production costs and prices are raised by taxes, social security taxes, wage controls, regulations of business for the protection of workers, limitations of the work day, as well as manipulation of prices (higher prices) that benefit particular producers (e.g., farm producers through a monopoly organisation acting as a syndicate), etc.* However, the intervention is due to government pursuit of the ideal of the nation's life, health and culture.

Lack of competitiveness in foreign markets may impact on both imports and exports. In the case of imports the government may protect itself to a degree by means of tariffs. We say, "to a degree" because other countries will erect tariff walls against our exports in retaliation to our erecting tariff walls against their exports. As for exports–if ours are more expensive–we can protect ourselves against less expensive foreign competition either by export subsidies (financed from tax revenues) or by syndicalisation (perhaps mandatory) of domestic industries, selling their output at high prices at home and using part of the profits from domestic sales to artificially reduce export prices. That is of course possible only when home consumption of the product largely dominates over exports. These methods too have their limitations and can only be used by countries that are small exporters. When competition in foreign markets is restricted, the volume of the country's foreign trade must sooner or later decline as well.

Because foreign trade and international division of labour are the cause of higher levels of economic welfare and because reducing the volume of foreign trade causes a decline of economic welfare, countries pay attention–when they intervene with the exchange economy–to the reactions of other countries. This leads to a sort of institutional parallelism of national legislation (legislation of individual countries in the area of taxation, social policy, etc.). In fact countries endeavour to conclude international agreements aimed at achieving such institutional parallelism in the area of social legislation, to promote competition in foreign trade (e.g., international agree-

---

* Translator's Note: The implied reference is to pre-war Czechoslovakia's *grain monopoly*, an organization sponsored by the government under the auspices of the Agrarian (Republican) Party for the benefit of farm producers.

ments concerning the length of the work day). When a government abandons this point of view, the result is inevitably a
closed economy, autarky (self-sufficiency). The country practically shuts itself off from international trade and becomes
dependent on the home market as outlet for its output. Complete autarky is only possible–regardless of the fact that it
lowers the level of economic welfare–in countries that need
nothing from abroad, i.e., countries that have their own raw
materials (to produce textiles) their own ores, etc., and have no
foreign debts, because to pay for raw materials and to service
foreign debt a country must export.

Why do some countries pursue a policy of autarky? Appar-
ently because they wish to pursue the national solidarist ideal.
This happens in particular when they feel threatened by
external enemies an wish to grow stronger domestically. In case
of war they do not wish to be dependent upon imports of raw
materials and foodstuffs and they compel domestic
producers–through shortages brought about by autarkic
policies–to search for substitute raw materials (synthetic rubber, synthetic petrol) to exploit mines with low ore content, to
cultivate land more intensively, etc. Shortages of imported
foodstuffs and raw materials would cause excessive increases
of prices at home. Price controls are therefore introduced and
raw materials and foodstuffs are allocated to users in accordance with objective needs (e.g., bread rations). Such country
sets up, already in peace time, a complete distribution organisation such as becomes necessary in war time. In this manner
the country uses autarky as preparation for war. It does so by
setting an exchange rate of its currency for deviates from the
rate that would maintain equilibrium in the balance of
payments–under conditions of completely free competition.
This restricts exports automatically, whereas imports must be
restricted artificially (by tariffs, by means of the clearing system,
etc.) so as to maintain equilibrium in the balance of payments.

When a country pursues autarkic policies, it naturally
impacts on the composition of other countries' product as well.
This follows from the fact that imports of the country that now

strives for autarky were previously other countries' exports. If the economy of the autarkic country is sufficiently large, its policies may indeed cause world wide disturbances. The trend toward world economic integration, international division of labour, and international exchange is disrupted and reversed by the emergence of closed national economies and economic nationalism that conflicts with free international economic competition.

A country that does not need to be concerned about its competitive position vis-a-vis other countries, need not be concerned either about institutional parallelism with other countries with respect to its financial, economic, and social systems. It may impart to its system a different character, more in line with its national ideal. National solidarism comes to play an increased role.

When the government must pay constant attention to the country's competitive position vis-a-vis other countries, it must limit its economic and social policies to establishing general conditions and norms that apply to all participants in economic activity–tariffs, limitations of the length of the work day, etc., i.e., enforcement of various regulations of domestic and foreign economic relations that are analogous in nature and extent to those of other countries.

When the government no longer needs to be concerned with foreign competition, as it has to be previously, it can manage the national economy by direct controls. In the individualist economic system there are three types of domestic equilibrium prices (prices of goods, interest rates, and wages) and one in the foreign sector (the exchange rate). They are the outcome of the operation of freely competitive markets and they determine the general equilibrium of the economy and practically also the entire distribution of the national product. This is so because prices determine the objective returns of business enterprises and their division between workers and capitalists, i.e., the formation of incomes as they emerge from the operation of competition in the market. The distribution of national product (the annual return of the nation's labour) is the outcome of the tendency toward general equilibrium (in the markets for goods, capital, and labour). It occurs however without consideration of equity or social utility.

We have noted that government uses controls to displace prices emerging from the operation of freely competitive markets to higher or lower levels, but that, in so doing it moves them away from their equilibrium position. Prices set by direct controls are no longer equilibrium prices. The government must then also control the determinants of prices (production, consumption, use of capital, use of labour, international payments) to restore and maintain balance.

However, when it does, the government not only maintains equilibrium but also assumes the second function of freely competitive market prices, distribution of the national product, because that can no longer be performed by prices that are not equilibrium prices. When direct controls were used during the First World War to benefit consumers by keeping the price of bread low (because bread was in short supply), many people would have bought bread at the lower price, but there was not enough bread available. Consumption had to be restricted to match available supply. However, the government did not restrict consumption in a merely mechanical way, to match it with available supply and thus restore balance between production and consumption. Instead it undertook to distribute bread, within this framework, paying attention to equity and social utility. There were different bread rations for children, for adults, for those performing heavy physical labour, i.e., in accordance with objective needs. And given equal needs the rations were the same. Raw materials prices can be controlled n the same way. Raw materials that are in short supply can be allocated to different uses in accordance with their importance. They can be allocated to different enterprises according to their importance and government priorities. International payments can also be controlled, given a particular volume of credit transactions, by permitting only those debit transactions that are of the greatest importance for the government. Similarly, investment can be controlled by assigning preference in employment to those workers who need work most, e.g., those who have been unemployed longest, those with large families, etc. The allocative mechanism of the unplanned competitive system is replaced by the allocative system of state controls concerned with equity and social utility. Solidarism increasingly replaces the individualist order as competition is set aside. However, the fundamental pillars of individualism–private property and the business enterprise system of production are preserved. This describes also the present economic system of our country, a system which replaces the equilibrium order of interaction of economic organisations formed in capitalism by the operation of competition in the four markets (for goods, capital, labour, and foreign exchange). That order depends on four types of pries (of goods, of capital, the wage rate, and the exchange rate). Competition is replaced by controls. This requires four main administrative agencies for the four markets–price administration, financial affairs, labour administration, and foreign exchange administration–to administer prices and their constituents in the corresponding markets. Such governmental organisations at the top implies as well the need for mandatory concentration and organisation at lower levels–mandatory organisation of producers, financial institutions, workers, trades and professions. This displaces the competitive struggle and its methods (strikes, lockouts) and therefore also the class struggle of employers and workers.

Such organisation of the national economy requires thorough and complex organisation not only of the state administrative apparatus, but also of the interactions of economic organisations and of the citizenry as such. Of course, governmental authority which thus assumes a major task, grows and suppresses the former autonomous system. To the earlier individualist system corresponding democracy (autonomy). In the controlled economy the centre of gravity is shifted to state authority.

PART FOUR

THE NATIONAL ECONOMY

EQUILIBRIUM OF THE NATIONAL ECONOMY

ECONOMIC DEPRESSION

A. THE NATIONAL ECONOMY

The aggregate of the nation's care to preserve and improve its life constitutes the national economy. It includes, first of all, a set of various institutions that come into being in individualist fashion as each individual exercises self-responsible care for himself (businesses, markets, prices, etc.). As we saw, this gives rise to the exchange economy. To this is added the government (and other public bodies within the state). It modifies–through legislation (directives and prohibitions)–the individualist economic system and individuals' care for themselves. By using the public sector it crates on the foundation of the individualist system (the exchange economy) a superstructure and a complement of care for preserving and improving the nation's life. It uses resources obtained from this base to provide a portion of the care for the nation according to its own wishes.

Care to preserve and improve the nation's life therefore originates in thousands of parallel points where it is guided, on one hand, by personal interest of individuals, and on the other, by a single point, superordinate to all the others, which guides and complements individuals' care according to the ideal of the nation's life, health and culture. The controlling authority of government and the public sector stands above thousands of economic organisations (businesses, cooperative, consumers). The two are dovetailed, the complement each other, they constitute a great entity–not one unitary economic organisation but an aggregate of private and public economic organisations. The aggregate does not represent a uniform order nor a unified will but a mix of the order which originates in the wills of thousands of individuals and that which originates in the will of the government. This mixed system reflects the person will to live and the personal interest (subjective satisfaction) of thousands of individuals and private economic organisations, and the will of the nation to preserve its life on a permanent basis, something that can only be achieved if the nation pursues simultaneously the ideal of life, health and culture.

The national economy is therefore a combination of individualist and solidarist orders. The nation's care to preserve and improve life originates in two focal points of will and purpose (interest). The two have been in conflict for thousands of years but it appears that only balance between the two assures continuation of national life and national culture.

B. ECONOMIC EQUILIBRIUM

To assure their continued existence all economic organisations must pay attention to balance. One a ongoing basis consumers cannot spend more than their income. If they did they would use up their substance or go into debt, until they exhausted their assets. Businesses cannot keep operating at a loss because the losses would use up their reserves and capital and they would go under. Nor can the government's annual expenditures continuously exceed its annual revenues.

There are other equilibria in addition to those mentioned, above all equilibrium of production and consumption of rather entire national economy. When consumption expenditures are less than the output of consumer goods, the unsaleable goods accumulate as inventories, and this may eventually lead to a temporary cessation of production. There is a tendency toward equilibrium not only in the goods market but also in the capital market and the labour market, and in market for foreign payments, the foreign exchange market. The tendency is due to the fact that disequilibrium results in losses or harmful developments for individual economic organisations.

There is therefore an equilibrium order between economic organisations in the exchange society as a whole, distinct from the purposive order within an individual economic organisation which is the outcome of the purposive plan and the ordering by the single will that rules it. The equilibrium order between individual economic organisations is not the outcome of a single will (which does not exist for the exchange society as a whole), nor a single plan. It is rather the automatic consequence of the fact that every economic organisation seeks its own disequilibrium, maximising utility and minimising cost. Of course it is a different matter in a controlled economy.

Finally a kind of equilibrium also exists in the relationship of the individualist base and the solidarist superstructure in that the superstructure does not subvert the base, that it respects what is materially possible, that it does not undermine or subvert the activity of business enterprises. This would be the case, e.g., if the tax system were to destroy the profitability of business, etc.

But the national economy is no always stable and therefore not always in equilibrium. When equilibrium is disturbed however, there immediately appear efforts to reestablish it.

C. DISTURBANCES OF EQUILIBRIUM OF THE NATIONAL ECONOMY

The more complex a piece of machinery the easier it breaks down–and we have seen that the "national economic engine" is very complex indeed. A particular state of affairs within economic organisations (what and how much is produced and consumed), between economic organisations (what quantities of labour, capital, and goods are traded in the market and at what "prices"), and in the international economic sphere (movement of persons, goods, and capital across international boundaries, changes in foreign exchange rates) depends on a particular set of conditions given by nature (climate, a region's fertility, underground wealth) or the human factor (man's will–what he desires to accomplish–and his intellect which changes both, what he wants to accomplish and what he succeeds in accomplishing). This applies also to the relationship between the private sector (individualist base) and the public sector (solidarist superstructure, fiscal system). From this follows a particular volume and structure of production and consumption, of capital formation, of the form and extent of wage labour, of the form and extent of international contacts, and of relationship between the private and public sectors. Every small part of this great engine, its structure (what it produces and sells, what it buys and uses) is important. A disturbance in one part is necessarily transferred, through the market, to all other parts. In the same way changes that occur in the market (of prices, interest rates, wage rates) produces changes in the structure of economic organisations that produce for the market and acquire what they use in the market.

Various events disturb, time and time again, the activities of economic organisations that strive toward order, and the organizations attempt in turn to re-establish equilibrium under the new circumstances, to achieve maximum utility with minimum cost. This includes disturbances caused by natural causes, such as crop failures, or earthquakes, disturbances caused by human will, such as fashion or preparation for national defence, disturbances caused by the human intellect, such as invention of the steam engine, disturbances that affect individual economic organisations, such as accident, death, or the formation of new businesses, disturbances that affect relations between economic organisations, and those that affect the market, such as price changes or changes in the purchasing power of money, disturbances that originate abroad such as competition from cheap labour or redemption of capital loans, and disturbances that originate in the solidarist sector, such as new taxation measures.

Economic order is like a water surface that is being exposed, over and over again, to sometimes large and sometimes small disturbances, but which seeks, again and again, a way to regain a position of rest. Disturbances of various equilibria are the cause of changes in economic activity, particularly business activity. Some disturbances stimulate business activity (bumper crops, rising prices) others dampen it (crop failures, deflation, overproduction). When they lead, overall, to decreased business activity, decreased output, exports and eventually declining welfare and employment, we speak of a recession or depression. The converse of recession is called expansion or prosperity.

The government monitors anxiously the level and change (development) of economic activity, recessions and expansions, their amplitude and external manifestations (unemployment, volume of railway freight carried, savings deposits, the volume of production and consumption). For this purpose it sets up special institutes for the study of business conditions. It monitors the level of economic activity and economic development to be able to assist in removing obstacles where activity is lagging, perhaps to care for the unemployed, and in general to formulate its productivity and social policies accordingly. The work of institutes for the study of business conditions can be compared with the work of meteorological stations, though the phenomena that they observe and the methods that they use are different.

Measurement of the volume of production and of business activity is undertaken. The measures attempt, for the most part, to describe a particular level by comparing it with an initial level designated as 100. Other levels that are being compared may then be e.g., 109, 107, 95, 83, etc. This way of stating and measuring a series is called the index number method, and the numerical expression of the series activity is termed an index number. An index that is continuously recorded yields arising and falling curve of development that exhibits a cyclical wave movement. These waves are observed over time in an effort to establish regularities and therefore also the possibility of forecasting economic development, though perhaps only over the very near future. Contrasted with the systemic science of economies which we have just come to examine (in outline form), there is therefore developmental economics, history of economics and the theory of economic boom.

[Bibliography of general works on economics in Czech]
[A number of the work listed are translations into Czech from other languages]

I. THE NATIONAL ECONOMY
II. FINANCIAL SCIENCE
III. HISTORY OF ECONOMIC THOUGHT

[A very detailed table of contents; includes the full text of all the marginal notes.]

ECONOMICS
written by
DR. KAREL ENGLIS
PUBLISHED IN 1946
BY THE AUTHOR

PRINTED
AS SECOND PRINTING OF THE 2ND EDITION
USING FOURNIER. MONOTYPE FONT
BY PRINTING HOUSE "ORBIS", PRAGUE XII
Price 80.00 Czechoslovak crowns [Kcs]

DATE DUE

			Printed in USA

Printed in USA